Dynamic Allocation and Pricing

Arne Ryde Memorial Lectures Series

1. *Seven Schools of Macroeconomic Thought*
   Edmund S. Phelps

2. *High Inflation*
   Daniel Heymann and Axel Leijonhufvud

3. *Bounded Rationality in Macroeconomics*
   Thomas J. Sargent

4. *Computable Economics*
   Kumaraswamy Vellupillai

5. *Rational Risk Policy*
   W. Kip Viscusi

6. *Strategic Learning and Its Limits*
   H. Peyton Young

7. *The Equilibrium Manifold: Postmodern Developments in the Theory of General Economic Equilibrium*
   Yves Balasko

8. *Empirical Model Discovery and Theory Evaluation: Automatic Selection Methods in Econometrics*
   David F. Hendry and Jurgen A. Doornik

9. *Dynamic Allocation and Pricing: A Mechanism Design Approach*
   Alex Gershkov and Benny Moldovanu

Dynamic Allocation and Pricing: A Mechanism Design Approach

Alex Gershkov and Benny Moldovanu

The MIT Press
Cambridge, Massachusetts
London, England

This book was set in Times Roman by diacriTech, Chennai.

Library of Congress Cataloging-in-Publication Data
Gershkov, Alex.
   Dynamic allocation and pricing: a mechanism design approach / Alex Gershkov and
      Benny Moldovanu.
      pages cm. – (Arne Ryde memorial lectures)
   Includes bibliographical references and index.
   ISBN 978-0-262-02840-0 (hardcover : alk. paper)
   ISBN 978-0-262-55244-8 (paperback) 1. Revenue management. 2. Pricing.
3. Assignment problems (Programming) I. Moldovanu, Benny. II. Title.
   HD60.7.G47 2014
   658.15'54—dc23

                            2014016709

I dedicate this book to my parents, Michael Gershkov and Hana Rafelson.—A.G.

I dedicate this book to my mother, Erna Moldovanu, and to the memory of my father, Liviu Moldovanu.—B.M.

Contents

About the Arne Ryde Foundation — ix

Acknowledgments — xi

1 Introduction — 1

2 The Sequential Assignment of Heterogeneous Objects — 11

3 Dynamic Revenue Maximization with Heterogeneous Objects — 41

4 The Stochastic and Dynamic Knapsack Model — 73

5 Learning and Dynamic Efficiency — 105

6 Long-lived Agents — 151

Bibliography — 181

Index — 191

About the Arne Ryde Foundation

Arne Ryde was an exceptionally promising student in the PhD program at the Department of Economics, Lund University. He was tragically killed in a car accident in 1968 at the age of twenty-three.

The Arne Ryde Foundation was established by his parents, pharmacist Sven Ryde and his wife Valborg, in commemoration of Arne Ryde. The aim of the Foundation, as given in the deed from 1971, is to foster and promote advanced economic research in cooperation with the Department of Economics at Lund University. The Foundation acts by lending support to conferences, symposia, lecture series, and publications that are initiated by faculty members of the department.

Acknowledgments

We are grateful to the European Research Council (Advanced Investigator Grant 246648DMD) and to the Arne Ryde foundation for financial support. We wish to thank Anders Borglin and Bo Larsson for organizing the lecture series on which this book is based. We thank Deniz Dizdar for the research cooperation on the topics covered in chapter 3. Andy Klein, Dimitry Knyazev, Holger Herbst, Benjamin Schickner, Wili Rivinius, and Michael Metzger read parts of the manuscript and made numerous comments. Kamil Lukas Dorn, Sebastian Elgass, Marius Beuth, and Marian Alexander Dreher assisted us with Tex formatting. We are also grateful to John Covell at the MIT Press and to three anonymous referees for their very helpful remarks that improved the quality of the exposition.

Alex Gershkov would like to thank his wife Marina, and his sons Ariel, Tomer, and Daniel for their continuing support. Benny Moldovanu would like to thank his mother Erna, his wife Iris, and his daughters Dana and Noa for their continuing support, and in particular, over the recent period of long illness.

1 Introduction

Dynamic allocation and pricing problems appear in numerous frameworks such as the retail of seasonal/style goods, the allocation of fixed capacities in the travel and leisure industries (e.g., airlines, hotels, rental cars, holiday resorts), the allocation of a fixed inventory of equipment in a given period of time (e.g., equipment for medical procedures, bandwidth or advertising space in online applications), and the assignment of personnel to incoming tasks. Although dynamic pricing is a very old technique (think about haggling in a bazaar!), modern revenue management (RM) techniques started with the US Airline Deregulation Act of 1978 (see McAfee and te Velde 2007). A major academic textbook is *The Theory and Practice of Revenue Management* by Talluri and van Ryzin (2004). According to these authors, the basic RM issues are as follows:

1. **Quantity decisions** How to allocate capacity/output to different segments, products or channels? When to withhold products from the market?
2. **Structural decisions** Which selling format to choose (posted prices, negotiations, auctions, etc.)? Which features to use for a particular format (segmentation, volume discounts, bundling, etc.)?
3. **Pricing decisions** How to set posted prices, reserve prices? How to price differentiate? How to price over time? How to mark down over life time?

Broadly speaking, all three questions deal with issues treated in the *auction/mechanism design* literature (e.g., see Milgrom's textbook; Milgrom 2004). Nevertheless, mechanism design has not been the tool of choice in RM: instead, most studies have focused on analyzing properties of restricted classes (sometime intuitive, sometimes rather ad hoc) of allocation/pricing schemes. One possible explanation for this gap is that the classical auction/mechanism design literature had a strong focus on static models, whereas the emphasis in RM is on dynamics.

Thus what is necessary for a modern theory of RM is a blend of elegant *dynamic models* from operations research, management science, and computer science literature (i.e., with historical focus on grand, centralized optimization and/or ad hoc mechanisms) with the classical mechanism design literature (i.e., with historical focus on information/incentives in static settings). Such a blend would have numerous valuable applications. Recently this challenge has been addressed by a more or less systematic body of work appearing under the heading of *dynamic mechanism design.*[1]

In this chapter we illustrate how this approach would work, based on our own recent efforts on the topic. We start with well-known, complete information, nonstrategic dynamic models directly taken from the OR/management science literature. For these models elegant, explicit solutions to the underlying dynamic optimization problems are available. We add privately informed, strategic agents and examine the consequences of these changes on the optimization problem of the designer. The present combination allows a clear, explicit picture of the delicate interplay between dynamic trade-offs and strategic incentives.[2] It is often the case that the ensuing design problems are relatively complex, requiring tools from advanced areas of mechanism design such as multidimensional signals, or interdependent values. The main topics discussed in the book are summarized below. We include a discussion of the related literature at the end of each chapter of point the header to many other relevant and important contributions that, due to space limitations, cannot be reviewed fully in the book.

1.1   Chapter 2: The Sequential Assignment of Heterogeneous Objects

Much of chapter 2 comes from Gershkov and Moldovanu (2010, 2012). In the chapter we present efficient, individual-rational and budget-balanced schemes for a specific dynamic mechanism design problem: the designer wants to assign a fixed, finite set of heterogeneous objects to a sequence of randomly arriving agents with privately known characteristics. Monetary transfers are feasible. The objects are substitutes, and each agent derives utility from at most one object. Moreover all agents share a common ranking over the available objects, and values for objects have a multiplicative structure, involving the agents' types and objects' qualities.

Examples of such settings include the dynamic allocation of limited resources among incoming projects, the allocation of limited research facilities among research units, the assignment of dormitory rooms to potential tenants, and the allocation of available positions to arriving candidates. It is often the case that positions in an organization's hierarchy cannot be re-assigned without very high penalties. The yield management literature has analyzed the simpler model of allocating identical objects (seats on an aeroplane, hotel rooms, etc.) from a revenue-maximization perspective. Our model also shares several common features with the classical job search models. The main difference is that in the search literature it is usually assumed that the stream of job offers is generated by a nonstrategic player, without private information. Hence implementation issues do not arise.[3]

The assumption of nonstrategic arrivals is an important limitation of the model. But many of the model's features do appear in practical situations of interest. For example, customers in duty-free or central railway station shops are impatient, "short-lived," and exhibit nonstrategic arrivals. Shopping in "mega-markets" situated outside population agglomerations (thus requiring long travel) present similar characteristics. Perishable items (flowers, food, seasonal apparel, etc.) sold in such shops have limited shelf lives. Similarly, every evening hotels face "last-minute" nonstrategic travelers in need of a room, so hotels' allocation/pricing policies change early in the evening based on their vacancy rates.

Compared to a static setting, the new trade-off is between an assignment today and the option of assigning it in the future, possibly to an agent who values it more. Since the arrival process of agents is stochastic, the "future" determining option value depends may never materialize (if there is a cutoff date), or it may be farther away in time and thus discounted. Incomplete information in a similar, but static model with nonrandom demand is introduced in the classic paper by Mussa and Rosen (1978) in whose analysis a monopolist faces price/quality decisions.

Efficient dynamic allocation under complete information is analyzed by Derman, Lieberman, and Ross (1972) for the discrete-time case, and via a system of differential equations by Albright (1974) for the continuous-time case. We derive associated menus of prices (one menu for each point in time, and for each subset of remaining objects) that implement their first-best solutions, yielding a dynamic version of the Vickrey–Clarke–Groves mechanism. For the study of efficient, individual rational and budget-balanced mechanisms in our frameworks, we distinguish between two scenarios: (1) both physical assignments and monetary payments must take place upon the agents' arrival; (2) payments can be postponed to later stages. While in the second scenario a balanced budget can always be reached, in the first scenario a balanced budget can only be reached asymptotically as the arrival rate (or the time up to the deadline) increases without bound.

1.2   Chapter 3: Dynamic Revenue Maximization with Heterogeneous Objects

Chapter 3 is mostly based on Gershkov and Moldovanu (2009a, 2010). We advance our analysis to revenue maximization while keeping the basic model of the preceding chapter fixed (with continuous time and a target date[4]). We show how certain features of the revenue-maximizing policy can be used to obtain a direct solution to the larger optimization problem where the designer must choose the size and quality composition of his/her inventory.

The main contributions are as follows:

1. By allowing for heterogeneous objects, we can combine quantity/quality optimization with the pricing considerations, analyzing optimization under stochastic demand conditions as have been traditionally the focus of the literature in economics and management science.

2. Out technical method has two components: A payoff equivalence principle with a focus on implementable policies rather than prices and a variational method that obtains new results even for the much studied case of dynamic revenue maximization of identical goods, and thus yields more insight than the traditional dynamic programming/Bellman's equation approach.

3. Our analysis yields testable implications about the pattern of prices in situations exhibiting fixed inventories of substitute goods that need to be sold by a certain date. An example of clearance sales for apparel is presented.

Unlike the large literature on yield and revenue management that has directly focused on revenue-maximizing pricing (as in the special case of our model where agents have linear, private values for identical objects), our approach is based on the characterization of all dynamically implementable, nonrandomized allocation policies. We compute the revenue generated by any individual—rational, deterministic, Markovian, and implementable allocation policy. Then we use variational arguments to characterize the revenue-maximizing allocation policy. The associated optimal prices are of secondary importance, since they are determined by the implementation conditions. This is an illustration of the famous payoff equivalence theorem, going back to the work of Vickrey (1961) and Myerson (1981).

Although the optimal prices generally depend on the composition of inventory, our main result is that at each point in time, the revenue-maximizing allocation policy depends only on the size of the available inventory, and not on its exact composition. We conclude with applications to the larger optimization problem where, before sales begin, the seller chooses both the size and composition of the inventory, and to a characterization of the price pattern for different qualities in clearance sales.

1.3 Chapter 4: The Stochastic Knapsack Model

Chapter 4 is mainly based on Dizdar, Gershkov, and Moldovanu (2011). We study revenue maximization in a model where agents have multi-unit demand. The nature of the complete-information optimization problem resembles the classical knapsack problem. The knapsack problem is a standard combinatorial optimization problem with numerous practical applications: several objects with known capacity needs (or weights) and known values must be packed in a "knapsack" of given capacity in order to maximize the total value of the included objects. In the dynamic and stochastic version (see Ross and Tsang 1989), objects sequentially arrive over time and their weight/value combination is stochastic but becomes known to the designer at arrival times. Objects cannot be recalled later, so it must be decided upon arrival whether or not an object is to be included. Several such applications are logistic decisions in the freight transportation industry, the allocation of fixed capacities in the travel and leisure industries (e.g., airlines, trains, hotels, and rental cars), the allocation of fixed equipment or personnel in a given period of time (e.g., equipment and personnel for medical procedures in an emergency), the allocation of fixed budgets to investment opportunities that appear sequentially, the allocation of R&D funds to emerging ideas, the allocation of dated advertising space on web portals.

Here we add incomplete information to the dynamic and stochastic setting with heterogeneous capacity requests. This way we obtain a dynamic monopolistic screening problem: there is a finite number of periods, and at each period a request for capacity arrives from an agent that is impatient and privately informed about both his valuation per unit of capacity and the needed capacity.[5] Each agent derives positive utility if he gets the needed capacity (or more), and zero utility otherwise. The designer accepts or rejects the requests in order to maximize the revenue obtained from the allocation.

We first characterize implementable policies, which requires us to deal with a model where information is multidimensional. The theory of multidimensional mechanism design is relatively complex: the main problem is that incentive compatibility—which in the one-dimensional case often reduces to a monotonicity constraint—imposes, besides a monotonicity requirement, an integrability constraint that is not easily included in maximization problems. Next, we solve the revenue-maximization problem for the case where there is private information about per-unit values but weights are observable. After that we derive conditions under which the revenue-maximizing policy for the case with observable weights is implementable, and thus optimal also for the case with two-dimensional private information.

We also construct—for general distributions of weights and values—a time-independent, nonlinear price schedule that is asymptotically revenue-maximizing when the available capacity and the time to the deadline both go to infinity. This extends an earlier result for the case of unit demand by Gallego and van Ryzin, and suggests that complicated dynamic pricing may not be that important for revenue maximization if the distribution of agents' types is known. Our result emphasizes though that nonlinear pricing remains asymptotically important in dynamic settings.

1.4   Chapter 5: Learning and Dynamic Efficiency

Chapter 5 is based on Gershkov and Moldovanu (2009b, 2012, 2013). Although rather rare in the mechanism design literature, the assumption of gradual learning about the environment (which replaces here the standard assumption whereby the agents' values are not known but their distribution is) seems to us descriptive of most real-life dynamic allocation problems. This feature is inconsequential in static models, where an efficient allocation is achieved by the dominant-strategy Vickrey–Clarke–Groves construction, but it leads to new and interesting phenomena in dynamic settings.

The allocation model studied in this part is again based on the classical model due to Derman, Lieberman, and Ross (1972). When learning about the environment takes place, the information revealed by a strategic agent affects both the current and the option values attached by the designer to various allocations. Since option values for the future serve as proxies for the values of allocating resources to other (future) agents, the private values model with learning indirectly generates informational externalities.

Efficient implementation is possible only if the efficient allocation satisfies a monotonicity condition. Intuitively, monotonicity will be satisfied if the optimism about the future distribution of values associated with higher current observation is not too unrealistic. An overly optimistic agent may reveal information and induce a failure of the truthful revelation—if the designer decides, in response, to restrict resources in order to keep them for a more auspious time.

We first derive the direct conditions—that can be checked in applications—on the exogenous parameters of the allocation-cum-learning environment (e.g., conditions on the initial beliefs about the environment and on the learning protocol) that enable the implementation of the first best. We use a Bayesian learning model and two adaptive, non-Bayesian learning models.

We next characterize the optimal policy respecting the incentive constraints (second best). The crucial insight is that the second-best policy is deterministic: instead of a lottery over several feasible qualities, it allocates to each agent type, at each point in time, a well-defined available quality.

Our analysis reveals close, formal connections between our dynamic allocation problems with incomplete information and learning and the classic problem of obtaining optimal stopping policies for search that are characterized by a *reservation price property*. However, our focus on dynamic welfare maximization differs from the extensive literature on dynamic revenue maximization. This literature excludes implementation issues and concentrates instead on intuitive pricing schemes. But, as we show, learning about the environment takes place simultaneously with allocation decisions: not all ad hoc pricing schemes will be generally implementable, and any revenue-maximization scheme must take this fact into account.

1.5 Chapter 6: Long-lived Agents

All models described above have assumed that agents are short lived (while goods are durable). This implies that physical allocations to agents can be made only at the point in time when they arrive. Moreover, because arrivals can be assumed to be observable, a short-lived agent cannot gain by faking (delaying) her arrival time. Allowing for long-lived, strategic agents adds a new layer of complexity, and allows us to describe many new and interesting phenomena that can arise in the different models.

Such distinctions have been neglected by the revenue management practitioners, who have mostly focused instead on short-lived, myopic agents. The reason seems to be technical: a unifying aspect of models with long-lived agents is the need to model information via multidimensional vectors (valuations and arrival times, valuations and departure times and/or deadlines, information at different points in time, etc.). A recurring difficulty is then to come up with general, sufficient conditions for optimality.

We first briefly study the polar case where agents are long lived but objects are short lived, before reviewing several models where both agents and goods are long lived. The analysis is structured the same as above (first we characterize the complete information policy and then discuss implementation issues under incomplete information), but here the basic model is search with recall, whereas the previous models involved search without recall.

One of the earliest and most elegant applications of dynamic mechanism design was made within the context of queue operations (Dolan 1978). In these environments randomly arriving, heterogeneous customers are awarded priorities for using a processing device that can only be used sequentially. We use such a setting to illustrate direct efficient dynamic mechanisms for queue management and the role of the curvature of waiting costs in auctions (indirect mechanisms) for priorities. Deadlines are extreme forms of convex waiting costs, and we also analyze a model where both valuations for the objects and deadlines by which the object must be consumed, are private information.

Finally, we consider another very important class of models where the population itself is fixed and static, while the private information available to the agents evolves dynamically over time. In this class of models we first offer a relatively general treatment of efficient dynamic implementation based on dynamic analogues to the Vickrey–Clarke–Groves mechanism. This treatment is based on the work of Bergemann and Välimäki (2010) and of Athey and Segal (2013). We close this section with the canonical setting of Courty and Li (2000) who considered the revenue-maximization problem of a monopolist seller facing buyers who gradually learn about their valuations over time. The monopolist could, in principle, wait until all information arrives, and then charge the standard monopoly price. But, when early information is related to later information, it turns out that the seller is able to extract additional revenue by a gradual screening of buyers.

Table 1.1 summarizes the main properties of the models analyzed in the various chapters

Table 1.1
Models analyzed in this book

	Designer's goal	Agents	Demand	Supply
Chapter 2	Efficiency	Short-lived, one-unit demand	Known process, stochastic	Heterogeneous objects, fixed
Chapter 3	Revenue	Short-lived, one-unit demand	Known process, stochastic	Heterogeneous objects, optimized
Chapter 4	Revenue	Short-lived, multi-unit demand	Known process, stochastic	Homogeneous objects, fixed
Chapter 5	Efficiency	Short-lived, one-unit demand	Unknown process with learning	Heterogeneous objects, fixed
Chapter 6	Efficiency, revenue	Long-lived, unit demand	Known process, learning, stochastic	Heterogeneous objects, stochastic

Notes

1. The more recent literature is surveyed in Bergemann and Said (2011), who differentiate among models where new agents or new information arrive over time. Of course, there were many antecedents, such as Dolan (1978), Riley and Zeckhauser (1983), or Wang (1993) on arriving agents, and Courty and Li (2000) on arriving information.

2. Several papers in the literature consider more general, abstract models where the solution to the optimization problem is not necessarily available. Thus some of the trade-offs remain implicit.

3. Other differences are the job search model corresponds here to the one object case, and sampling has an explicit cost.

4. Simpler techniques can be applied to the setting where the horizon is infinite and where there is time discounting. We do present below the equivalent of our main result for this situation.

5. Our results are easily extended to the setting where arrivals are stochastic and/or time is continuous.

2 The Sequential Assignment of Heterogeneous Objects

2.1 Introduction

The basic model takes the following form. The designer wants to assign a fixed, finite set of heterogeneous objects to a sequence of randomly arriving agents with privately known characteristics. Monetary transfers are feasible. The objects are substitutes, and each agent derives utility from at most one object. Moreover all agents share a common ranking over the available objects, and values for objects have a multiplicative structure involving the agents' types and objects' qualities.

We first study the discrete-time, complete information case analyzed by Derman, Lieberman, and Ross (1972), and then via *majorization* the relation between the cutoffs appearing in the optimal policy and the order statistics associated with the distribution of values. In continuous time, the efficient dynamic allocation under complete information was subsequently characterized—via a system of differential equations—by Albright (1974). This policy involves partitioning the set of possible agent types. Then an arriving agent gets the first-best available object if his type lies in the highest interval of the partition, the second-best available object if his type lies in the second highest interval, and so on. The intervals depend on the point in time of the arrival, and on the composition of the set of available objects at that point in time.

We next introduce continuous-time models with stochastic arrivals, with both finite and infinite horizons. The cutoff curves defining the efficient policy are derived using appropriate differential equations. We show that an increase in the variability of values or of inter-arrival times leads to an increase in expected welfare in the dynamic assignment problem. The proof of these results uses several simple insights from majorization theory. Majorization by a vector of weighted sums of order statistics plays is also the main way we assess the welfare loss due to the sequential nature of the allocation process versus the scenario where the allocation can be delayed until all arrivals and types have been observed.

We derive associated menus of prices (one menu for each point in time, and for each subset of remaining objects) that implement the efficient allocation. We show that these menus have an appealing recursive structure: each agent who is assigned an object has to pay the value he displaces in terms of the chosen allocation. Thus we obtain a dynamic version of the Vickrey–Clarke–Groves (VCG) mechanism.

Nevertheless, it is not enough to focus on the physical allocation in order to ensure efficiency; one also has to describe what happens to the monetary payments. In some frameworks these accrue to a third party (e.g., a seller in an auction) and physical efficiency is thus what matters. In other settings, the implementation of the efficient physical allocation generates a deficit or a surplus. If there is no third party, then full efficiency calls for a balanced budget. It is well known that in the static setup no VCG mechanism can generally be both individually rational and budget balanced.

For the study of efficient, individually rational and budget-balanced mechanisms in our frameworks, we distinguish between two scenarios: (1) both physical assignments and monetary payments must take place upon the agents' arrival, and (2) payments can be postponed to later stages.

2.2 Models with Complete Information

We start our analysis with a paradigmatic model due to Derman, Lieberman, and Ross (1972). In their model several heterogeneous objects, ordered—in terms of quality, are allocated over time to sequentially arriving agents. The designer maximizes the expected welfare of agents, which is sum of their utilities. There is complete information and the only "friction" is due to the sequentiality: allocating an object today means that it cannot be allocated in the future, possibly to an agent that values it more.

2.2.1 Discrete-Time Model

We start with the original, discrete-time formulation where one agent arrives per period, before analyzing the continuous-time version with random arrivals.

We let period n denote the first period, period $n-1$ denote the second period, and period 1 denote the last period. There are n agents who arrive sequentially, one agent per period. There are m items. Each item $i = 1, \ldots, m$ is characterized by a "quality" q_i with $0 \leq q_m \leq q_{m-1} \leq \ldots \leq q_1$. Without loss of generality, we can assume that $n = m$. (If $m > n$, then only the n items with highest qualities are relevant for our study; if $m < n$, then we add $n - m$ dummy objects with quality $q = 0$.)

The agents can be served only upon arrival. After an item is assigned, it cannot be reallocated. Each agent is characterized by a "type" x_j, and agents' types are governed by IID random variables $X_i = X$ on $[0, +\infty)$ with a common cdf, F. We assume that X has a finite mean, denoted by μ, and a finite variance.

Types are observable to the designer upon the agents' respective arrival (thus at each point in time there is uncertainty about the types of agents arriving in the future). If an item with type $q_i \geq 0$ is assigned to an agent with type x_j, this agent enjoys a utility of $q_i x_j$. The designer wants to assign the items to the arriving agents in such a way as to maximize the expectation of the sum of agents' utilities.

Theorem 1 (Derman, Lieberman, and Ross 1972) *Consider the arrival of an agent with type x_k in period $k \geq 1$. There exist $k + 1$ constants $0 = a_{k,k} \leq a_{k-1,k} \leq \ldots \leq a_{1,k} \leq a_{0,k} = \infty$ such that:*

1. *the dynamically efficient policy assigns the item with quality q_i if $x_k \in (a_{i,k}, a_{i-1,k}]$, where q_i is the ith highest quality among the available objects in period k;*

2. *in a problem with n periods the total expected welfare is given by*

$$W_n = \sum_{i=1}^{n} q_i a_{i,n+1}. \tag{2.1}$$

The remarkable part of the preceding result is that the precise values of the available qualities do not play any role for the allocation policy. It is also interesting to compare the characterization above to the one in the static case where all agents arrive at once. In that case we obtain a standard matching problem, and the efficient assignment among types and objects is *assortative*, meaning that the agent with the i-highest type gets the object with the i-highest quality. Thus the expected welfare in the static case is given by

$$W_n^s = \sum_{i=1}^{n} q_i \mu_{i,n}, \tag{2.2}$$

where $\mu_{i,k}$ denotes the expectation of the ith highest order statistic out of k copies of X. For the comparison between the dynamic and static case we need the following definition of vector variability, due to Hardy, Littlewood, and Pólya (1934):

Definition 1

1. *For any vector* $\gamma = (\gamma_1, \gamma_2, \ldots, \gamma_k)$, *let* $\gamma_{(j)}$, *denote the jth largest co-ordinate so that* $\gamma_{(k)} \leq \gamma_{(k-1)} \leq \ldots \leq \gamma_{(1)}$. *We say that vector* $\alpha = (\alpha_1, \alpha_2, \ldots, \alpha_n)$ *is* majorized *by vector* $\beta = (\beta_1, \beta_2, \ldots, \beta_n)$, *and we write* $\alpha \prec \beta$ *if the following system of* $n - 1$ *inequalities and one equality is satisfied:*

$$\alpha_{(1)} \leq \beta_{(1)},$$
$$\alpha_{(1)} + \alpha_{(2)} \leq \beta_{(1)} + \beta_{(2)},$$
$$\ldots, \alpha_{(1)} + \alpha_{(2)} + \ldots \alpha_{(n-1)} \leq \beta_{(1)} + \beta_{(2)} + \beta_{(n-1)}$$
$$\alpha_{(1)} + \alpha_{(2)} + \ldots + \alpha_{(n)} = \beta_{(1)} + \beta_{(2)} + \ldots + \beta_{(n)}$$

2. *We say that* α *is* weakly sub-majorized *by* β *and we write* $\alpha \prec_w \beta$ *if all relations above hold with weak inequality.*

3. *Let* $S \subseteq \mathbb{R}^n$. *A function* $\Psi : S \to \mathbb{R}$ *is called* Schur-convex *on the domain* S *if* $\alpha \prec \beta \Rightarrow \Psi(\alpha) \leq \Psi(\beta)$ *for* $\alpha, \beta \in S$.

A well-known characterization of Schur-convexity is the following:

Theorem 2 (Marshall and Olkin 1979) *Assume that* $\Psi : \mathbb{R}^n \to \mathbb{R}$ *is symmetric and has continuous partial derivatives. Then* Ψ *is Schur-convex if and only if for all* $(y_1, \ldots, y_n) \in \mathbb{R}^n$ *and all* $i, j \in \{1, \ldots, n\}$ *it holds that*

$$\left(\frac{\partial \Psi(y_1, \ldots, y_n)}{\partial y_i} - \frac{\partial \Psi(y_1, \ldots, y_n)}{\partial y_j} \right)(y_i - y_j) \geq 0.$$

We can now state:

Theorem 3 *For each* n, *the vector* $\{a_{i,n+1}\}_{i=1}^n$ *is majorized by the vector* $\{\mu_{i,n}\}_{i=1}^n$.

Proof Assume first that all available qualities are equal, say $q_i = 1$ for all i. Then sequential arrivals do not impose any loss of welfare. Thus formulas (2.1) and (2.2) yield the one equality needed in the definition of majorization. In order to prove that all required inequalities hold, note that expected welfare in the dynamic case—where assignment "mistakes" occur because of the sequential arrival—can never be higher than the welfare attained in the static case. The result follows by applying formulas (2.1) and (2.2) to the $n - 1$ vector of qualities of the form $(1, 0, \ldots, 0), (1, 1, 0, \ldots, 0), \ldots, (1, 1, 1, \ldots, 0)$. ∎

2.2.2 Continuous-Time Model with Stochastic Arrivals

We assume now that time is continuous, and that agents arrive according to a (possibly nonhomogeneous) Poisson arrival process with intensity $\lambda(t)$, and each can only be served upon arrival (i.e., agents are impatient). **Here we count time chronologically; that is the process starts at time 0.** For some results we relax the Poisson assumption, and we allow for a more general renewal stochastic process to describe arrivals.

If an item of quality q_i is assigned to an agent with type x_j at time t, then the utility for the designer is given by $r(t)q_i x_j$, where r is a piecewise continuous, nonnegative, nonincreasing discount function that satisfies $r(0) = 1$. We denote by $q_{(i:\Pi_t)}$ the ith highest element of Π_t, which is the set of the available objects at time t. We denote by k_t the cardinality of Π_t.

Albright (1974) characterized the allocation policy that maximizes the total expected welfare from the designer's point of view . His main result is:

Theorem 4 (Albright 1974)   *There exist m unique functions $y_m(t) \leq y_{n-1}(t) \leq \ldots \leq y_1(t)$, $\forall t$, that do not depend on the q's such that:*

1. if an agent with type x arrives at a time t, it is optimal to assign to that agent $q_{(j:\Pi_t)}$ if $x \in [y_j(t), y_{j-1}(t))$, where $y_0 \equiv \infty$, and not to assign any object if $x < y_{k_t}(t)$;

2. for each k, the function $y_k(t)$ satisfies

    a. $\lim_{t\to\infty} r(t)y_k(t) = 0$;

    b. $\frac{d[r(t)y_k(t)]}{dt} = -\lambda(t)r(t) \int\limits_{y_k}^{y_{k-1}} (1 - F(x))dx \leq 0$;

3. the expected welfare starting from time t is given by $\left[r(t) \sum_{i=1}^{k_t} q_{(i:\Pi_t)} y_i(t) \right]$.

Again, the interesting element in the preceding result is that the dynamic welfare-maximizing cutoff curves $y_j(t)$ do not depend on the items' characteristics. Since selling one object is equivalent to exchanging one of the currently available items with an item having a type equal to zero, the observation above implies that after any sale at time t, the $k_t - 1$ curves that determine the optimal allocation from time t on, coincide with the $k_t - 1$ highest curves that were relevant for the decision at time t.

Deadline Model   We assume here that there is a deadline T after which all objects perish. The discount rate satisfies

$$r(t) = \begin{cases} 1 & \text{if } 0 \leq t \leq T, \\ 0 & \text{if } t > T. \end{cases}$$

It is then obvious that the dynamically efficient policy needs to satisfy

$$y_1(T) = y_2(T) = \ldots = y_m(T) = 0.$$

Example 1 *Assume that there are three objects, that the arrival process is homogeneous with rate $\lambda(t) = 1$, and that the distribution of agents' types is exponential, meaning $F(x) = 1 - e^{-x}$. By theorem 4, we obtain the following system of differential equations that characterize the cutoff curves in the dynamic welfare-maximizing policy:*

$$y_1' = -\int_{y_1}^{\infty} e^{-x} dx = -e^{-y_1},$$

$$y_2' = -\int_{y_2}^{y_1} e^{-x} dx = e^{-y_1} - e^{-y_2},$$

$$y_3' = -\int_{y_3}^{y_2} e^{-x} dx = e^{-y_2} - e^{-y_3},$$

with initial conditions $y_1(T) = y_2(T) = y_3(T) = 0$. The solution to this system is given by

$$y_1(t) = \ln(1 + T - t),$$
$$y_2(t) = \ln\left(1 + \frac{(T-t)^2}{2(1+T-t)}\right),$$
$$y_3(t) = \ln\left(1 + \frac{(T-t)^3}{3[(T-t)^2 + 2(1+T-t)]}\right).$$

Figure 2.1 depicts the solution for $T = 5$.

Our main result here shows that an increase in the variability of the distribution of the agents' values (while keeping a constant mean) increases expected welfare. We want to emphasize here that this result holds even if all available objects are identical! For the proof, which again uses majorization, we first need a well-known lemma:

Lemma 1 *Let $\alpha = (\alpha_1, \alpha_2, \ldots, \alpha_n)$ and $\beta = (\beta_1, \beta_2, \ldots, \beta_n)$ be two n-tuples such that $\sum_{i=1}^{n} \alpha_i = \sum_{i=1}^{n} \beta_i$. Then $\alpha \prec \beta$ if and only if $\sum_{i=1}^{n} q_i \alpha_{(i)} \leq \sum_{i=1}^{n} q_i \beta_{(i)}$ for any constants $q_n \leq q_{n-1} \leq \cdots \leq q_1$.*

Proof Assume that $\sum_{i=1}^{n} q_i \alpha_{(i)} \leq \sum_{i=1}^{n} q_i \beta_{(i)}$ for any $q_n \leq q_{n-1} \leq \cdots \leq q_1$. For each $k = 1, 2, \ldots, n-1$ consider $q^k = (q_1^k, q_2^k, \ldots, q_n^k)$, where $q_i^k = 1$ for $i = 1, 2, \ldots k$, and $q_i^k = 0$ for $i = k+1, k+2, \ldots, n$. Then for each k

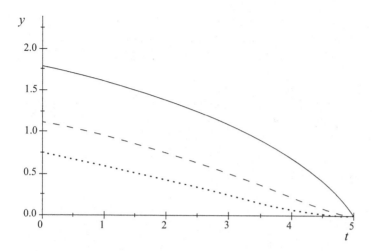

Figure 2.1
y_1 solid line; y_2 dashed line; y_3 dotted line

we obtain

$$\sum_{i=1}^{n} q_i^k \alpha_{(i)} \leq \sum_{i=1}^{n} q_i^k \beta_{(i)} \Leftrightarrow \sum_{i=1}^{k} \alpha_{(i)} \leq \sum_{i=1}^{k} \beta_{(i)},$$

and thus $\alpha \prec \beta$.

Assume $\alpha \prec \beta$, and let $q_n \leq q_{n-1} \leq \ldots \leq q_1$. Then we have the following chain:

$$\sum_{i=1}^{n} q_i [\beta_{(i)} - \alpha_{(i)}] = q_n \sum_{i=1}^{n} [\beta_{(i)} - \alpha_{(i)}] + \sum_{i=1}^{n-1} (q_i - q_n)[\beta_{(i)} - \alpha_{(i)}]$$

$$= q_n \sum_{i=1}^{n} [\beta_{(i)} - \alpha_{(i)}] + (q_{n-1} - q_n) \sum_{i=1}^{n-1} [\beta_{(i)} - \alpha_{(i)}]$$

$$+ \sum_{i=1}^{n-2} (q_i - q_{n-1})[\beta_{(i)} - \alpha_{(i)}]$$

$$\vdots$$

$$= q_n \sum_{i=1}^{n} [\beta_{(i)} - \alpha_{(i)}] + \sum_{j=1}^{n-1} (q_j - q_{j+1})(\sum_{i=1}^{j} [\beta_{(i)} - \alpha_{(i)}])$$

$$\geq 0.$$

The last inequality follows since (1) $\sum_{i=1}^{n} [\beta_{(i)} - \alpha_{(i)}] = \sum_{i=1}^{n} \beta_i - \sum_{i=1}^{n} \alpha_i = 0$ by definition, (2) $\forall j$, $q_j - q_{j-1} \geq 0$ by definition, and (3) $\forall j$, $\sum_{i=1}^{j} [\beta_{(i)} - \alpha_{(i)}] \geq 0$ by majorization. ∎

Theorem 5 *Consider two distributions of agents' types F and G such that $\mu_F = \mu_G = \mu$ and such that F second-order stochastically dominates G (in particular F has a lower variance than G). Then it holds that:*

1. $\sum_{i=1}^{k} y_i^F(t) \leq \sum_{i=1}^{k} y_i^G(t), \forall k, t;$
2. *for any time t and for any set of available objects at $t, \Pi_t \neq \emptyset$, the expected welfare in the efficient dynamic allocation under F is lower than that under G.*

Proof (1) By theorem 4, we know that

$$\frac{d(\sum_{i=1}^{k} y_i^F(t))}{dt} = -\lambda(t) \int_{y_k^F(t)}^{\infty} (1 - F(x)) dx,$$

$$\frac{d(\sum_{i=1}^{k} y_i^G(t))}{dt} = -\lambda(t) \int_{y_k^G(t)}^{\infty} (1 - G(x)) dx.$$

Define first $H_F(s) = \int_s^{\infty} (1 - F(x)) dx$ and $H_G(s) = \int_s^{\infty} (1 - G(x)) dx.$ These are both positive, decreasing functions with $H_F(0) = H_G(0) = \mu$. By SSD, for any $s \geq 0$ it holds that

$$\int_0^s F(x) dx \leq \int_0^s G(x) dx \Leftrightarrow \int_0^s (1 - F(x))) \, dx \geq \int_0^s (1 - G(x))) \, dx$$

$$\Leftrightarrow \int_s^{\infty} (1 - F(x)) dx \leq \int_s^{\infty} (1 - G(x)) dx \Leftrightarrow H_F(s) \leq H_G(s),$$

where the second line follows because

$$\int_0^{\infty} (1 - F(x)) dx = \mu_F = \mu_G = \int_0^{\infty} (1 - G(x)) dx.$$

Thus the curve H_F is always below H_G. Consider now $y_1^F(t)$ and $y_1^G(t)$. These are, respectively, the solutions to the differential equations

$$y' = -\lambda(t) H_F(y) \quad \text{and} \quad y' = -\lambda(t) H_G(y)$$

with boundary condition $y(T) = 0$. Integrating these equations from t to T, and using the boundary condition, we get the integral equations

$$y(T) - y(t) = -\int_t^T \lambda(s)H_F(y(s))ds \Leftrightarrow y(t) = \int_t^T \lambda(s)H_F(y(s))ds \quad \text{and}$$

$$y(T) - y(t) = -\int_t^T \lambda(s)H_G(y(s))ds \Leftrightarrow y(t) = \int_t^T \lambda(s)H_G(y(s))ds.$$

Because H_F is always below H_G and because these are decreasing functions, we obtain $y_1^F(t) \le y_1^G(t)$.

Consider now $y_1^F(t) + y_2^F(t)$ and $y_1^G(t) + y_2^G(t)$. These functions satisfy the differential equations

$$y' = -\lambda(t) \int_{y-y_1^F(t)}^\infty (1 - F(x))dx \quad \text{and} \quad y' = -\lambda(t) \int_{y-y_1^G(t)}^\infty (1 - F(x))dx$$

with boundary condition $y(T) = 0$. Integrating from t to T yields the equations

$$y(t) = \int_t^T \lambda(s)\left[\int_{y(s)-y_1^F(s)}^\infty (1 - F(x))dx\right]ds = \int_t^T \lambda(s)H_F[(y(s) - y_1^F(s)]\,ds,$$

$$y(t) = \int_t^T \lambda(s)\left[\int_{y(s)-y_1^G(s)}^\infty (1 - G(x))dx\right]ds = \int_t^T \lambda(s)H_G[(y(s) - y_1^G(s)]\,ds.$$

We have

$$H_F[(y(t) - y_1^F(t)] \le H_F[(y(t) - y_1^G(t)] \le H_G[(y(t) - y_1^G(t)], \qquad \forall t,$$

where the first inequality follows because $y_1^F(t) \le y_1^G(t) \Leftrightarrow y(t) - y_1^F(t) \ge y(t) - y_1^G(t)$ and because the function H_F is decreasing, and the second inequality follows because H_F is always below H_G. This yields $y_1^F(t) + y_2^F(t) \le y_1^G(t) + y_2^G(t)$, as required. The rest of the proof follows analogously.

(2) The expected welfare terms at time t if there are $|\Pi_t| = k$ are given by $\sum_{i=1}^k q_{(i:\Pi_t)}y_i^F(t)$ and by $\sum_{i=1}^k q_{(i:\Pi_t)}y_i^G(t)$, respectively. By point 1, we know that for each k and for each time t, $y^{kF}(t) = (y_1^F(t), y_2^F(t), \ldots, y_k^F(t)) \prec_w (y_1^G(t), y_2^G(t), \ldots, y_k^G(t)) := y^{kG}(t)$. By result (12.5 b) in Pecaric, Proschan, and Tong (1992), for each k and each t there exists a k-vector $z(t)$

such that $z(t) \prec y^{kG}(t)$ and such that $z_i(t) \geq y_i^F$, $\forall i$. We obtain then

$$\sum_{i=1}^{k} q_{(i:\Pi_t)} y_i^F(t) \leq \sum_{i=1}^{k} q_{(i:\Pi_t)} z_i(t) \leq \sum_{i=1}^{k} q_{(i:\Pi_t)} y_i^G(t), \qquad \forall k, t,$$

where the last inequality follows since $\alpha \prec \beta$ if and only if $\sum_{i=1}^{n} q_i \alpha_{(i)} \leq \sum_{i=1}^{n} q_i \beta_{(i)}$ for any constants $q_n \leq q_{n-1} \leq \ldots \leq q_1$ by lemma 1.   ∎

A main application of theorem 5 follows. For a constant arrival rate, the system of differential equations that characterizes the efficient dynamic allocation can be solved explicitly for any number of objects if the distribution of the agents' types is exponential (see the example above), while this is rarely the case for other distributions. Together with the preceding result, that solution can be used to bound the optimal policy and the associated welfare for large, nonparametric classes of distributions. We first need the following definition:

Definition 2 *A nonnegative random variable X is said to be new better than used in expectation (NBUE, new worse than used in expectation, NWUE) if*

$$E[X - a \mid X > a] \leq (\geq) E[X], \qquad \forall a \geq 0.$$

A nonnegative random variable X is said to have an increasing failure rate (IFR; decreasing failure rate, DFR) if the function $\frac{f(a)}{1-F(a)}$ is increasing (decreasing), where F is the cumulative distribution function governing X, and where f is the associated density.

The concepts comes from *reliability theory* where X represents the stochastic lifetime of a certain component. The term $E[X - a \mid X > a]$ is the expected remaining lifetime given that the component has functioned for a given period a. The failure rate $\frac{f(a)}{1-F(a)}$ is the instantaneous probability that the component fails at time a given that it has functioned so far. The classes of NBUE (NWUE) distributions are large and contain many of the distributions that appear in applications. Any distribution with an *increasing failure (or hazard) rate* is NBUE, while any distribution with a *decreasing failure rate* is NWUE. The exponential distribution belongs to the intersection of all these classes.

Corollary 1 *Let F, the distribution of agents' types, be NBUE (NWUE) with mean μ. Then, for any t and $\Pi_t \neq \varnothing$, the expected welfare in the efficient dynamic allocation under F is lower (higher) than that under the exponential distribution $G(x) = 1 - e^{-\frac{x}{\mu}}$.*

Proof The result follows directly from theorem 5 by noting that F second-order stochastically dominates $G(x) = 1 - e^{-x/\mu}$ (is second-order stochastically dominated by $G(x) = 1 - e^{-x/\mu}$) if and only if F is NBUE (NWUE). This is theorem 8.6.1 in Ross (1983). In other words,

$$\forall y \geq 0, \int_y^\infty (1 - F(x))dx \leq (\geq)\mu e^{-x/\mu} \text{ if } F \text{ is NBUE (NWUE)}.$$

■

Example 2 *Let $F(x) = x$ on $[0, 1]$ so that F is IFR, and thus NBUE, and let $\lambda(t) = 1$. Assume that there is one object with type $p_1 = 1$. The optimal cutoff curve satisfies*

$$y'_F = -\int_{y_F}^1 (1 - x)dx = -\frac{1}{2} + y_F - \frac{y_F^2}{2}$$

with initial condition $y_F(T) = 0$. The solution to this differential equation is

$$y_F(t) = 1 - \frac{2}{T - t + 2}.$$

Figure 2.2 illustrates the corollary for $T = 5$: $y_F(t) = 1 - \frac{2}{7-t}$ is the dashed line, $y_G(t) = \frac{1}{2}\ln[6 - t]$ is the solid line corresponding to the exponential distribution $G(x) = 1 - e^{-2x}$ with mean $\frac{1}{2}$.

Loss due to Sequentiality Suppose that at time t there are m objects left, with qualities $q_1 \geq q_2 \geq \ldots \geq q_m$. Instead of the original formulation,

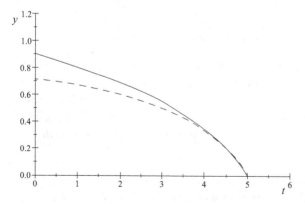

Figure 2.2
$y_F(t) = 1 - \frac{2}{7-t}$ dashed line; $y_G(t) = \frac{1}{2}\ln[6 - t]$ solid line

consider now the scenario where the allocation decision to all subsequently arriving agents can be made at time T (the deadline) where their precise number and types are known. At time T a welfare-maximizing designer will allocate the object with the highest quality to the agent with the highest type, the object with the second highest quality to the agent with the second highest type, and so on (assortative matching). This means that the expected welfare at time t is given by $\sum_{i=1}^{m} q_i z_i(t)$, where $z_i(t)$ represents the expected type of an agent that arrives after t and that get assigned to the object with the ith highest quality. In order to calculate the $z_i(t)$ terms, let $X_{(i,l)}$ denote the ith-order statistic out of l copies of X, and denote by $\mu_{i,l}$ its expectation (note that $\mu_{l,l}$ is the expectation of the maximum or highest order statistic).

We assume here for simplicity that arrivals follow a homogeneous Poisson process with rate λ. The argument is easily extended to non-homogeneous processes.

Let $\Pr_l(t) = e^{-\lambda(T-t)} \frac{\lambda^l(T-t)^l}{l!}$ be the probability that there will be l arrivals, $l \geq 1$, after time t. Given assortative matching at time T, we obtain[1]

$$z_i(t) = \sum_{l=i}^{\infty} \Pr_l(t) \mu_{l-i+1,l}$$

$$= e^{-\lambda(T-t)} \sum_{l=i}^{\infty} \frac{\lambda^l(T-t)^l \mu_{l-i+1,l}}{l!}, \qquad i = 1, 2, \ldots, m.$$

Our next result establishes a relation between the m-vector of optimal dynamic cutoffs $\{y_i(t)\}_{i=1}^{m}$ and the m-vector of the corresponding static expected types $\{z_i(t)\}_{i=1}^{m}$. Intuitively,

$$\sum_{i=1}^{m} q_i[y_i(t) - z_i(t)]$$

measures the welfare loss due to the sequentiality constraint.

Theorem 6 *For any period t, and for any n, the vector $\{y_i(t)\}_{i=1}^{m}$ of optimal cutoffs in the welfare-maximizing sequential allocation of m objects to agents arriving according to a Poisson process with parameter λ is weakly sub-majorized by the vector $\{z_i(t)\}_{i=1}^{m}$. Moreover $\lim_{m \to \infty} \sum_{i=1}^{m} y_i(t) = \lim_{m \to \infty} \sum_{i=1}^{m} z_i(t) = \lambda(T-t)\mu$, where μ is the mean of the distribution of agents' types.*

Proof Consider a situation with $k \leq m$ identical objects available at time t. For any particular realization of arrivals and agents' types from period t on, welfare in the case where the decision can be delayed until the entire realization has been observed is given by $\sum_{i=1}^{k} z_i(t)$. Consider now the original sequential assignment problem where agents arrive according to a Poisson process, and allocations must be made upon arrival. By theorem 4, the expected total welfare is then given by $\sum_{i=1}^{k} y_i(t)$. For any realization of arrivals and types, this total welfare cannot be larger than that obtained in the previous scenario where allocations can be delayed since mistakes may have occurred due to the constraints of sequentiality, meaning an agent with a lower type was served although there was another arrival with a higher type. In other words, any allocation obtained in the sequential process can be replicated when delayed allocations are possible. This yields $\sum_{i=1}^{k} y_i(t) \leq \sum_{i=1}^{k} z_i(t), \forall k \leq m$, as required.

The second part follows by considering the limit when the number of identical objects tends to infinity. In that limit, all arriving agents should be served, and there is no welfare loss due to the sequentiality constraint. By theorem 4, we know that

$$\frac{d[\sum_{i=1}^{m} y_i(s)]}{ds} = -\lambda \int_{y_m(s)}^{\infty} (1 - F(x))dx.$$

Integrating the expression above between t and T and recalling that $\sum_{i=1}^{m} y_i(T) = 0$ yields

$$\sum_{i=1}^{m} y_i(t) = \lambda \int_t^T \left(\int_{y_m(s)}^{\infty} (1 - F(x))dx \right) ds.$$

Taking the limit with respect to m, we finally obtain

$$\lim_{m \to \infty} \sum_{i=1}^{m} y_i(t) = \lim_{m \to \infty} \lambda \int_t^T \left(\int_{y_m(s)}^{\infty} (1 - F(x))dx \right) ds$$

$$= \lambda \int_t^T \left(\int_0^{\infty} (1 - F(x))dx \right) ds = \lambda(T - t)\mu,$$

where the second line follows since $\lim_{m \to \infty} y_m(t) = 0$ uniformly. ∎

If the number of homogeneous objects m is large, sequentiality does not cause any welfare loss, since any arriving agent should get an object. The limit expression is intuitive: for each arrival, expected welfare is given by the average type μ, and $\lambda(T - t)$ is the expected number of arrivals.

Finally, we note here that theorem 5 has an analogous counterpart for the static cutoffs $z_i(t)$. The proof uses then a recent result about majorization of mean order statistics due to De La Cal and Caracamo (2006).

Infinite Horizon Model   Let us assume that the time horizon is potentially infinite and that $r(t) = e^{-\alpha t}$. Given this "memoryless" specification, the arrival process can be more general, and it is assumed here to be a *renewal* process with a general inter-arrival distribution B.This is a generalization of the Poisson process where the inter-arrival distribution is assumed to be exponential.[2] We start with a simple example that illustrates the main insight: the *stationarity* of the welfare-maximizing dynamic policy. We first need the following definition:

Definition 3   *Let* $t \geq 0$. *The Laplace transform of a function* $g(t)$ *is defined by*

$$G(s) = \int\limits_0^\infty e^{-st} g(t) dt.$$

Example 3   *Let the arrival process be Poisson with rate* λ, *that is,* $B(t) = 1 - e^{-\lambda t}$, *and let* $\widetilde{B}$ *denote the Laplace transform of the inter-arrival distribution* B. *Note that*

$$\widetilde{B}(\alpha) = \int\limits_0^\infty e^{-\alpha t} \lambda e^{-\lambda t} dt = \frac{\lambda}{\alpha + \lambda}$$

and that

$$\frac{\widetilde{B}(\alpha)}{1 - \widetilde{B}(\alpha)} = \frac{\lambda}{\alpha}.$$

The Laplace transform $\widetilde{B}(\alpha)$ *acts here as the effective discount rate. It represents the discounted value of one unit at the expected time of the next arrival. Consider now the the differential equation (see theorem 4) defining the efficient allocation curve for the case of one object* $y_1(t)$:

$$\frac{d[r(t) y_1(t)]}{dt} = -\lambda r(t) \int\limits_{y_1}^\infty (1 - F(x)) dx.$$

Plugging $r(t) = e^{-\alpha t}$, *we get*

$$(y_1' - \alpha y_1) = -\lambda \int\limits_{y_1}^\infty (1 - F(x)) dx.$$

Assuming now that $y_1' = 0$ yields

$$y_1 = \frac{\lambda}{\alpha} \int_{y_1}^{\infty} (1 - F(x))dx = \frac{\widetilde{B}(\alpha)}{1 - \widetilde{B}(\alpha)} \int_{y_1}^{\infty} (1 - F(x))dx.$$

On $[0, \tau]$, the interval of definition of the distribution of types F the identity function on the left-hand side, y_1, increases from 0 to τ while the function $\frac{\lambda}{\alpha} \int_{y_1}^{\infty} (1 - F(x))dx$ decreases in y_1 from $\frac{\lambda}{\alpha}\mu$ (where μ is the mean of F) to 0. Thus there is a unique intersection point, and the equation above has a unique solution y_1^*. Since $\lim_{t \to \infty} e^{-\alpha t} y_1^* = 0$, we obtain that the efficient dynamic cutoff curve is indeed described by the constant y_1^*. The derivations for more items follow analogously.

More generally, the complete-information efficient dynamic assignment turns out to be stationary, and it is characterized in the following theorem:

Theorem 7 (Albright 1974) *Assume that $r(t) = e^{-\alpha t}$. The efficient allocation curves are constants (i.e., independent of time) $y_m \le y_{n-1} \le \ldots \le y_1$. These constants do not depend on the q's, and are given by the implicit recursion:*

$$(y_k + y_{k-1} + \ldots + y_1) = \frac{\widetilde{B}(\alpha)}{1 - \widetilde{B}(\alpha)} \int_{y_k}^{\infty} (1 - F(x))dx, \qquad 1 \le k \le m,$$

where $\widetilde{B}$ is the Laplace-transform of the inter-arrival distribution B.

The analogue of theorem 5 for this case is:

Theorem 8 *Consider two distributions of agents' types F and G such that $\mu_F = \mu_G = \mu$ and such that F second-order stochastically dominates G (in particular F has a lower variance than G). Then, for any fixed inter-arrival distribution B, it holds that:*

1. $\sum_{i=1}^{k} y_i^F \le \sum_{i=1}^{k} y_i^G, \forall k$;

2. for any t and any $\Pi_t \ne \emptyset$ the expected welfare in the efficient dynamic allocation under F is lower than that under G.

Proof (1) Define first $H_F(s) = \frac{\tilde{B}(\alpha)}{1-\tilde{B}(\alpha)} \int\limits_s^\infty (1 - F(x))dx$ and $H_G(s) =$

$\frac{\tilde{B}(\alpha)}{1-\tilde{B}(\alpha)} \int\limits_s^\infty (1 - G(x))dx$. These are both decreasing functions and

$$H_F(0) = H_G(0) = \frac{\tilde{B}(\alpha)}{1 - \tilde{B}(\alpha)} \mu.$$

Consider now y_1^F and y_1^G. These are, respectively, the solutions to the equations:

$$s = H_F(s) \quad \text{and} \quad s = H_G(s)$$

By SSD, for any $s \geq 0$ it holds that

$$\int\limits_0^s F(x))dx \leq \int\limits_0^s G(x))dx \Leftrightarrow \int\limits_0^s (1 - F(x))) \, dx \geq \int\limits_0^s (1 - G(x))) \, dx$$

$$\Leftrightarrow \int\limits_s^\infty (1 - F(x))dx \leq \int\limits_s^\infty (1 - G(x))dx \Leftrightarrow H_F(s) \leq H_G(s)$$

Thus the decreasing curve $H_F(s)$ is always below the decreasing curve $H_G(s)$, so we obtain $y_F^1 \leq y_G^1$. Consider now y_2^F and y_2^G, which are defined by the equations

$$y_2^F + y_1^F = \frac{\tilde{B}(\alpha)}{1 - \tilde{B}(\alpha)} \int\limits_{y_2^F}^\infty (1 - F(x))dx,$$

$$y_2^G + y_1^G = \frac{\tilde{B}(\alpha)}{1 - \tilde{B}(\alpha)} \int\limits_{y_2^G}^\infty (1 - G(x))dx.$$

Equivalently, $y_2^F + y_2^F$ and $y_2^G + y_1^G$ are, respectively, the solutions of

$$s = H_F(s - y_1^F) \quad \text{and} \quad s = H_G(s - y_1^G).$$

Recalling that $y_1^F \leq y_1^G$, we obtain $s - y_1^F \geq s - y_1^G$, $\forall s$. This yields

$$H_F(s - y_1^F) \leq H_F(s - y_1^G) \leq H_G(s - y_1^G),$$

where the first inequality follows because the function H_F is decreasing, and the second inequality follows by SSD. Thus the curve $H_F(s - y_1^G)$ is always below the curve $H_G(s - y_1^G)$ and the result follows as above. The rest of the proof is completely analogous.

(2) The expected welfare terms from time t on if k objects left are given by $e^{-\alpha t}\left[\sum_{i=1}^{k} q_{(i)} y_i^F\right]$ and by $e^{-\alpha t}\left[\sum_{i=1}^{k} q_{(i)} y_i^G\right]$, respectively. The proof proceeds exactly as that of theorem 5, condition 2. ∎

In addition to theorem 8 on the benefits of increased variability in the agents' types, we now obtain a comparative-statics result about the benefits of variability in arrival times. Interestingly, this next result holds for a stochastic order that is much weaker than second-order stochastic dominance.

Definition 4 (Shaked and Shanthikumar 2007) *Let X, Y be two nonnegative random variables. X is said to be smaller than Y in the Laplace transform order, denoted by $X \leq_{Lt} Y$, if*

$$E[e^{-sX}] \geq E[e^{-sY}] \qquad \text{for all } s > 0.$$

Theorem 9 *Consider two inter-arrival distributions B and E such that $B \geq_{Lt} E$. Then, for any fixed distribution of agents' characteristics F, it holds that*

1. $\sum_{i=1}^{k} y_i^B \leq \sum_{i=1}^{k} y_i^E, \forall k$;
2. *for any t and for any $\Pi_t \neq \emptyset$, the expected welfare in the efficient dynamic allocation under B is lower than that under E.*

Proof (1) Let

$$H_B(s) = \frac{\widetilde{B}(\alpha)}{1 - \widetilde{B}(\alpha)} \int_s^{\infty} (1 - F(x))dx,$$

$$H_E(s) = \frac{\widetilde{E}(\alpha)}{1 - \widetilde{E}(\alpha)} \int_s^{\infty} (1 - F(x))dx,$$

where $\widetilde{B}$ and $\widetilde{E}$ are the respective Laplace transforms. By the definition of the Laplace transform, and by the assumption that $B \geq_{Lt} E$, we know that $\widetilde{B}(\alpha) \leq \widetilde{E}(\alpha)$. This yields

$$\widetilde{B}(\alpha) \leq \widetilde{E}(\alpha) \Leftrightarrow \frac{\widetilde{B}(\alpha)}{1 - \widetilde{B}(\alpha)} \leq \frac{\widetilde{E}(\alpha)}{1 - \widetilde{E}(\alpha)} \Leftrightarrow H_B(s) \leq H_E(s).$$

The first equivalence follows because the function $x/(1 - x)$ is increasing on the interval $[0, 1)$ with $\lim_{x \to 1} x/(1 - x) = \infty$, and because Laplace transforms take values in the interval $[0, 1]$.

Thus we have learned that the decreasing function $H_B(s)$ is always below the decreasing function $H_E(s)$. Consider first y_1^B and y_1^E. These are, respectively, the solutions to the equations $s = H_B(s)$ and $s = H_E(s)$. The rest of the proof continues analogously to the proof of theorem 5.   ∎

Again, we can apply the comparative-static results above in order to bound the optimal cutoff curves and the associated expected welfare for large classes of distributions of the agents' types and of the inter-arrival times.

Corollary 2 *For any t and for any $\Pi_t \neq \emptyset$ we have the following welfare comparisons:*

1. *for any fixed distribution of inter-arrival times, the expected welfare under an NBUE(NWUE) distribution of agents' types with mean μ is lower (higher) than the expected welfare under the exponential distribution $G(t) = 1 - e^{-t/\mu}$;*

2. *for any fixed distribution of agents' types, the expected welfare under an NBUE(NWUE) distribution of inter-arrival times with mean μ is lower (higher) than the expected welfare under a Poisson arrival process with rate $1/\mu$.*

Proof The first claims follows from theorems 8, from the fact that NBUE (NWUE) distributions second-order stochastically dominate (are dominated by) an exponential distribution with the same mean (see also the proof of corollary 1). The second claim follows from theorem 9, from the observation above, and from the fact that second-order stochastic dominance implies domination in the Laplace transform order.   ∎

Example 4 *Assume that there is one object with $q_1 = 1$, and consider a situation with an NBUE(NWUE) distribution of agents' types with mean μ, and another NBUE(NWUE) distribution of inter-arrival times with mean ω. Let the discount rate be α. Then the expected welfare under the efficient sequential allocation policy is lower (higher) than*

$$\mu \text{LambertW} \left(\frac{1}{\omega \alpha} \right),$$

where the increasing function $\text{LambertW}(x)$ is implicitly defined by

$$\text{LambertW}(x) e^{\text{LambertW}(x)} = x.$$

To show this, consider the exponential distributions $G_\mu = 1 - e^{-t/\mu}$ for the agents' types and $G_\omega = 1 - e^{-t/\omega}$ for the inter-arrival times. For these

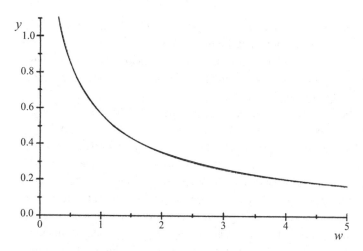

Figure 2.3
Solution as a function of ω for $\mu = \alpha = 1$

distributions, the optimal cutoff point y_1 solves

$$y_1 = \frac{\widetilde{G}_\omega(\alpha)}{1 - \widetilde{G}_\omega(\alpha)} \int_{y_1}^{\infty} e^{-t/\mu} dt = \mu/\omega\alpha e^{-y_1/\mu}.$$

The solution to this equation is given by

$$y_1 = \mu \text{LambertW}\left(\frac{1}{\omega\alpha}\right),$$

and the result follows by corollary 2. Note that the solution is linear in μ, the mean of the agents' distribution of types. Figure 2.3 plots the solution as a function of ω for $\mu = \alpha = 1$ (note that ω, the mean inter-arrival time, and α, the discount factor, play here analogous roles).

2.3   Incomplete–Information Model and the Dynamic Vickrey–Clarke–Groves Mechanism

2.3.1   Private Information

We consider the basic dynamic allocation model outlined above, but we now assume that the arriving agents' types are private information. Thus the designer does not observe types.

The main question here is whether the designer is able to implement the dynamic efficient policy characterized in theorem 4. We answer this question in the affirmative by allowing monetary transfers, and by constructing a dynamic analogue of the celebrated Vickrey–Clarke–Groves (VCG) mechanism. With monetary transfers, we assume that the utility functions are *quasi-linear:* that is, an agent with type x who obtains an item with quality q at price p has a utility of $(qx - p)$, and an agent that makes a payment p without receiving an object has a utility of $(-p)$.

We focus here on the continuous-time case with a deadline. The analysis for the other cases is completely analogous.

Without loss of generality, we restrict attention to *direct mechanisms* where every agent, upon arrival, reports his characteristic x_i and where the mechanism specifies an allocation (which item, if any, the agent gets) and a payment. The schemes we develop also have an obvious and immediate interpretation as *indirect mechanisms*, where the designer sets a time-dependent menu of prices, one for each item, and where arriving agents choose an item out that menu.

An allocation policy is called *deterministic* and *Markovian* if, at any time t, and for any possible type of agent arriving at t, it uses a nonrandom allocation rule that only depends on the arrival time t, on the declared type of the arriving agent, and on the set of items available at t, denoted by Π_t. Thus the policy depends on past decisions only via the state variable Π_t. We also restrict attention to interim-individually rational policies, where no agent ever pays more than the utility obtained from the physical allocation.

Denote by $Q_t : [0, +\infty) \times 2^{\Pi_0} \to \Pi_0 \cup \emptyset$ a deterministic Markovian allocation policy for time t with an additional requirement that for any $A \in 2^{\Pi_0}$ and $x \in [0, +\infty)$, $Q_t(x, A) \in A \cup \emptyset$. That is for any set of the available objects, the allocation policy will assign either one of the available objects or no object at all. Denote by $P_t : [0, +\infty) \times 2^{\Pi_0} \to \mathbb{R}$ the associated payment rule. Recall that we denote by k_t the cardinality of set Π_t and by $q_{(j:\Pi_t)}$ the jth highest element of the set Π_t.

The next proposition shows that a deterministic, Markovian allocation policy is *implementable* if and only if it is based on a partition of the agents' type space.[3] In other words, implementability reduces here to setting a menu of prices, one for which object, from which the arriving agent has to choose.

Proposition 1 *Assume that Π_t is the set of objects available at time t, and assume that $q_j \neq q_k$ for any $q_j, q_k \in \Pi_t$, $j \neq k$.*

1. *A deterministic, Markovian policy Q_t is implementable if and only if there exist $k_t + 1$ functions*

$$\infty = y_{0,\Pi_t}(t) \geq y_{1,\Pi_t}(t) \geq y_{2,\Pi_t}(t) \geq \cdots \geq y_{k_t,\Pi_t}(t) \geq 0,$$

such that $x \in [y_{j,\Pi_t}(t), y_{j-1,\Pi_t}(t)) \Rightarrow Q_t(x, \Pi_t) = q_{(j:\Pi_t)}$ and $x < y_{k_t,\Pi_t}(t) \Rightarrow Q_t(x, \Pi_t) = \emptyset$.[4]

2. *In the associated payment scheme, an agent with type x that arrives at time t obtains an amount $S(t)$ where $S(t)$ is some allocation- and type-independent function. In addition, if $x \in [y_{j,\Pi_t}(t), y_{j-1,\Pi_t}(t))$, then the agent pays for the object with the j-highest quality (among the remaining objects) a price given by*

$$P_t^j(x, \Pi_t) = \sum_{i=j}^{k_t}(q_{(i:\Pi_t)} - q_{(i+1:\Pi_t)})y_{i,\Pi_t}(t),$$

where $\forall t,\ q_{(k_t+1:\Pi_t)} = 0$.[5]

Proof (1) If two reports of the agent that arrives at t lead to the same physical allocation, then, in any incentive compatible mechanism, the associated payments should be the same as well. With some abuse of notation, denote by P^j the payment that will be charged for the object with the j-highest quality q_j. A direct mechanism is equivalent to a mechanism where the agent arriving at time t chooses an object and a payment from a menu $(q_j, P^j)_{j=1}^{k_t}$. If some type x prefers the pair (q_k, P^k) over any other pair (q_l, P^l) with $q_k > q_l$, then any type $\tilde{x} > x$ also prefers (q_k, P^k) over (q_l, P^l). This implies that $Q_t(\tilde{x}, \Pi_t) \geq Q_t(x, \Pi_t)$ for any t and Π_t. Finally, noting that $Q_t(x, \Pi_t) = \emptyset$ is equivalent to allocating an object with quality equal to zero, implies that an agent who arrives at time t gets object $q_{(k)}$ if he reports a type contained in the interval $(y_{k,\Pi_t}(t), y_{k-1,\Pi_t}(t))$. A similar argument shows that $Q_t(y_{i,\Pi_t}(t), \Pi_t) \in \{q_{(i+1:\Pi_t)}, q_{(i:\Pi_t)}\}$ for $i \in \{1, 2, \ldots, k_t\}$.

(2) The proof is constructive: given a partition-based policy, we design a payment scheme that, for any $j \in \{1, \ldots, k_t\}$, induces type $x \in [y_{j,\Pi_t}(t), y_{j-1,\Pi_t}(t))$ to choose the object with type $q_{(j:\Pi_t)}$. Without loss of generality, we assume that an agent whose type is on the boundary between two intervals in the partition chooses the item with higher type. Consider then the following payment scheme where an agent who arrives at t obtains $S(t)$, and in addition pays

$$P_t^j(x, \Pi_t) = \sum_{i=j}^{k_t}(q_{(i:\Pi_t)} - q_{(i+1:\Pi_t)})y_{i,\Pi_t}(t) \qquad \text{if } x \in [y_{j,\Pi_t}(t), y_{j-1,\Pi_t}(t)),$$

$$(2.3)$$

that is, if he is allocated the object with the j-highest quality among the remaining ones. Note that $S(t)$ does not affect incentives. Note also that type $x = y_{j,\Pi_t}(t)$ is indifferent between $(q_{(j:\Pi_t)}, P^j)$ and $(q_{(j+1:\Pi_t)}, P^{j+1})$. Moreover any type above $y_{j,\Pi_t}(t)$ prefers $(q_{(j:\Pi_t)}, P^j)$ over $(q_{(j+1:\Pi_t)}, P^{j+1})$, while any type below prefers $(q_{(j+1:\Pi_t)}, P^{j+1})$ over $(q_{(j:\Pi_t)}, P^j)$. Therefore any type $x \in [y_{j,\Pi_t}(t), y_{j-1,\Pi_t}(t))$ prefers $\left(q_{(j:\Pi_t)}, P^j\right)$ over any other pairs in the menu.   ∎

It is important to note that, although the cutoff curves determining an implementable allocation are independent of the objects's qualities, the prices that implement this allocation do depend on the exact values of these qualities. This insight will be heavily used in the next chapter where we study the revenue maximizing allocation and the associated prices: it is much easier to maximize over the quality-independent implementable allocations rather than directly over prices.

For our present purpose of dynamic efficient implementation, the desired allocation rule is clear: the agent who arrives at time t gets the object with the i'th highest characteristic if and only if he reports a type $x \in [y_i(t), y_{i-1}(t))$, where the cutoff $y_i(t)$ is given by theorem 4. Since this allocation has the partition form described in the result above, we obtain:

Corollary 3 *The complete information dynamically efficient allocation policy is implementable also under incomplete information by the following payment scheme: any agent that arrives at time t obtains an amount $S(t)$. In addition the price at period t for the object with the jth highest quality (among the remaining objects) is given by*

$$P_t^j(\Pi_t) = \sum_{i=j}^{k_t} (q_{(i:\Pi_t)} - q_{(i+1:\Pi_t)}) y_{i,\Pi_t}(t), \tag{2.4}$$

where the cutoff functions $\{y_{i,\Pi_t}(t)\}_{i,t}$ are given in theorem 4 and where $\forall t$, $q_{(k_t+1:\Pi_t)} = 0$. This mechanism is individually rational if $S(t) \geq 0$.

Proof It only remains to prove that the mechanism is individually rational when $S(t) \geq 0$. To see this, note first that an agent with type x that arrives at time t has in any case utility of $S(t) \geq 0$. In addition, if he purchases the object with the j-highest characteristic among the remaining ones, he obtains an additional utility of

$$x q_{(j:\Pi_t)} - \sum_{i=j}^{k_t} (q_{(i:\Pi_t)} - q_{(i+1:\Pi_t)}) y_{i,\Pi_t}(t)$$

$$= q_{(j:\Pi_t)}(x - y_{j,\Pi_t}(t)) - \sum_{i=j+1}^{k_t} q_{(i:\Pi_t)}(y_{i+1,\Pi_t}(t) - y_{i,\Pi_t}(t)) \geq 0.$$

The last inequality holds because $y_{i+1,\Pi_t}(t) - y_{i,\Pi_t}(t) \leq 0$, $\forall i$, and because $x - y_{j,\Pi_t}(t) \geq 0$, since we have assumed that the agent gets the object with the j-highest characteristic among the remaining ones ∎

The payment scheme has an intuitive interpretation. Assume, for the moment, that the analyzed setup is the static one with k_t objects and $k_t + 1$ agents, where in addition to an agent with type x, there are k_t "dummy" agents with types $y_{1,\Pi_t}(t), y_{2,\Pi_t}(t), \ldots, y_{k_t,\Pi_t}(t)$. The payment for the object with the j-highest quality, $\sum_{i=j}^{k_t}(q_{(i:\Pi_t)} - q_{(i+1:\Pi_t)})y_{i,\Pi_t}(t)$, represents the externality imposed by the agent with type x_i on the dummy agents in the corresponding efficient allocation.

2.3.2 Budget-Balancedness

The preceding analysis was solely concerned with physical allocational efficiency. As remarked above, the employed mechanisms that implemented the efficient allocation were also individual rational. On the one hand, if there are no alternative resources to subsidize the allocation process, we must require that the total money amount collected by the designer be nonnegative. This can be easily achieved, for example, by choosing $S(t) \equiv 0$. On the other, an inability to redistribute the raised money among agents reduces their welfare and hence prevents reaching a fully efficient outcome. Roughly speaking, in an allocatively efficient mechanism, the payment of a buyer is tied to the externality he imposes on other agents, and hence it depends on the values of others. A redistribution of this payment to others is therefore bound to affect their incentives, and full redistribution is impossible while insisting on individual rationality, allocative efficiency, and incentive compatibility.

Nevertheless, in our dynamic setting, budget-balancedness is easier to achieve due to the sequential nature of the allocation process: the amount each agent pays depends on the imposed *expected* externality, and hence it is not affected by the realized reports of the agents that should get this amount as a refund. In other words, the "future" acts here as a nonstrategic agent that can receive transfers without affecting her incentives.

We propose below mechanisms that reallocate the gathered money among the agents without distorting their incentives. We restrict attention to the more interesting scenario with a deadline and with random arrivals (for simplicity, we also restrict attention to a homogeneous, Poisson arrival process with parameter λ). The results can be easily extended to the other cases.

We consider two types of mechanisms: (1) *online mechanisms*, where monetary transfers pertaining to a specific transaction need to be completed at the same time as the physical allocation, and (2) *offline mechanisms*, where payments can be postponed to later stages. Ex post budget-balancedness is attainable by offline mechanisms, but it can be only asymptotically achieved by online mechanisms.

Online Mechanisms   Denote by $B(t)$ the budget surplus accumulated by time t when using a mechanism that implements the efficient physical allocation and never runs a deficit (thus $B(t) \geq 0$, $\forall t$). While it is impossible here to precisely obtain ex post budget-balancedness, we describe below a scheme where the expected surplus vanishes asymptotically, as $\lambda \longrightarrow \infty$.

Definition 5   (Online redistribution mechanism) *A scheme that implements the efficient allocation such that the type-independent part of the payment scheme for the agent arriving at t is $S(t) = B(t)$ will be called a dynamically efficient online redistribution mechanism (DEON).*

By definitions, then, each agent's payment consists of two parts: first, a nonnegative fee for the object he gets, which is determined by the report and by the efficient cutoffs, and second, a refund equal to the payment of the previously arrived agent. Clearly, the *DEON* mechanism never runs a budget deficit, but it may run a surplus if, after the last sale, no agent arrives till the deadline. The next result shows that the expected surplus goes to zero if the rate of the Poisson process goes to infinity, that is if $\lambda \to \infty$. Note that increasing λ has two opposite effects on the expected surplus: On the one hand, both prices and the expected surplus in case no agent arrives after the last sale go up. On the other hand, the probability of no arrival after the last sale goes down. The next theorem shows that the second effect dominates.[6]

We denote by σ the expected surplus generated by the DEON mechanism. Note that it is positive only if the last agent that arrived before T obtained one of the objects, in which case the payment made by this agent cannot be reallocated any further.

Theorem 10   *For any distribution of values, and for any deadline T, $\lim_{\lambda \to \infty} \sigma = 0$.*

Proof   In the *DEON* mechanism, if an agent arrives at time t and reports type $x_t \in [y_{j,\Pi_t}(t), y_{j-1,\Pi_t}(t))$, and if the previous agent arrived at $\tau < t$ and reported a type $x_\tau \in [y_{l,\Pi_\tau}(\tau), y_{l-1,\Pi_\tau}(\tau))$, then the time t agent's monetray transfer is given by

$$\sum_{i=j}^{k_t}(q_{(i:\Pi_t)} - q_{(i+1:\Pi_t)})y_{i,\Pi_t}(t) - \sum_{i=l}^{k_\tau}(q_{(i:\Pi_\tau)} - q_{(i+1:\Pi_\tau)})y_{i,\Pi_\tau}(\tau).$$

Since the probability that no agent arrives between periods s and T is $e^{-\lambda(T-s)}$, the expected surplus of the mechanism is given by

$$\sigma = \sum_{\Pi_s \subseteq \Pi} \int_0^T \Pr_s (\Pi_s) \sum_{j=1}^{k_s} \sum_{i=j}^{k_s} (q_{(i,\Pi_s)} - q_{(i+1,\Pi_s)})$$
$$\times \, y_{i,\Pi_s}(s) \, g_{i,\Pi_s}(s) \, e^{-\lambda(T-s)} ds,$$

where $\Pr_\tau (\Pi_s)$ is the probability that at time τ the set of the objects still available is Π_s, $q_{(j,\Pi_s)}$ is the jth highest quality out of Π_s, and $g_{i,\Pi_s}(s)$ is the density that at time s an agent arrives with a type that leads to the allocation of the jth highest quality out of Π_s

Let $k_0 = 1$. That is, initially there is only one object available of quality q normalized to be one. The expected surplus of the *DEON* mechanism is given by

$$\int_0^T y_1(t) \, \lambda \, [1 - F(y_1(t))] \, e^{-\lambda \int_0^t [1 - F(y_1(z))] dz} e^{-\lambda(T-t)} dt.$$

Since $[1 - F(y_1(t))] \leq 1$, it is sufficient to show that

$$\lim_{\lambda \to \infty} \int_0^T \frac{\lambda y_1(t)}{e^{\lambda \left(T - t + \int_0^t [1 - F(y_1(z))] dz \right)}} dt = 0.$$

The claim will follow by showing that for any $t \in [0, T]$, the integrand goes to 0 when $\lambda \to \infty$. If $t = T$, then the result follows immediately, since $y(T) = 0$. Assume that $t < T$, and recall that

$$y_1'(t) = -\lambda \int_{y_1(t)}^\infty [1 - F(x)] \, dx.$$

Integrating both sides between t and T yields

$$y_1(t) = \lambda \int_t^T \int_{y_1(s)}^\infty [1 - F(x)] \, dx \, ds \leq \lambda (T - t) E(x),$$

where the last inequality follows from $\int_0^\infty [1 - F(x)] \, dx = E(x)$. In addition, for any $t < T$, there exists a constant $A > 0$ such that $T - t + \int_0^t [1 - F(y_1(z))] \, dz > A$. Therefore it is sufficient to show that $\lim_{\lambda \to \infty} \lambda^2 (T - t) E(x) / e^{\lambda A} = 0$. Twice applying L'Hospital's rule to this ratio provides the required results.

If $k_0 = 2$, then the expected surplus of the *DEON* mechanism is

$$
\int_0^T \frac{\lambda\left((q_1 - q_2)\, y_1\,(t) + q_2 y_2\,(t)\right)\left[1 - F\left(y_1\,(t)\right)\right]}{e^{\lambda\left(T - t + \int_0^t [1 - F(y_2(z))]dz\right)}}\, dt
$$

$$
+\, q_2 \int_0^T \frac{y_2\,(t)\,\lambda\left[F\left(y_1\,(t)\right) - F\left(y_2\,(t)\right)\right]}{e^{\lambda\left(T - t + \int_0^t [1 - F(y_2(z))]dz\right)}}\, dt
$$

$$
+\, q_1 \int_0^T \int_s^T \frac{\lambda^2 y_1\,(t)\left[1 - F\left(y_1\,(t)\right)\right]\left[F\left(y_1\,(s)\right) - F\left(y_2\,(s)\right)\right]}{e^{\lambda\left(T - t + \int_s^t [1 - F(y_1(z))]dz + \int_0^s [1 - F(y_2(z))]dz\right)}}\, dt ds
$$

$$
+\, q_2 \int_0^T \int_s^T \frac{\lambda^2 y_1\,(t)\left[1 - F\left(y_1\,(s)\right)\right]\left[1 - F\left(y_1\,(t)\right)\right]}{e^{\lambda\left(T - t + \int_0^s [1 - F(y_2(z))]dz + \int_s^t [1 - F(y_2(z))]dz\right)}}\, dt ds
$$

Similarly to the argument above, each element in the summation goes to 0 as λ goes to infinity, and the result follows analogously.   ∎

Implicitly, the assumption of nonstrategic arrivals plays a significant role in the DEON mechanism. If an agent can split her identity, then she will find it optimal to arrive "again" immediately after a sale, and to claim type zero, say, which allows her to collect the payment from the last sale. Note though that analogous manipulations also afflict static budget balanced mechanisms. For example, in the well-known static mechanism due to Arrow, D'Aspremont, and Gerard Varet, an agent would benefit from creating and controlling additional dummy agents since monetary receipts are evenly distributed.[7] The specific mechanism exhibited above (and the offline mechanism described below) is, of course, a theoretical construct, tailored to the assumptions made here. One can envisage variations that go some—but not all—of the way in the direction of a balanced budget and that could be used in practice, such as that the available budget surplus need not be observable to outsiders or that refunds may be made randomly.

Offline Mechanism   We now show how to construct a mechanism that satisfies ex post budget-balancedness for any λ and T by relaxing the "online" requirement that all monetary transfers need to be implemented upon arrival. There are many examples where the physical part of the allocation is a matter of urgency to the agents, but where there is a possibility to delay final monetary payoffs until more information arrives (e.g., electricity or heat is continuously supplied in large apartment houses, but the precise cost allocation among tenants is done—at least in Germany—at the end of the year and is a function of later information on vacancy rates, average temperature, fuel costs, etc.). It is of practical interest to determine where such offline schemes are feasible and less prone to moral hazard problems.

We sketch here the case where there is one object, with quality $q = 1$, but the generalization to the case with several heterogeneous objects is straightforward. The designer can now observe the number of the agents that eventually arrive, and may ex post refund the entire fee to the buyer who paid it if nobody else shows up. But, in order not to distort that buyer's incentives, he has to pay a higher net price if additional agents subsequently arrive.

Consider a time t where the object is still available, and the direct mechanism where (1) the arriving agent at t does not get the object and pays nothing if his reported type is below $y_1(t)$, or (2) the arriving agent at t gets the object and pays $P(t)$ if his reported type is above $y_1(t)$. Moreover, at time T, the designer distributes the raised revenue equally among all agents that arrived after the sale. Obviously, this mechanism is budget-balanced. Denote by $\mathrm{Pr}_l(t)$ the probability that exactly l additional agents arrive after period t. In order to implement the efficient allocation, the type $y_1(t)$ should be indifferent between getting the object, which yields utility of $y_1(t) - P(t) + \sum_{l=0}^{\infty} \frac{P(t)\,\mathrm{Pr}_l(t)}{1+l}$, and not getting the object, which generates utility of zero. Noting that $\sum_{l=0}^{\infty} \frac{\mathrm{Pr}_l(t)}{1+l} = \frac{1-e^{-\lambda(T-t)}}{\lambda(T-t)}$ for the Poisson arrival process, yields

$$P(t) = \frac{\lambda(T-t)\,y_1(t)}{\lambda(T-t) + e^{-\lambda(T-t)} - 1}. \tag{2.5}$$

Although the proposed mechanism is interim individually rational, it is not individually rational ex post. It is impossible to attain ex post individual rationality if the designer insists on an efficient allocation and on budget-balancedness. To see this, observe that if a buyer is the only arriving agent, he should ultimately pay zero (by budget-balancedness); since, by efficiency, the type $y_1(t)$ should be indifferent between buying and not, we obtain that sometimes this type needs to pay strictly more than his valuation.

It can be easily shown that $\lim_{t \to T} P(t) = 2\mu$. Thus the payment $P(t)$ does not "explode" as one gets near the deadline: on the one hand, an agent that buys the good near the deadline is almost sure to get the fee back, so he will be willing to pay a high amount for it, on the other, the fee is calculated to generate indifference between buying or not for an agent with a very low type.

2.4 Related Literature

An early paper that uses optimal stopping theory to characterize the efficient assignment of a single object to randomly arriving agents in continuous time is Elving (1967). In a model with several identical objects, McAfee and te Velde (2008) compute the dynamic welfare maximizing policy for a Pareto distributions of agents' values, and show that it coincides then with the revenue optimizing policy. Majorization is introduced in Hardy, Littlewood, and Pólya (1934).

Dolan (1978) was the first to use a dynamic version of the Vickrey–Clarke–Groves mechanism in order to achieve welfare maximization in queues with random arrivals and with incomplete information about the agents' characteristics. Dynamic extensions of VCG schemes (for more general situations than those considered here) have been offered by Athey and Segal (2013), Bergeman and Välimäki (2010), and Parkes and Singh (2003). Guo and Conitzer (2009) and Moulin (2009) analyze surplus minimizing VCG schemes in the static environment, and derive bounds on the ensuing efficiency loss.

Notes

1. An object remains unassigned if there are not sufficient arrivals, yielding a zero reward.

2. The derived controlled stochastic process is *semi-Markov* since the Markov property is preserved only at decision points, but not between them. See Puterman (2005) for solution approaches to such problems by an *uniformization* procedure, and for conditions guaranteeing that optimal policies are deterministic and Markovian.

3. The result holds for any nonrandom policy. But, since the rest of the analysis focuses on the Markov case, and in order to save on notational complexity, we consider only this case here.

4. Types at the boundary between two intervals can be assigned to either one of the neighboring elements of the partition. That is, if $x_i \in \{y_{k_t, \Pi_t}(t), y_{k_t-1, \Pi_t}(t), \ldots, y_{2, \Pi_t}(t), y_{1, \Pi_t}(t)\}$, then $Q_t(y_{i, \Pi_t}(t), \Pi_t) \in \{q_{(i:\Pi_t)}, q_{(i+1:\Pi_t)}\}, i = 1, 2, \ldots, k_t$.

5. If there are some identical objects, there exist implementable policies that do not take the form of partitions. But, for each such policy, there exists another implementable policy that is based on a partition, and that generates the same expected utility for all agents and for the designer.

6. Since λ governs the number of arrivals per unit of time, a similar result holds if λ is constant but $T \to \infty$.

7. For problems created by false identities in VCG mechanisms, see also Yokoo, Sakurai, and Matsubara (2004).

3 Dynamic Revenue Maximization with Heterogeneous Objects

3.1 Introduction

We now shift attention to revenue maximization. Whereas the large literature on yield or revenue management has directly focused on revenue-maximizing pricing (mostly for the special case of our model where agents have linear, private values for identical objects), our approach is based on the characterization of all dynamically implementable, nonrandomized allocation policies (see the previous chapter). As we have already seen, such policies are described by partitions of the set of possible agent types: an arriving agent gets the best available object if his type lies in the highest interval of the partition, the second-best available object if his type lies in the second highest interval, and so on. These intervals may depend on the point in time of the arrival, and on the composition of the set of available objects at that point in time.

For any implementable allocation policy we also derived the associated menus of prices (one menu for each point in time, and for each subset of remaining objects). We implement these menus, and showed that they have an appealing recursive structure.

In this chapter we use several basic results about the Poisson stochastic process, and we compute the revenue generated by any individual-rational, deterministic, Markovian, and implementable allocation policy. We show that, we can directly use variational arguments to characterize the revenue-maximizing allocation policy. The associated optimal prices are of "secondary importance" because they are determined by the implementation conditions. This is an illustration of the famous "payoff equivalence theorem," going back to the work of Vickrey (1961) and Myerson (1981).

Whereas the optimal prices necessarily depend on the composition of inventory, our main result is that at each point in time, the revenue-maximizing allocation policy depends only on the size of the available inventory and not on its exact composition. To understand the meaning of this result, consider the same model but with identical objects. For each size of available inventory then, and for each point in time, the revenue-maximizing allocation policy is characterized by a single cutoff type: only an arriving agent with type above that cutoff obtains one of the objects. In contrast, when objects are heterogeneous, the revenue-maximizing policy is, at each point in time and for each subset of available objects, characterized by several cutoff types that determine if the arriving agent gets the best available object, the second best, and so on. Our result says that for any subset of k available heterogeneous objects and for any point in time, the highest cutoff coincides with the optimal cutoff in a situation with one available object, the second-highest cutoff coincides with the optimal cutoff in a situation with two identical objects, and so on, till the lowest cutoff that coincides with the optimal cutoff in a situation with an inventory of k identical objects. We also compare these cutoff curves with those obtained for a designer who wishes to maximize allocative efficiency, as in the previous chapter.

We conclude this chapter with two applications that use the characterization result described above:

1. We embed revenue maximization in the larger optimization problem where, before sales begin, the seller chooses the size and composition of the inventory. A good illustration is offered by the move of several US supermarket chains to reduce "shrink"—the amount of fresh food that needs to be dumped because it is not sold by the expiration date. Obviously the amount and variety of food on display and the temporal pricing pattern will affect shrink. Although some "intentional" waste is part of revenue maximization, the US shrink rate is twice as large as that of European retailers, suggesting that at least one of them may not be optimal.[1]
   We show how the formulas we derived for revenue maximization (together with information about marginal costs) directly yield a set of intuitive equations that characterize the optimal number of objects and their qualities.

2. We derive some testable inferences about the pattern of observed prices for different qualities in clearance sales, and pair them with available data. Compared to standard models that only cover identical objects, our analysis obtains a somewhat more convincing explanation for several well-known observed regularities. For example, we see why the average clearance markdown (in percentage terms) is higher for higher quality, more expensive product lines, as empirically observed in a variety of settings (see the literature review below).

3.2   The Model

We focus first on the incomplete-information, continuous-time scenario with a deadline T, where arrivals are governed by a homogeneous Poisson process with intensity λ.[2] Agents can be served only upon arrival. As before, there are m items with qualities $0 \leq q_m \leq q_{m-1} \leq ... \leq q_1$. After an item is assigned, it cannot be reallocated.

Each agent is characterized by a privately observed "type" x_j, and agents' types are governed by IID random variables $X_i = X$ on $[0, +\infty)$ with a common cumulative distribution function F that is known to the designer. We assume that X has a finite mean, denoted by μ, and a finite variance. Additionally, we assume that the distribution F is twice differentiable with density $0 < f(x) < \infty$. Finally, we assume that the *virtual type* $x - \frac{1-F(x)}{f(x)}$ is increasing in x.[3] The utilities of the agents are quasi-linear, as defined in the previous chapter. But the designer's goal is now maximization of revenue.

3.3   Revenue Maximization

In this section we solve the dynamic revenue-maximization problem. A main feature that differentiates our analysis from previous ones is the fact that we use the mechanism design approach, and the insight behind the celebrated payoff/revenue equivalence theorem. This theorem implies that the expected payments in an incentive-compatible mechanism are determined, up to a constant, by the implemented allocation. Accordingly we focus on the dynamic allocation policy that underlies revenue maximization. Incentive-compatible pricing plays only a "secondary" role. This is because, once the allocation is fixed, it is automatically induced by the implementation requirements.

Without loss of generality, we can restrict attention to Markovian, deterministic policies where the state includes the set of available objects Π_t, the period of time t, and the type of the agent that arrives at t. The optimality of Markovian, possibly randomized, policies is standard for all models where, as is the case here, the instantaneous rewards and transition probabilities are history independent (e.g., see theorem 11.1.1 in Puterman 2005, which shows that for any history-dependent policy, there is a Markovian, possibly randomized, policy with the same payoff).[4] Given a Markovian policy, at each period t the designer's problem is equivalent to a static problem where one object out of a given inventory needs to be allocated to a privately informed agent, and where the seller has certain salvage values for the remaining possible inventories (the salvage values correspond to the various continuation values in the dynamic case). Analogously to Myerson (1981), the static revenue-maximization problem has a nonrandomized solution: if at all, the agent should get the object for which virtual valuation plus salvage value is highest. The expected revenue from any incentive compatible mechanism in the static problem is given by

$$\int \sum_{q_i \in \Pi_t \cup \varnothing} \Pr{}_i (x) \left[q_i \left(x - \frac{1 - F(x)}{f(x)} \right) + SV (\Pi_t \backslash q_i) \right] dx,$$

where $\Pr_i(x)$ is the probability that the designer assigns to type x the object of quality q_i and where $SV(\Pi_t \backslash q_i)$ is the salvage value of the set of objects $\Pi_t \backslash q_i$. Thus at each period t in the dynamic problem the seller has a deterministic optimal policy as well.

We first calculate the expected revenue for any given Markovian, deterministic allocation policy. Then we use a variational argument to derive the cutoff curves describing the revenue-maximizing dynamic policy.

Recall from proposition 1 that in order to implement a Markovian, deterministic allocation, which is given by $\infty = y_{0,\Pi_t}(t) \geq y_{1,\Pi_t}(t) \geq y_{2,\Pi_t}(t) \geq \cdots \geq y_{k_t,\Pi_t}(t) > 0, \forall t$, an agent that arrives at t obtains a transfer of $S(t)$. The price at period t for the object with the jth highest characteristic (among the remaining objects) needs to be

$$P_t^{(j)}(\Pi_t) = \sum_{i=j}^{k_t} (q_{(i:\Pi_t)} - q_{(i+1:\Pi_t)}) y_{i,\Pi_t}(t). \tag{3.1}$$

In any interim individually rational mechanism the agent must have $S(t) \geq 0$ for any t, and in order to maximize the revenue, the seller must clearly have $\forall t, \ S(t) = 0$. Thus agents are never subsidized in the revenue-maximizing mechanism.

After using simple properties of sampling out of Poisson processes (see the proof of proposition 2 below), the expected revenue at time t where $\Pi_t \neq \emptyset$ takes the form

$$R(\Pi_t, t) = \sum_{i=1}^{k_t} \int_t^T \left(P_s^{(i)}(\Pi_t) + R(\Pi_t \backslash \{q_{(i:\Pi_t)}\}, s) \right) h_{i,\Pi_t}(s) \, ds,$$

where

$$h_{i,\Pi_t}(s) = \lambda \left[F(y_{i-1,\Pi_t}(s)) - F(y_{i,\Pi_t}(s)) \right] e^{-\int_t^s \lambda [1 - F(y_{k_t,\Pi_t}(z))] dz}$$

is the density of the waiting time till the first arrival of an agent with a type in the interval $[y_{i,\Pi_t}(s), y_{i-1,\Pi_t}(s))$ given that no arrival that leads to a sale (e.g., type above $y_{k_t}(s)$) has occurred.

Recall that a Markovian, determinsistic policy must specify an allocation decision for each possible state, meaning for each possible subset of objects $\Pi_t \neq \emptyset$ available at time t. Moreover, for each state, the policy consists of $k_t = |\Pi_t|$ cutoff curves that describe the partition of the set of agents' types—generally these curves depend on the precise composition of the set Π_t. The number of curves needed if there are m objects is $\sum_{k=1}^{m} k \binom{m}{k} = m2^{m-1}$. This yields 4 cutoff curves for two objects, 12 curves for three objects, 32 curves for 4 objects, and so on. In order to save on notation and to keep the somewhat involved proofs more transparent, we assume below that there are only two objects with characteristics $q_1 \geq q_2$. But we will describe the completely analogous solution to the revenue maximization problem for the general case with any number of distinct objects. A main result is that the dynamic revenue-maximizing policy for m (possibly distinct) objects is in fact completely described by only m cutoff curves. In particular, it shows that this policy is independent of the characteristics of the available objects.

With slight abuse of notation, we write "2" in place of $\Pi_t = \{q_1, q_2\}$ at the second subscript of the allocation functions $y_{i,\Pi_t}(t)$ whenever $k_t = 2$. This should not lead to any confusion.

Theorem 11 *The dynamic revenue-maximizing allocation policy is indepen-dent of the qualities of available objects q_1 and q_2. In particular, we have:*

1. $y_{1,q_1}(t) = y_{1,q_2}(t) = y_{1,2}(t) := y_1(t)$ where $y_1(t)$ is a solution of

$$y_1(t) = \frac{1 - F(y_1(t))}{f(y_1(t))} + \lambda \int_t^T \frac{[1 - F(y_1(s))]^2}{f(y_1(s))} ds;$$

2. $y_{2,2}(t) := y_2(t)$ is a solution of

$$y_2(t) = \frac{1 - F(y_2(t))}{f(y_2(t))} + \lambda \int_t^T \frac{[1 - F(y_2(s))]^2}{f(y_2(s))} ds - R(1,t),$$

where

$$R(1,t) = \lambda \int_t^T \frac{[1 - F(y_1(s))]^2}{f(y_1(s))} ds$$

is the expected revenue at time t if there is one available object with $q = 1$ and the optimal policy will be followed from time t on.

The proof of these results proceeds by a sequence of three arguments: first, we derive the expected revenue for any Markovian, deterministic allocation policy (proposition 2); second, we derive the revenue-maximizing allocation policy when only one object remains (claim 1); finally, we derive the revenue-maximizing allocation policy if two objects are left (claim 2).

Proposition 2 *Assume the following:*

1. *If $k_t = 2$, the designer uses the dynamic allocation cutoff curves $y_{2,2}(t) \leq y_{1,2}(t)$. That is, the agent that arrives at time t gets: the object with quality q_1 if his type is $x_i \geq y_{1,2}(t)$; the object with quality q_2, if his type is $x_i \in [y_{2,2}(t), y_{1,2}(t))$; no object if $x_i < y_{2,2}(t)$.*

2. *If $k_t = 1$, the designer uses the dynamic cutoff curves $y_{1,q_j}(t)$. That is, the agent that arrives at time t gets the remaining object with characteristic q_j if $x_i \geq y_{1,q_j}(t)$, and no object otherwise. Then the expected revenue from this policy is given by*

$$\int_0^T (q_2 y_{2,2}(t) + R(q_1, t)) \lambda (1 - F(y_{2,2}(t))) e^{-\int_0^t \lambda(1-F(y_{2,2}(s)))ds} dt$$

$$+ \int_0^T ((q_1 - q_2) y_{1,2}(t) + R(q_2, t) - R(q_1, t))$$

$$\cdot \lambda (1 - F(y_{1,2}(t))) e^{-\int_0^t \lambda(1-F(y_{2,2}(s)))ds} dt,$$

where

$$R(q_j, t) = q_j \int_t^T y_{1,q_j}(s) \lambda (1 - F(y_{1,q_j}(s))) e^{-\int_t^s \lambda[1-F(y_{1,q_j}(z))]dz} ds \quad (3.2)$$

is the expected revenue at time t if only one object with quality q_j remains, given that the dynamic allocation function y_{1,q_j} is used from t on.

Proof If only one object with characteristic q_i is available at time t, then the expected revenue is given by

$$q_i \int_t^T y_{1,q_i}(s) h_{1,q_i}(s) ds$$

where $h_{1,q_i}(s)$ represents the density of the waiting time till the first arrival of an agent with a value that is at least $y_{1,q_i}(s)$. Note that this density is equal to the density of the first arrival in a nonhomogeneous Poisson process with rate $\lambda(s)(1 - F(y_{1,q_i}(s)))$. The density of the time of the nth arrival in a nonhomogeneous Poisson process with rate $\delta(s)$ is given by (see Ross 1983)

$$g_n(s) = \delta(s)e^{-m(s)}\frac{m(s)^{n-1}}{(n-1)!},$$ (3.3)

where $m(s) = \int_t^s \delta(z)dz$. Thus, we obtain

$$h_{1,q_i}(s) = \lambda(s)(1 - F(y_{1,q_i}(s)))e^{-\int_t^s \lambda(z)[1-F(y(z))]dz} \qquad \text{for } t \le s \le T,$$

and (3.2) follows.

If two objects are still available, the expected revenue is given by

$$\int_0^T \left[P_t^{(2)}(\{q_1,q_2\}) + R(q_1,t)\right]h_{2,2}(t)dt$$

$$+ \int_0^T \left[P_t^{(1)}(\{q_1,q_2\}) + R(q_2,t)\right]h_{1,2}(t)dt.$$ (3.4)

Here $h_{1,2}(t)$ represents the density of the waiting time till the first arrival of an agent with a value that is at least $y_{1,2}(t)$ if no arrival of an agent with value in the interval $[y_{2,2}(t), y_{1,2}(t))$ has occurred. Similarly $h_{2,2}(t)$ represents the density of the waiting time till the first arrival of an agent with a value in the interval $[y_{2,2}(t), y_{1,2}(t))$ if no arrival of an agent with value in the interval $[y_{1,2}(t), \infty)$ has occurred. Since the arrival processes of agents with types in the intervals $[y_{2,2}(t), y_{1,2}(t))$ and $[y_{1,2}(t), \infty)$, respectively, are independent nonhomogeneous Poisson processes (see proposition 2.3.2 in Ross 1983), using (3.3) we obtain

$$h_{1,2}(t) = \lambda(1 - F(y_{1,2}(t)))e^{-\int_0^t \lambda[1-F(y_{1,2}(s))]ds}$$

$$e^{-\int_0^t \lambda[F(y_{1,2}(s))-F(y_{2,2}(s))]ds}$$

$$= \lambda(1 - F(y_{1,2}(t)))e^{-\int_0^t \lambda[1-F(y_{2,2}(s))]ds}$$

and

$$h_{2,2}(t) = \lambda \left(F(y_{1,2}(t)) \right.$$
$$\left. -F(y_{2,2}(t)) \right) e^{-\int_0^t \lambda [F(y_{1,2}(s)) - F(y_{2,2}(s)) + 1 - F(y_{1,2}(s))] ds}$$
$$= \lambda \left(F(y_{1,2}(t)) - F(y_{2,2}(t)) \right) e^{-\int_0^t \lambda [1 - F(y_{2,2}(s))] ds}.$$

Finally, recall that incentive compatibility implies that

$$P_t^{(2)}(\{q_1, q_2\}) = q_2 y_{2,2}(t) \quad \text{and} \quad P_t^{(1)}(\{q_1, q_2\}) = q_2 y_{2,2}(t)$$
$$+ (q_1 - q_2) y_{1,2}(t).$$

Plugging the expressions for $P_t^{(2)}(\{q_1, q_2\})$, $P_t^{(1)}(\{q_1, q_2\})$, $h_{1,2}(t)$, and $h_{2,2}(t)$ into the expression for expected revenue (3.4) yields the required formula. ∎

Claim 1 *If only one object remains, the dynamic revenue-maximizing allocation curve $y_1(t)$ solves*

$$y_1(t) = \frac{1 - F(y_1(t))}{f(y_1(t))} + \lambda \int_t^T \frac{[1 - F(y_1(s))]^2}{f(y_1(s))} ds. \tag{3.5}$$

The expected revenue at time t where $\Pi_t = q_j$ is given by $R(q_j, t) = q_j R(1, t)$ where

$$R(1, t) = \lambda \int_t^T \frac{[1 - F(y_1(s))]^2}{f(y_1(s))} ds. \tag{3.6}$$

Proof If only the object with characteristic q_j is available, it follows from Proposition 2 that the expected revenue at time t is given by

$$R(q_j, t) = q_j \int_t^T y_{1,q_j}(s) \lambda (1 - F(y_{1,q_j}(s))) e^{-\int_t^s \lambda [1 - F(y_{1,q_j}(z))] dz} ds.$$

Let $H(s) = \int_t^s \lambda [1 - F(y_{1,q_j}(z))] dz$. Then we obtain

$$R(q_j, t) = q_j \int_t^T F^{-1} \left[1 - \frac{H'(s)}{\lambda} \right] H'(s) e^{-H(s)} ds.$$

This expression for revenue is appropriate for using a variational argument with respect to the function H. The corresponding necessary condition for the variational problem (i.e., the Euler–Lagrange condition) is

$$- (H'(s))^2 + 2H''(s) + \frac{H'(s)H''(s)f'\left[F^{-1}(1 - (H'(s)/\lambda))\right]}{\lambda f\left[F^{-1}(1 - H'(s)/\lambda)\right]^2} = 0.$$

Plugging back the expression for $H(s)$ gives

$$- \lambda[1 - F(y_{1,q_j}(s))]^2 - 2f(y_{1,q_j}(s))y'_{1,q_j}(s)$$
$$- \frac{[1 - F(y_{1,q_j}(s))]f'(y_{1,q_j}(s))y'_{1,q_j}(s)}{f(y_{1,q_j}(s))} = 0.$$

This implies that for any $s \in [0, T]$, the solution $y_{1,q_j}(s)$ should satisfy

$$- y'_{1,q_j}(s) - y'_{1,q_j}(s) \left\{ 1 + \frac{[1 - F(y_{1,q_j}(s))]f'(y_{1,q_j}(s))}{[f(y_{1,q_j}(s))]^2} \right\}$$
$$= \lambda \frac{[1 - F(y_{1,q_j}(s))]^2}{f(y_{1,q_j}(s))}.$$

Since for any t, and for any differentiable $y(t)$ it holds that

$$-y'(t) \left\{ 1 + \frac{[1 - F(y(t))]f'(y(t))}{[f(y(t))]^2} \right\} = \frac{d}{dt}\left[\frac{1 - F(y(t))}{f(y(t))} \right],$$

we can rewrite the necessary condition as

$$y'_{1,q_j}(s) + \lambda \frac{[1 - F(y_{1,q_j}(s))]^2}{f(y_{1,q_j}(s))} = \frac{d}{ds}\left[\frac{1 - F(y_{1,q_j}(s))}{f(y_{1,q_j}(s))} \right].$$

Taking now the integral between t and T yields

$$\int_t^T y'_{1,q_j}(s)\,ds + \lambda \int_t^T \frac{[1 - F(y_{1,q_j}(s))]^2}{f(y_{1,q_j}(s))}\,ds$$
$$= \int_t^T \frac{d}{ds}\left[\frac{1 - F(y_{1,q_j}(s))}{f(y_{1,q_j}(s))} \right] ds.$$

This is equivalent to

$$y_{1,q_j}(T) - y_{1,q_j}(t) + \lambda \int_t^T \frac{[1 - F(y_{1,q_j}(s))]^2}{f(y_{1,q_j}(s))}\,ds$$
$$= \frac{1 - F(y_{1,q_j}(T))}{f(y_{1,q_j}(T))} - \frac{1 - F(y_{1,q_j}(t))}{f(y_{1,q_j}(t))}.$$

Together with the boundary condition

$$y_{1,q_j}(T) - \frac{1 - F(y_{1,q_j}(T))}{f(y_{1,q_j}(T))} = 0$$

we get (3.5). The assumptions of increasing virtual type and finite density ensure that a solution to (3.5) exists for any t.

To complete the proof and obtain the expression for revenue (3.6), note that the expected revenue is given by $R(q_j, t) = q_j R(1, t)$, where

$$R(1,t) = \int_t^T y_1(s)\lambda(1 - F(y_1(s)))e^{-\int_t^s \lambda[1 - F(y_1(z))]dz}\, ds.$$

Differentiating the expression above with respect to t gives

$$R'(1,t) = \lambda(1 - F(y_1(t)))(R(1,t) - y_1(t)).$$

It is then straightforward to verify that the function $\lambda \int_t^T \frac{[1 - F(y_1(s))]^2}{f(y_1(s))}\, ds$ satisfies the above differential equation with the boundary condition $R(1,T) = 0$.   ∎

We proceed now to characterize the revenue-maximizing allocation policy if there are two objects left.

Claim 2 *If two objects remain, then the dynamic revenue-maximizing policy is characterized by two cutoff curves, $y_1(t)$ and $y_2(t)$, where $y_1(t)$ satisfies equation (3.5) and where $y_2(t)$ satisfies*

$$y_2(t) = \frac{1 - F(y_2(t))}{f(y_2(t))} + \lambda \int_t^T \frac{[1 - F(y_2(s))]^2}{f(y_2(s))}\, ds - R(1, t). \tag{3.7}$$

Moreover the expected revenue at time t for the case $\Pi_t = \{1, 1\}$ is given by

$$R(\{1,1\}, t) = \lambda \int_t^T \frac{[1 - F(y_2(s))]^2}{f(y_2(s))}\, ds. \tag{3.8}$$

Proof We split the proof into two cases:

Case 1. We consider first the case where $q_1 > q_2$. That is, the seller needs to specify two different prices, and hence two different cutoff curves, $y_{1,2}(t)$ and

$y_{2,2}(t)$. We can rewrite the expected revenue given by proposition 2 as

$$\int\limits_0^T \left(q_2 F^{-1}\left(1 - \frac{H'(t)}{\lambda}\right) + q_1 R(1,t) \right) H'(t) e^{-H(t)} dt$$

$$+ (q_1 - q_2) \int\limits_0^T \left[F^{-1}\left(1 - \frac{G'(t)}{\lambda}\right) - R(1,t) \right] G'(t) e^{-H(t)} dt,$$

where

$$\int\limits_0^t \lambda\left[1 - F(y_{2,2}(s))\right] ds := H(t)$$

$$\int\limits_0^t \lambda\left[1 - F(y_{1,2}(s))\right] ds := G(t).$$

The necessary conditions for the variational problem (i.e., the Euler–Lagrange equation) with respect to the functions $H(t)$ and $G(t)$, respectively, are

$$- (q_1 - q_2) G'(t) \left[F^{-1}\left(1 - \frac{G'(t)}{\lambda}\right) - R(1,t) \right] - q_2 \frac{\frac{1}{\lambda}(H'(t))^2}{f\left(F^{-1}\left(1 - \frac{H'(t)}{\lambda}\right)\right)}$$

$$+ 2q_2 \frac{\frac{1}{\lambda}H''(t)}{f\left(F^{-1}\left(1 - \frac{H'(t)}{\lambda}\right)\right)} - q_1 R'(1,t)$$

$$+ q_2 \frac{\frac{1}{\lambda^2} H'(t) H''(t) f'\left(F^{-1}\left(1 - \frac{H'(t)}{\lambda}\right)\right)}{\left[f\left(F^{-1}\left(1 - \frac{H'(t)}{\lambda}\right)\right) \right]^3} = 0$$

and

$$- \frac{2\frac{1}{\lambda}G''(t)}{f\left(F^{-1}\left(1 - \frac{G'(t)}{\lambda}\right)\right)} - R'(1,t) - \frac{\frac{1}{\lambda^2}G'(t)G''(t)f'\left(F^{-1}\left(1 - \frac{G'(t)}{\lambda}\right)\right)}{\left[f\left(F^{-1}\left(1 - \frac{G'(t)}{\lambda}\right)\right) \right]^3}$$

$$- H'(t) \left[-\frac{\frac{1}{\lambda}G'(t)}{f\left(F^{-1}\left(1 - \frac{G'(t)}{\lambda}\right)\right)} + F^{-1}\left(1 - \frac{G'(t)}{\lambda}\right) - R(1,t) \right] = 0.$$

Plugging in the expressions for $H(t)$ and $G(t)$ allows us to write the necessary conditions in the following way:

$$- (q_1 - q_2) \lambda [1 - F(y_{1,2}(t))] (y_{1,2}(t) - R(1,t)) - q_2 \frac{\lambda [1 - F(y_{2,2}(t))]^2}{f(y_{2,2}(t))}$$

$$\hspace{11cm} (3.9)$$

$$-2q_2 y'_{2,2}(t) - q_1 R'(1,t) - q_2 \frac{y'_{2,2}(t) [1 - F(y_{2,2}(t))] f'(y_{2,2}(t))}{[f(y_{2,2}(t))]^2} = 0$$

and

$$\lambda [1 - F(y_{2,2}(t))] \left[\frac{1 - F(y_{1,2}(t))}{f(y_{1,2}(t))} - y_{1,2}(t) + R(1,t) \right] + 2y'_{1,2}(t) \hspace{1cm} (3.10)$$

$$-R'(1,t) + \frac{y'_{1,2}(t) [1 - F(y_{1,2}(t))] f'(y_{1,2}(t))}{[f(y_{1,2}(t))]^2} = 0.$$

Next we show that a solution to the system of differential equations (3.9) and (3.10) is given by $y_{1,2}(t) = y_1(t)$ and $y_{2,2}(t) = y_2(t)$, where $y_1(t)$ and $y_2(t)$ solve the system of equations:

$$y_1(t) = \frac{1 - F(y_1(t))}{f(y_1(t))} + \lambda \int_t^T \frac{[1 - F(y_1(s))]^2}{f(y_1(s))} ds \hspace{1cm} (3.11)$$

$$y_2(t) = \frac{1 - F(y_2(t))}{f(y_2(t))} + \lambda \int_t^T \frac{[1 - F(y_2(s))]^2}{f(y_2(s))} ds - R(1,t). \hspace{1cm} (3.12)$$

Again, the assumptions of increasing virtual types and finite density guarantee the existence of solutions for (3.11) and (3.12). Note also that since $R(1,t) \geq 0$, we must have $y_2(t) \leq y_1(t)$, $\forall t$.

Differentiation of (3.11) with respect to t gives

$$2y'_1(t) = -y'_1(t) \frac{[1 - F(y_1(t))] f'(y_1(t))}{[f(y_1(t))]^2} - \lambda \frac{[1 - F(y_1(t))]^2}{f(y_1(t))}.$$

Plugging the expression above into (3.10), and using the fact that

$$R'(1,t) = -y_1(t)\lambda (1 - F(y_1(t))) + \lambda (1 - F(y_1(t))) R(1,t) \hspace{1cm} (3.13)$$

yields

$$\left[\lambda \int_t^T \frac{[1 - F(y_1(s))]^2}{f(y_1(s))} ds - R(1,t) \right] [\lambda (1 - F(y_1(t)))$$

$$-\lambda (1 - F(y_{2,2}(t)))] = 0,$$

where the last equality follows from Claim 1. Thus we have shown that $y_{1,2}(t) = y_1(t)$ solves (3.10) for any $y_{2,2}(t)$. We still need to show that $y_{1,2}(t) = y_1(t)$ and $y_{2,2}(t) = y_2(t)$ solve equation (3.9). Differentiation of (3.12) with respect to t gives

$$2y_2'(t) = -y_2'(t)\frac{[1 - F(y_2(t))]\, f'(y_2(t))}{[f(y_2(t))]^2} - \lambda\frac{[1 - F(y_2(t))]^2}{f(y_2(t))} - R'(1,t).$$

Plugging this equality into (3.9), we have to show that

$$- (q_1 - q_2)\,\lambda\,[1 - F(y_{1,2}(t))]\,(y_{1,2}(t) - R(1,t)) - (q_1 - q_2)R'(1,t) = 0.$$

For $y_{1,2}(t) = y_1(t)$, this equality holds by (3.13).

Case 2. We now consider the case with $q_1 = q_2 = q$. Since $R(q,t) = qR(1,t)$, proposition 2 implies that we can rewrite the expected revenue as

$$q\int_0^T (y_{2,2}(t) + R(1,t))\,\lambda\,(1 - F(y_{2,2}(t)))\,e^{-\int_0^t \lambda(1 - F(y_{2,2}(s)))ds}\,dt.$$

The proof that the revenue-maximizing cutoff curves are given by $y_1(t)$ and $y_2(t)$ is analogous to the preceding case, and we omit it here.

Proposition 2 implies then that

$$R(\{1,1\},t) = \int_t^T (y_2(s) + R(1,s))\,\lambda\,(1 - F(y_2(s)))\,e^{-\int_t^s \lambda(1 - F(y_2(z)))dz}\,ds.$$

Differentiation with respect to t yields

$$R'(\{1,1\},t) = \lambda\,(1 - F(y_2(t)))\,(R(\{1,1\},t) - y_2(t) - R(1,t)). \qquad (3.14)$$

Recall that $y_2(t)$ solves

$$y_2(t) + R(1,t) = \frac{1 - F(y_2(t))}{f(y_2(t))} + \lambda\int_t^T \frac{[1 - F(y_2(s))]^2}{f(y_2(s))}ds. \qquad (3.15)$$

Using equation (3.15), it is easy to verify that $R(\{1,1\},t)$ given by equation (3.8) satisfies differential equation (3.14) with the boundary condition $R(\{1,1\},T) = 0$.

To complete the proof of the proposition, we have to show that the resulting cutoffs are implementable, meaning $y_2(t) \le y_1(t)$ for any $t \le T$. Note that (3.11) and (3.12) imply that $y_1(t)$ is the solution to $y(t) = L(y(t))$, while $y_2(t)$ is the solution to $y(t) = M(y(t))$. Since $M(y) \le L(y)$ holds for any y, the result follows. ∎

Remark 1 *Let us explore in some detail the intuition for the result whereby the optimal cutoffs do not depend on qualities. Assume that there are two available objects $q_1 > q_2$, and that at time t the cutoffs are $y_1^o > y_2^o$. Consider the effect of small shift in the highest cutoff from y_1^o to $y_1^o + \epsilon$. This shift has any effect only if some agent arrives at t. Moreover the shift has no effect on the expected revenue if the arriving agent has value below y_1^o. If at time t an agent with value y_1^o arrives, then the shift switches the object he gets from q_1 to q_2— which implies that he has to pay $P_t^{(2)}(\{q_1, q_2\})$ instead of $P_t^{(1)}(\{q_1, q_2\})$—and also switches the object that remains available for the future allocation from q_2 to q_1. The infinitesimal effect is*

$$f(y_1^o)\left(P_t^{(2)}(\{q_1, q_2\}) + q_1 R(1, t) - P_t^{(1)}(\{q_1, q_2\}) - q_2 R(1, t)\right)$$
$$= (q_1 - q_2) f(y_1^o)(R(1, t) - y_1^o).$$

The equality in the equation above follows here from the fact that in any incentive-compatible mechanism we must have $P_t^{(2)}(\{q_1, q_2\}) - P_t^{(1)}(\{q_1, q_2\}) = (q_2 - q_1) y_1^o$. Recall also that $P_t^{(1)}(\{q_1, q_2\}) = (q_1 - q_2) y_1^o + q_2 y_2^o$. Therefore the shift increases the price that will be charged to all agents with type above $y_1^o + \epsilon$, since supporting a more conservative allocation of the best available object requires charging a higher price to all types that should get this object. Increasing the cutoff y_1^o also yields a higher revenue if an agent with value above $y_1^o + \epsilon$ arrives. This effect is

$$[1 - F(y_1^o + \epsilon)][(q_1 - q_2)(y_1^o + \epsilon) + q_2(y_2^o + R(1, t))]$$
$$- (1 - F(y_1^o + \epsilon))[(q_1 - q_2)y_1^o + q_2(y_2^o + R(1, t))]$$
$$= (q_1 - q_2)[1 - F(y_1^o + \epsilon)]\epsilon.$$

For an infinitesimal change this effect becomes $(q_1 - q_2)(1 - F(y_1^o))$. To sum up, the total effect of the shift on expected revenue is

$$(q_1 - q_2)[1 - F(y_1^o)] - f(y_1^o)[y_1^o - R(1, t)].$$

The expression is linear in the difference $(q_1 - q_2)$ and the optimal y_1^o—where the total effect of the shift should be equal to zero—does not depend on the characteristics of the available objects.

Remark 2 *The equations for the revenue-maximizing cutoff curves have an intuitive interpretation. Assume first that only one object with $q = 1$ is* *available. The allocation policy is described by the equation*

$$y_1(t) - \frac{1 - F(y_1(t))}{f(y_1(t))} = \lambda \int_t^T \frac{[1 - F(y_1(s))]^2}{f(y_1(s))} ds = R(1, t).$$

On the left-hand side, we have the virtual valuation of an agent with type $y_1(t)$. As claim 1 showed, the right-hand side represents the expected revenue from time t on if the object is not sold at t, given that an optimal allocation policy is followed from time t on. Since the seller is able to extract as revenue only the virtual valuation of an arriving buyer, the equation shows that the optimal cutoff curve satisfies an indifference condition between immediate selling and a continuation that uses the optimal policy.

In the general case, if there are $k_t = |\Pi_t|$ available objects, then, no matter what their types are, the ith cutoff curve, $1 \leq i \leq k_t$, in the dynamic revenue-maximizing policy is given by

$$y_i(t) - \frac{1 - F(y_i(t))}{f(y_i(t))} + \lambda \int_t^T \frac{[1 - F(y_{i-1}(s))]^2}{f(y_{i-1}(s))} ds = \lambda \int_t^T \frac{[1 - F(y_i(s))]^2}{f(y_i(s))} ds$$

$$(3.16)$$

or, equivalently, by

$$y_i(t) - \frac{1 - F(y_i(t))}{f(y_i(t))} + R(1_{i-1}, t) = R(1_i, t), \qquad (3.17)$$

where 1_i is the set of 1's of cardinality i and

$$R(1_j, t) = \lambda \int_t^T \frac{[1 - F(y_j(s))]^2}{f(y_j(s))} ds \qquad (3.18)$$

is the expected revenue at time t from the optimal cutoff policy if j identical objects with $q = 1$ are still available. Since there will be sales only to the agents with positive virtual valuations, equation (3.17) implies that $R(1_i, t) > R(1_j, t)$ for any $i > j \geq 0$ and $t < T$.

While equation (3.17) has been obtained for the case of identical objects in the revenue-management literature (e.g., see Gallego and Ryzin 1994 Bitran and Mondschein 1997 for a discrete-time model), equation (3.18) is new, and an explicit expression of the fact that our analysis focused on the allocation policy rather than on prices.

For the general case with several distinct objects, note also that if an object is sold at time t, then the lowest among the current optimal cutoffs becomes

irrelevant regardless of the characteristic of the sold object, while all the other
$k_t - 1$ *cutoffs do not change and remain relevant for the future allocation deci-*
sions. That is, the optimal cutoffs depend only on the cardinality of Π_t, k_t. *For*
any two sets of available objects Π_t^1 *and* Π_t^2 *with* $k_t^1 = \left|\Pi_t^1\right|$ *and* $k_t^2 = \left|\Pi_t^2\right|$,
and for any $1 \leq i \leq \min\left\{k_t^1, k_t^2\right\}$, *it holds that*

$$y_{i,\Pi_t^1}(t) = y_{i,\Pi_t^2}(t).$$

If Π_t *is a set of identical objects, then only the lowest cutoff* $y_{k_t}(t)$, *where*
$k_t = \left|\Pi_t\right|$, *is relevant for the allocation decision.*

Note that in the optimal mechanism, prices for the remaining objects
increase after each sale. This follows because (1) the invariance property
implies that the allocation policy after a sale of any of k available objects
will be based on the $k - 1$ pre-sale highest cutoffs. (this more conservative
allocation is implemented via higher prices for all objects) and (2) each sale
increases the difference between the remaining qualities, which in turn leads
to an increase in the prices of all objects with qualities higher than the one just
sold. As a consequence, arriving buyers do not necessarily have an incentive
to delay their purchases because the average price may well go up for a period
of time, before inevitably going down if the good is not sold and the deadline
approaches.

We conclude this section with an example:

Example 5 *Let* $F(x) = x$ *on* $[0,1]$, *let* $\lambda(t) = 1$, *and assume that there are*
two objects. Then, the revenue-maximizing policy is characterized by:

$$y_1(t) = 1 - \frac{2}{4 + T - t},$$

$$y_2(t) = 1 - \frac{1 - \sqrt{5} + \left(1 + \sqrt{5}\right) c \left(T - t + 4\right)^{\sqrt{5}}}{T - t + 4 + c \left(T - t + 4\right)^{1+\sqrt{5}}},$$

where $c = \frac{\sqrt{5}+1}{4^{\sqrt{5}}\left(\sqrt{5}-1\right)}$.

Figure 3.1 plots these cutoffs for $T = 5$. *The optimal mechanism can be*
described as follows: Assume first that both objects are still available at time t,
and consider an agent arriving at t. *If his type is* $x_i \in [y_2(t), y_1(t))$, *he gets*
the object q_2 *and pays* $q_2 y_2(t)$; *if his type is* $x_i \in [y_1(t), 1]$, *he gets object* q_1
and pays $q_2 y_2(t) + (q_1 - q_2) y_1(t)$; *if his type is* $x < y_2(t)$, *he gets nothing*
and pays nothing. Assume now that one object is sold at time τ. *Then the other*
object will be sold at some time $t > \tau$, *which is the time of the first arrival*
of an agent with type $x_i \in [y_1(t), 1]$ *(assuming that this arrival is before the*

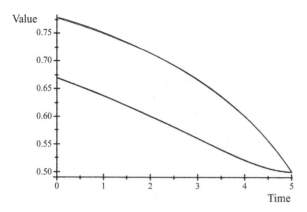

Figure 3.1
Cutoffs for $T = 5$

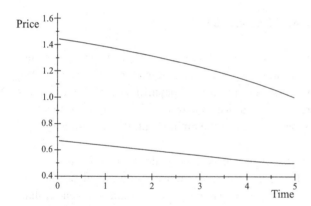

Figure 3.2
Cutoffs for $T = 5$, $q_1 = 2$, and $q_2 = 1$

deadline). The charged price depends then on the type of the available object and is given by $q_i y_1(t)$, $i = 1, 2$.

Assume now that $T = 5$, $q_1 = 2$, and $q_2 = 1$. Figure 3.2 plots the **price dynamics** if both objects are still available. Note that the prices of both objects jump after a sale, even if the upper cutoff in the revenue-maximizing allocation policy remains the same.

Figure 3.3 plots the **price dynamics** if only one object is available. The upper curve describes the offered price if only q_1 is available, while the lower curve corresponds to the offered price if only q_2 is available.

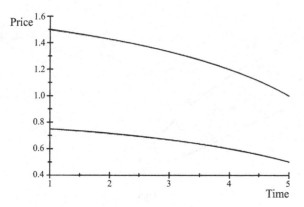

Figure 3.3
Prices when only one object is available

3.4   Infinite Horizon with Discounting

In this section we very briefly present the characterization of the dynamic revenue-maximizing allocation scheme in an infinite horizon setting. We assume that the utility of the designer from a payment at time t is discounted at rate $e^{-\alpha t}$, where $\alpha > 0$ is a discount factor. For the case of identical objects, Gallien (2006) has shown that the optimal cutoffs are stationary (i.e., time independent).

We show below that the revenue-maximizing allocation policy for several distinct objects does not depend on the characteristics of the available objects. The analysis of the discounted, infinite horizon case is similar and easier than the one we performed for the deadline case, therefore we omit the proof of the next proposition.

Theorem 12   *The dynamic revenue-maximizing policy consists of $m + 1$ constants $y_m \leq y_{m-1} \leq \ldots \leq y_1 \leq y_0 \equiv \infty$ that do not depend on the q's such that:*

1. *if an agent with type x arrives at time t, then it is optimal to assign to that agent the j'th highest element of Π_t if $x \in [y_j, y_{j-1})$, and not to assign any object if $x < y_{k_t}$, where $k_t = |\Pi_t|$;*

2. *the constants y_j satisfy*

$$y_j - \frac{1 - F(y_j)}{f(y_j)} + \frac{\lambda}{\alpha} \frac{[1 - F(y_{j-1})]^2}{f(y_{j-1})} = \frac{\lambda}{\alpha} \frac{[1 - F(y_j)]^2}{f(y_j)},$$

where

$$R(1_j) = \frac{\lambda}{\alpha} \frac{[1 - F(y_j)]^2}{f(y_j)}$$

is the expected revenue at time t if j identical objects with $q_1 = q_2 = \ldots = q_j = 1$ are available at time t, given that the designer uses the optimal allocation policy from time t on.

An important observation is that in the infinite horizon model prices only go up while the inventory is gradually depleted. Thus, even if buyers are long-lived, they do not have an incentive to delay their purchase after the arrival time.

The next example illustrates the proposition:

Example 6 *Assume that there are three objects. Let $F(x) = x$ on $[0,1]$ and let $\alpha = \lambda = 1$. Then the constant cutoffs defining the revenue-maximizing policy are*

$$y_1 = 2 - \sqrt{2} \approx 0.585\,79,$$

$$y_2 = 2 - \sqrt{5 - 2\sqrt{2}} \approx 0.526\,37,$$

$$y_3 = 2 - \sqrt{2}\frac{\sqrt{2\sqrt{2}\sqrt{5 - 2\sqrt{2}} - 5\sqrt{5 - 2\sqrt{2}} - 13\sqrt{2} + 24}}{\sqrt{5 - 2\sqrt{2}}} \approx 0.508\,58.$$

3.5 Comparison of the Efficient and the Revenue-Maximizing Policies

In this section we compare the efficient and revenue-maximizing dynamic allocation policies for the case where there is a deadline (the discounted infinite horizon case is analogous). Our main result in this section shows that the curves describing the revenue-maximizing allocation are always above the respective curves describing the efficient allocation if the agents' types follow a distribution with an increasing failure rate. In other words, at any point in time, the revenue-maximizing policy is more "conservative." Denote by $y_i^e(t)$ $(y_i^o(t))$ the efficient (revenue-maximizing) cutoff for the object with the ith highest characteristic.

Theorem 13 *Assume that $\lambda(t) = \lambda$ and that the distribution of values F has an increasing failure rate. Then for any $t \in [0,T]$, $y_i^e(t) < y_i^o(t)$, $i = 1, 2, \ldots, n$.*

Proof   We start with the proof for $i = 1$. By proposition 11, we know that

$$y_1^o(t) = \frac{1 - F\left(y_1^o(t)\right)}{f\left(y_1^o(t)\right)} + \lambda \int_t^T \frac{\left[1 - F\left(y_1^o(s)\right)\right]^2}{f\left(y_1^o(s)\right)} ds,$$

and by theorem 4, we know that

$$-y_1^{e\prime}(s) = \lambda \int_{y_1^e(s)}^\infty (1 - F(x)) dx$$

and that $y_1^e(T) = 0$. Integrating both sides between t and T of the differential equation above, and using the boundary condition, yields

$$y_1^e(t) = \lambda \int_t^T \left[\int_{y_1^e(s)}^\infty (1 - F(x)) dx \right] ds.$$

We now argue that

$$\frac{1 - F\left(y_1^o(t)\right)}{f\left(y_1^o(t)\right)} > 0 \qquad \text{for any } t \in [0, T]. \tag{3.19}$$

Assume that there exists t^* such that

$$\frac{1 - F\left(y_1^o(t^*)\right)}{f\left(y_1^o(t^*)\right)} = 0. \tag{3.20}$$

Then, since $f(x) < \infty$ for any x, (3.20) implies that $F\left(y_1^o(t^*)\right) = 1$. That is, the probability that an agent who arrives at time t^* has a type above $y_1^o(t^*)$ is zero. By proposition 11, we can assume that $q_1 = 1$. This yields

$$0 < R(1, t^*) < y_1^o(t^*). \tag{3.21}$$

Consider then decreasing $y_1^o(t^*)$ to $R(1, t^*) + \epsilon$, where $y_1^o(t^*) - R(1, t^*) > \epsilon > 0$ (inequality 3.21 implies that such ϵ exists). This change matters only if at t^* some agent arrives. But in this case the proposed change increases the revenue, since the object can be sold to that agent at the price $R(1, t^*) + \epsilon$ while prior to the change the probability of a sale was zero. This yields a contradiction that $y_1^o(t^*)$ was chosen optimally.

In order to complete the proof for the one-object case, it is enough (given inequality 3.19) to show that

$$\forall y, \quad \frac{(1 - F(y))^2}{f(y)} \geq \int_y^\infty (1 - F(x)) dx.$$

This follows from

$$\int\limits_y^\infty (1 - F(x))dx = \int\limits_y^\infty \frac{1 - F(x)}{f(x)} f(x)\, dx \leq \frac{1 - F(y)}{f(y)} (1 - F(y)),$$

where the last inequality follows from the increasing failure rate (IFR) assumption.

We now proceed to the proof for two objects. After plugging in the expression for $R(1,t)$, we know, by proposition 11, that $y_2^o(t)$ solves

$$y_2^o(t) = \frac{1 - F(y_2^o(t))}{f(y_2^o(t))} + \lambda \int\limits_t^T \left[\frac{[1 - F(y_2^o(s))]^2}{f(y_2^o(s))} - \frac{[1 - F(y_1^o(s))]^2}{f(y_1^o(s))} \right] ds.$$

By theorem 4, we know that

$$-y_2^{e\prime}(s) = \lambda \int\limits_{y_2^e(s)}^{y_1^e(s)} (1 - F(x))dx.$$

Integrating again both sides between t and T yields

$$y_2^e(t) = \lambda \int\limits_t^T \left[\int\limits_{y_2^e(s)}^{y_1^e(s)} (1 - F(x))dx \right] ds.$$

By theorem 4, we also know that $y_2^e(t) < y_1^e(t)$. Together with the result for the one-object case (see the proof above), we obtain that $y_2^e(t) < y_1^o(t)$.

Let $y_2^e(t)$ be the solution to

$$y(t) = L(y(t)),$$

and let $y_2^o(t)$ be the solution to

$$y(t) = M(y(t)).$$

We are now going to show that $M\left(y\left(t\right)\right) > L\left(y\left(t\right)\right)$ for any $y\left(t\right) < y_1^o(t)$. Together with $y_2^e\left(t\right) < y_1^o(t)$, this will complete the proof. Note that

$$L(y\left(t\right)) = \int\limits_t^T \left[\int\limits_{y(s)}^{y_1^e(s)} (1 - F(x))dx \right] ds \tag{3.22}$$

$$= \int\limits_t^T \left[\int\limits_{y(s)}^{y_1^e(s)} \frac{1 - F(x)}{f(x)} f\left(x\right) dx \right] ds$$

$$\leq \int\limits_t^T \frac{1 - F\left(y\left(s\right)\right)}{f\left(y\left(s\right)\right)} \left([1 - F\left(y\left(s\right)\right)] - [1 - F\left(y_1^e\left(s\right)\right)] \right) ds$$

$$= \int\limits_t^T \left(\frac{\left(1 - F\left(y\left(s\right)\right)\right)^2}{f\left(y\left(s\right)\right)} - \frac{\left(1 - F\left(y\left(s\right)\right)\right)\left(1 - F\left(y_1^e\left(s\right)\right)\right)}{f\left(y\left(s\right)\right)} \right) ds$$

$$\leq \int\limits_t^T \left(\frac{\left(1 - F\left(y\left(s\right)\right)\right)^2}{f\left(y\left(s\right)\right)} - \frac{\left(1 - F\left(y_1^o(s)\right)\right)^2}{f\left(y_1^o(s)\right)} \right) ds < M(y\left(t\right)).$$

The third line follows from IFR assumption, and the fifth line follows from IFR, from the assumption $y\left(t\right) < y_1^o(t)$ and from $y_1^e\left(s\right) < y_1^o(t)$. The last inequality follows by the same argument as in the one object case, since $\frac{1 - F(y_2^o(t))}{f(y_2^o(t))} > 0$. Also note that the IFR assumption implies that M is a decreasing function.

Assume now, by contradiction, that there exists some t such that $y_2^e\left(t\right) > y_2^o\left(t\right)$. Then

$$y_2^e\left(t\right) = L\left(y_2^e\left(t\right)\right) < M\left(y_2^e\left(t\right)\right) < M\left(y_2^o\left(t\right)\right) = y_2^o\left(t\right),$$

where the first inequality follows from (3.22), while monotonicity of M implies the second inequality. Therefore we got that $y_2^e\left(t\right) < y_2^o\left(t\right)$, which is a contradiction. The proof for $n > 2$ follows analogously. ∎

The next example illustrates the theorem:

Example 7 *Assume that there are two objects, that the arrival process is homogeneous with rate $\lambda(t) = 1$, and that the distribution of agents' types is* *exponential, meaning, $F(x) = 1 - e^{-x}$. The efficient policy is described by the cutoff functions*

$$y_1^e(t) = \ln(1 + T - t),$$
$$y_2^e(t) = \ln\left(1 + \frac{(T-t)^2}{2(1+T-t)}\right),$$

while the revenue-maximizing policy is given by

$$y_1^o(t) = \ln(e + T - t)$$
$$y_2^o(t) = \ln\left(\frac{1}{2}(e + T - t) + \frac{1}{2}\frac{e^2}{(e+T-t)}\right).$$

Figure 3.4 plots the solutions for $T = 5$. The solid lines represent the revenue-maximizing cutoffs and the dashed lines represent the efficient cutoffs.

Our last example shows that the efficient and revenue-maximizing cutoffs may coincide if the IFR assumption is not satisfied. In particular, an increasing virtual valuation is not sufficient for the preceding result.

Example 8 *(McAfee and te Velde 2008)   Assume that there is one object, that the arrival process is Poisson with rate $\lambda(t) = 1$, and that values are distributed according to a Pareto distribution, that is, $F(x) = 1 - x^{-\epsilon}$ for $x \geq 1$, $\epsilon > 1$.*

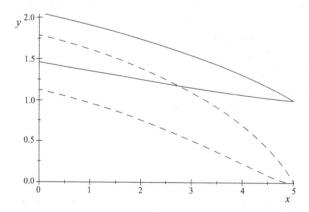

Figure 3.4
Revenue-maximizing cutoffs (solid lines) and efficient cutoffs (dashed lines)

The failure rate is given by $\frac{f(x)}{1-F(x)} = \frac{\epsilon}{x}$, which is decreasing. McAfee and te Velde showed for this case that the efficient and revenue-maximizing cutoffs coincide:

$$y_1^e(t) = y_1^o(t) = \left[\frac{\epsilon}{\epsilon - 1}(T - t)\right]^{1/\epsilon}.$$

Note that the virtual valuation is given by $x - \frac{1-F(x)}{f(x)} = x(1 - \frac{1}{\epsilon})$, which is increasing in x since $\epsilon > 1$. This shows that an increasing virtual valuation is not sufficient for the result of theorem 13.

3.6   Dynamic Pricing and Optimal Inventory Choice

The preceding analysis was based on the assumption that the inventory's size and composition are exogenously given. In practice, and important issue is the determination and composition of the inventory itself, for example, in the airline industry, the decision on the partition in classes first, business, and economy and number of seats in each class. In this section we show how our previous insights can be used as a building block for a more general analysis where the seller can choose both the number of objects and the spectrum of offered qualities before sales start. This timing assumption is appropriate in cases where the necessary production lead-times are significant in comparison to the retail period. Our present treatment extends the seminal Mussa and Rosen (1978) analysis to the framework with random arrivals. Gallego and Ryzin (1994) characterized the optimal inventory size in a model with deterministic demand, and showed that the solution coincides with the optimal size of the inventory in the original problem if the horizon goes to infinity. In contrast, we are able to characterize the optimal inventory size (and its composition) in the original problem for any finite horizon.

Since our analysis identified an invariant of the optimal selling scheme—the allocation policy—we can easily solve the larger problem backward and characterize the optimal quality choice. Formally, the decision of the monopolist is to choose the optimal package of qualities Π_0:

$$\max_{\Pi_0} R(\Pi_0, 0) - C(\Pi_0),$$

where $C(\Pi)$ denotes cost of producing the package of qualities Π. It is plausible to assume that the cost function is convex and symmetric (symmetry means here that the cost of producing any permutation of a given package of qualities is the same as the cost of producing the original package). Note that any convex and symmetric function is *Schur-convex*. Schur-convexity guarantees that a higher marginal revenue is associated with a higher chosen quality for the respective object.

We assume below a very simple, separable form of Schur-convexity for the cost function, but the reader will have no difficulty adding the technical details needed for the more general result that does not assume separability.

Theorem 14 *Let* $y = \{y_i(t)\}_{i=1}^m$ *denote the allocation underlying the revenue-maximizing policy with* m *objects, and assume that for all* m *and for all vectors of qualities* $(q_1, q_2, \ldots, q_m)$, $C(q_1, q_2, \ldots, q_m) = \sum_{i=1}^m \phi(q_i)$, *where the function* $\phi : R \to R$ *is strictly increasing, convex and satisfies* $\phi(0) = 0$. *Then:*

1. *the optimal number of objects* m^* *is characterized by[5]*

$$\phi'(0) \in \left[y_{m^*+1}(0) - \frac{1 - F\left(y_{m^*+1}(0)\right)}{f\left(y_{m^*+1}(0)\right)}, \ y_{m^*}(0) - \frac{1 - F\left(y_{m^*}(0)\right)}{f\left(y_{m^*}(0)\right)} \right];$$

$$(3.23)$$

2. *the optimal qualities* q_i^* *are given by*

$$\phi'(q_i^*) = y_i(0) - \frac{1 - F\left(y_i(0)\right)}{f\left(y_i(0)\right)}, \qquad i = 1, \ldots, m^*. \tag{3.24}$$

Proof We start by showing that the expected revenue from the optimal mechanism is linear in the q's. That is, if at time $t \leq T$ the set Π_t of the object is still available, then the expected revenue is given by

$$R(\Pi_t, t) = \sum_{i=1}^{k_t} q_{(i:\Pi_t)} \left(y_i(t) - \frac{1 - F\left(y_i(t)\right)}{f\left(y_i(t)\right)} \right).$$

Our first step toward the above-mentioned result consists of showing, by induction on the number of objects, that there exist factors that depend on time but not on the qualities, $a_1(t), \ldots, a_{k_t}(t)$, such that

$$R(\Pi_t, t) = \sum_{i=1}^{k_t} q_{(i:\Pi_t)} a_i(t). \tag{3.25}$$

When only one object of quality q is available, the price for the object is given by $qy_1(t)$, and from claim 1 it follows that the expected revenue is given by

$$R(q, t) = q\lambda \int_t^T \frac{\left[1 - F\left(y_1(s)\right)\right]^2}{f\left(y_1(s)\right)} ds.$$

Assume then that if at time t there are k objects with qualities $\Pi_t = (q_1, q_2, \ldots, q_k)$, the expected revenue is given by

$$R(\Pi_t, t) = \sum_{i=1}^{k_t} q_{(i:\Pi_t)} a_i.$$

Consider now a situation with $k + 1$ objects at time t. Recall that

$$R(\Pi_t, t) = \sum_{i=1}^{k_t} \int_t^T P_s^i(\Pi_t) h_{i,\Pi_t}(s) \, ds$$

$$+ \sum_{i=1}^{k_t} \int_t^T R\left(\Pi_t \backslash \{q_{(i:\Pi_t)}\}, s\right) h_{i,\Pi_t}(s) \, ds.$$

The second element of the sum is linear in qualities by the induction argument, while the first element is linear by the definition of $P_s^i(\Pi_t)$ (see equation 3.1).

To see that $a_i(t) = y_i(t) - \frac{1 - F(y_i(t))}{f(y_i(t))}$, note that, since $a_i(t)$ does not depend on Π_t, equations (3.25) and (3.17) imply that

$$a_i(t) = R(\mathbf{1}_i, t) - R(\mathbf{1}_{i-1}, t) = y_i(t) - \frac{1 - F(y_i(t))}{f(y_i(t))}.$$

By this argument, at time $t = 0$ the marginal returns to qualities are ordered, with the i-highest produced quality having also the i-highest marginal return $y_i(0) - \frac{1 - F(y_i(0))}{f(y_i(0))}$. By the convexity of ϕ, the i-highest quality will have the i-highest marginal cost as well, and the characterization of the optimal produced qualities follows. As soon as the marginal return drops below $\phi'(0)$, the cost of producing another object with a positive quality cannot be recovered, and this determines the optimal number of produced objects.   ∎

The preceding result and its analogue for welfare maximization can be used to compare the quality choices in the two regimes. For example, it is intuitive that a revenue-maximizing monopolist will produce lower qualities than a welfare-maximizing one, as in the Mussa–Rosen framework. Note, though, that some insights will differ from Mussa and Rosen's due to a difference in timing: while we assume that qualities are produced in advance—before buyers' characteristics get revealed—Mussa and Rosen implicitly assume that quality can be produced contingent on these. For instance, in our setup there is a distortion even in the quality provided to the highest type.

3.7 The Pattern of Prices in Clearance Sales

Our characterization generates a wealth of empirically testable implications about the pattern of observed prices associated with the revenue-maximizing policy. These implications can be compared to available data for relevant situations. For example, an important finding in the well-known empirical study of clearance sales for apparel conducted by Pashigian and Bowen (1991) is that: "More expensive apparel items within each product line are frequently sold at a higher average percentage markdown."

Pashigian and Bowen attempt to explain this phenomenon by using Lazear's (1986) theory of retail pricing and clearance sales. Lazear's theory only deals with the sale of homogeneous products, and it cannot incorporate the parallel sale of several substitutes, as is common practice in most stores. Thus the offered theoretical explanation for the empirical finding is not entirely convincing.[6] The next result shows how the empirical observation agrees with a fairly general prediction of our model that holds for any two different qualities, for any positive levels of inventories before and after the clearance sale, and for any distribution of values.

Proposition 3 *Assume that the seller uses the revenue-maximizing policy in a situation where at time $t = 0$ there are $n_1 > 0$ items of quality q and $n_2 > 0$ items of quality s, $s < q$. Assume also that at time $t = T$ there are $0 < l_1 \leq n_1$ items of quality q and $0 < l_2 \leq n_2$ items of quality s left unsold. Then the percentage markdown—defined as the difference between the prices of the same product at $t = 0$ and $t = T$ divided by the price at $t = 0$—is always higher for the higher quality.*

Proof Denote by $y = \{y_i\}_{i=1}^{n_1+n_2}$ the optimal policy given the inventory in period $t = 0$. Our previous results imply that

$$P_T^{(l_1+l_2)}(\Pi_T) = sy_{l_1+l_2}(T); \; P_0^{(n_1+n_2)}(\Pi_0) = sy_{n_1+n_2}(0),$$

$$P_T^{(l_1)}(\Pi_T) = sy_{l_1+l_2}(T) + (q - s)y_{l_1}(T);$$

$$P_0^{(n_1)}(\Pi_0) = sy_{n_1+n_2}(0) + (q - s)y_{n_1}(0).$$

We obtain the following chain:

$$\frac{P_0^{(n_1)}(\Pi_0) - P_T^{(l_1)}(\Pi_T)}{P_0^{(n_1)}(\Pi_0)} \geq \frac{P_0^{(n_1+n_2)}(\Pi_0) - P_T^{(l_1+l_2)}(\Pi_T)}{P_0^{(n_1+n_2)}(\Pi_0)} \Leftrightarrow$$

$$\frac{P_T^{(l_1)}(\Pi_T)}{P_0^{(n_1)}(\Pi_0)} \leq \frac{P_T^{(l_1+l_2)}(\Pi_T)}{P_0^{(n_1+n_2)}(\Pi_0)} \Leftrightarrow$$

$$\frac{sy_{l_1+l_2}(T) + (q-s)y_{l_1}(T)}{sy_{n_1+n_2}(0) + (q-s)y_{n_1}(0)} \leq \frac{sy_{l_1+l_2}(T)}{sy_{n_1+n_2}(0)} \Leftrightarrow$$

$$\frac{qy_{l_1+l_2}(T)}{sy_{n_1+n_2}(0) + (q-s)y_{n_1}(0)} \leq \frac{y_{l_1+l_2}(T)}{y_{n_1+n_2}(0)} \Leftrightarrow$$

$$\frac{q}{sy_{n_1+n_2}(0) + (q-s)y_{n_1}(0)} \leq \frac{1}{y_{n_1+n_2}(0)} \Leftrightarrow$$

$$qy_{n_1+n_2}(0) \leq sy_{n_1+n_2}(0) + (q-s)y_{n_1}(0) \Leftrightarrow$$

$$(q-s)y_{n_1+n_2}(0) \leq (q-s)y_{n_1}(0) \Leftrightarrow y_{n_1+n_2}(0) \leq y_{n_1}(0).$$

The third line uses proposition 1 and remark 2. The fourth line uses the fact that for all $1 \leq i, j \leq n_1 + n_2$, $y_i(T) = y_j(T)$, which is a consequence of equation (3.16). The last inequality follows from proposition 1.   ∎

We conclude this section with another related observation that can also be taken to the data:

Proposition 4 *Consider the revenue-maximizing policy. At any point in time t where two different qualities are available, the price of the higher quality decreases quicker than the price of the lower quality.*

Proof Assume that the inventory at time t is Π_t, and consider two different qualities $q_{(j_1:\Pi_t)}$ and $q_{(j_2:\Pi_t)}$ such that $q_{(j_1:\Pi_t)} > q_{(j_2:\Pi_t)}$. Recall that the prices associated with each quality satisfy

$$P_t^{(j_l)}(\Pi_t) = \sum_{i=j_l}^{k_t} (q_{(i:\Pi_t)} - q_{(i+1:\Pi_t)})y_{i,\Pi_t}(t), \qquad l = 1, 2,$$

where y denotes the (quality-independent) revenue-maximizing allocation policy. Thus

$$P_t^{(j_1)}(\Pi_t) = P_t^{(j_2)}(\Pi_t) + \sum_{i=j_1}^{j_2-1} (q_{(i:\Pi_t)} - q_{(i+1:\Pi_t)})y_{i,\Pi_t}(t),$$

which implies that

$$\frac{dP_t^{(j_1)}(\Pi_t)}{dt} = \frac{dP_t^{(j_2)}(\Pi_t)}{dt} + \frac{d[\sum_{i=j_1}^{j_2-1}(q_{(i:\Pi_t)} - q_{(i+1:\Pi_t)})y_{i,\Pi_t}(t)]}{dt}.$$

Lemma 2 (proved below) yields

$$\frac{dy_{i,\Pi_t}(t)}{dt} \leq 0, \qquad \forall i,$$

which implies that

$$\frac{dP_t^{(j_1)}(\Pi_t)}{dt} \leq \frac{dP_t^{(j_2)}(\Pi_t)}{dt}.$$

Since these last derivatives are negative (as is implied again by lemma 2), the result follows.[7] ∎

Lemma 2 *In the revenue-maximizing mechanism, the cutoffs determining the allocation policy are decreasing with time. That is,*

$$y_i'(t) \leq 0 \qquad for\ i \in \{1, ..., k_t\}\ and\ t \in [0, T).$$

Proof We prove the result by induction on the number of the available objects k_t. If $k_t = 1$, differentiating (3.5) with respect to t gives

$$y_1'(t) \frac{\partial}{\partial y_1(t)} \left(y_1(t) - \frac{1 - F(y_1(t))}{f(y_1(t))} \right) = -\lambda \frac{[1 - F(y_1(t))]^2}{f(y_1(t))}.$$

The result follows then since the right-hand side is negative, and since the virtual valuation is assumed to be increasing. Assume then that the statement holds for $k_t = l$, and consider the case where $k_t = l + 1$. The properties of the revenue-maximizing mechanism imply that l highest curves $y_i(t)$ coincide with those relevant for the case where $k_t = l$. Thus $y_i'(t) \leq 0$ for $i \in \{1, ..., l\}$. Differentiating with respect to t the expression (3.16) for $y_{l+1}(t)$ gives

$$y_{l+1}'(t) \frac{\partial}{\partial y_{l+1}(t)} \left(y_{l+1}(t) - \frac{1 - F(y_{l+1}(t))}{f(y_{l+1}(t))} \right)$$
$$= \lambda \left[\frac{[1 - F(y_l(t))]^2}{f(y_l(t))} - \frac{[1 - F(y_{l+1}(t))]^2}{f(y_{l+1}(t))} \right]. \qquad (3.26)$$

Proposition 1 implies that $y_{l+1}(t) \leq y_l(t)$ for any $t \in [0, T)$. There are two cases:

Case 1. There exists $t \in [0, T)$ such that $y_{l+1}(t) = y_l(t)$. Then (3.26) implies that $y_{l+1}'(t) = 0$.

Case 2. For any $t \in [0, T)$ we have $y_{l+1}(t) < y_l(t)$. Notice that the function $\frac{[1-F(y)]^2}{f(y)}$ is decreasing if and only if the virtual valuation is increasing. Therefore an increasing virtual valuation implies that the right-hand side of (3.26) is negative and that $\frac{\partial}{\partial y_{l+1}(t)} \left(y_{l+1}(t) - \frac{1-F(y_{l+1}(t))}{f(y_{l+1}(t))} \right) > 0$. This yields $y_{l+1}'(t) < 0$, and completes the proof. ∎

3.8 Related Literature

There are very large theoretical and applied literatures on dynamic pricing of inventories (sometimes called *revenue or yield management*) both in economics and in the fields of management and operations research. The general goal in this literature is revenue maximization. We refer the reader to the excellent literature surveys and discussions of involved issues by Bitran and Caldentey (2003) and Elmaghraby and Keskinocak (2003), and to the comprehensive book by Talluri and van Ryzin (2004). McAfee and te Velde (2007) survey the applications to the airline industry that has pioneered many of the modern practices in revenue management.

Riley and Zeckhauser (1983) considered a single-object revenue-maximizing procedure where there is learning about the distribution of the agents' values. In their model, the optimal mechanism is a sequence of take-it-or-leave-it offers. Lazear (1986) offers a theory of clearance sales that allows for several identical units. In his model all customers have the same value, and the seller learns about this value over time. It is shown that a pattern of decreasing prices is optimal. Pashigian (1988), Pashigian and Bowen (1991), and Pashigian, Bowen, and Gould (1995) test some of the empirical implications of Lazear's analysis based on data obtained from several industries.

In a continuous-time framework with stochastic arrivals of agents, Kincaid and Darling (1963), and Gallego and Ryzin (1994) use dynamic programming in order to characterize—implicitly via Bellman's equations—the revenue-maximizing pricing policy for a set of identical objects that need to be sold before a deadline. A main result is that the expected revenue in the optimal policy—which is characterized for each size of inventory by a single posted price—is increasing and concave both in the number of objects and in the length of time left till the deadline. Moreover each relevant cutoff price drops with time as long as there is no sale, but jumps up after each sale.[8] These authors were able to calculate in closed form the solution for what amounts (in our terms) to an exponential distribution of agents' values. McAfee and te Velde (2008) find an explicit solution for a Pareto distribution of agents' values, and show that it coincides with the welfare-maximizing policy. Generally, a closed-form solution is not available, and even the expression of expected revenue as a function of the optimal cutoff prices is not available in the literature.

Arnold and Lippman (2001), Das Varma and Vettas (2001), and Gallien (2006) consider the same basic problem as above, but in a framework with an infinite horizon and discounting. In this case the revenue-maximizing posted prices—again one price for each size of inventory—turn out to be stationary: they do not depend on time.[9] This stationarity allows Gallien to offer a reasonable sufficient condition ensuring that all sales occur immediately upon arrival, even if the arriving agents can strategically delay their purchase. Also in an infinite horizon model, Wang (1993) compares a posted-price regime with an auction regime. In his framework, the auction option is costly.

Lazear (1986) argues that delayed purchases by strategic consumers is not likely to be significant if the number of consumers is large, but a more recent, still small, strand of the literature focuses on strategic buyer behavior in models with fixed inventories.[10] Nocke and Peitz (2007) exhibit conditions for a decreasing price path to be optimal even if consumers are strategic about the timing of purchases in a model with identical units and fixed demand. These authors do not consider pricing policies that condition on past realized sales. Aviv and Pazgal (2008) assume that prices must be declining (which is not innocuous) in a two-period model with stochastic arrivals, but they derive analytic results only for policies that do not depend on past realized sales. Su (2007) allows more general policies but assumes a deterministic demand flow.

To conclude, as Bitran and Caldentey (2003) noted, due to the technical complexity, the literature on dynamic revenue maximization with stochastic demand has focused on models with identical objects, contrasting the present framework.[11]

Notes

1. The estimate is that $20 billion worth of shrink is wasted annually in the Unite States, about 10 percent of sales. See "Shrink rapped," *The Economist,* May 17, 2008, p. 75.

2. The generalization to nonhomogeneous Poisson processes is straightforward.

3. For a detailed discussion of this assumption, see Myerson (1981) and Bulow and Roberts (1989).

4. If the optimal policy is non-Markov, there are different histories after which the state is the same but the taken action differs. For each state s and for any history H, let $p(H|s)$ be the *exante* probability that history H occurs, conditional on the reached state being s. Modify now the policy in the following way: at time t the new policy uses a lottery where the action used in the original policy after history H is taken with probability $p(H|s)$. If the original policy was optimal, then it need to be incentive compatible for **any** history H. By construction, the modified policy will be incentive compatible as well.

5. It should be obvious how to adjust the formula in order to deal with the extreme cases where $m^* = 0, \infty$.

6. For some special forms of the distribution of values, Lazear's theory predicts that increasing the dispersion in values for the product will lead to an increased markdown. Pashigian and Bowen identify more expensive items (which contain more elements of fashion and style) with an increased dispersion.

7. The same argument also shows that the difference between the two prices is monotonically decreasing.

8. Bitran and Mondschein (1997) obtain similar results in a discrete time framework.

9. Das Varma and Vettas consider a model with discrete-time and deterministic arrivals, whereas Gallien and Arnold and Lippman have continuous-time models with stochastic arrivals. The latter authors assume (rather than derive) the stationarity of posted prices, and also compare these to reservation prices in a model where arriving agents announce bids.

10. This should be contrasted with the earlier literature on the so-called Coase conjecture where by the inventory can be replenished. McAfee and Wiseman (2008) show that the introduction of capacity costs counters the Coasian insight. For other papers that examine the relationship between limited inventories and pricing schemes, see Harris and Raviv (1981) and Wilson (1988).

11. See Gallego and Ryzin (1997) for an exception. Some models assume that customers belong to several known classes, which allows the use of third-degree price discrimination.

4 The Stochastic and Dynamic Knapsack Model

4.1 Introduction

In this chapter we add incomplete information to the dynamic and stochastic knapsack problem with heterogeneous capacity requests. This way we obtain a dynamic monopolistic screening problem: there is a finite number of periods, and at each period a request for capacity arrives from an agent that is impatient and privately informed about both his valuation per unit of capacity and the needed capacity.[1] Each agent derives positive utility if he gets the needed capacity (or more), and zero utility otherwise. The designer accepts or rejects the requests in order to maximize the revenue obtained from the allocation. The main difference to the models in the previous chapters is that agents have multi-unit demand and also multidimensional privately known types.

We first characterize implementable policies. Our implementation problem is special because useful deviations in the weight dimension can only be one-sided (upward). This feature allows here, relative to standard multidimensional private information models, a less cumbersome characterization of implementable policies. This characterization can be embedded then in the dynamic analysis under certain conditions on the joint distribution of values and weights of the arriving agents.

We first solve the revenue-maximization problem for the case where there is private information about per-unit values, but weights are observable. We will sometimes refer to this as the *relaxed* problem. Under a standard monotonicity assumption on virtual values, this is the virtual value analogue of the problem solved by Papastavrou, Rajagopalan, and Kleywegt (1996). The resulting optimal policy is Markovian, deterministic, and has a threshold property with respect to virtual values. It is important to emphasize that this policy need not be implementable for the case where both values and weights are unobservable, unless additional conditions are imposed. Our main results in the first part of the chapter demonstrate the implementability of the relaxed optimal solution: we derive two sets of additional conditions on the joint distribution of values and weights under which the revenue-maximizing policy for the case with observable weights is implementable, and thus optimal also for the case with two-dimensional private information. The first condition—which is satisfied in a variety of intuitive settings—is a hazard rate ordering that expresses a form of positive correlation between weights and values. It ensures that the incentive constraint in the capacity dimension is never binding.

We also draw a connection between incentive compatibility and the structural property of concavity of revenue in capacity. Concavity of optimal revenue in the relaxed problem creates a tendency to set higher virtual value thresholds for higher capacity requests. It is then less attractive for agents to overstate their capacity needs, which facilitates the implementation of the relaxed solution by relaxing the incentive constraints. We quantify this relation in our second set of additional conditions: concavity of revenue combined with a (substantial) weakening of the hazard rate order imply implementability of the relaxed solution. For completeness, we also briefly translate to our model the sufficient condition for concavity of revenue due to Papastavrou, Rajagopalan, and Kleywegt (1996) in order to obtain a condition on the model's primitives.

Finally, we construct—for general distributions of weights and values—a time-independent, nonlinear price schedule that is asymptotically revenue maximizing when the available capacity and the time to the deadline both go to infinity, and when weights are observable. Our result suggests that complicated dynamic pricing may not be that important for revenue maximization if the distribution of agents' types is known. Our result emphasizes, though, that nonlinear pricing remains asymptotically important in dynamic settings. As a nice link to the first part described above, the constructed nonlinear price schedule turns out to be implementable for the case with two-dimensional private information if the weakened hazard rate condition employed in our discussion of concavity is satisfied.

Since prices are time-independent, the policy is also immune to strategic buyer arrivals (which we do not model here explicitly). We also point out that a policy that varies with time but not with requested weight (whose asymptotic optimality in the complete information case has been established by Lin, Lu, and Yao 2008) is usually not optimal under incomplete information.

4.2   The Model

The designer has a "knapsack" of given capacity $C \in \mathbb{R}$ that he wants to allocate in a revenue-maximizing way to several agents in at most $T < \infty$ periods. In this chapter we count periods chronologically, meaning the first period is period 1, the second period is period 2, and so on. In each period an impatient agent arrives with a demand for capacity characterized by a weight (or quantity request) w, and by a per-unit value v.[2] While the realization of the random vector (w, v) is private information to the arriving agent, its distribution is assumed to be common knowledge and given by the joint cumulative distribution function $F(w, v)$, with continuously differentiable density $f(w, v) > 0$, defined on $[0, \infty)^2$. Demands are independent across different periods.[3]

In each period the designer decides on a capacity to be allocated to the arriving agent (possibly none) and on a monetary payment. Type (w, v)'s utility is given by $wv - p$ if at price p he is allocated a capacity $w' \geq w$ and by $-p$ if he is assigned an insufficient capacity $w' < w$. Each agent observes the remaining capacity of the designer.[4] Finally, we assume that for all w, the conditional virtual value functions $\hat{v}(v, w) := v - \frac{1 - F(v|w)}{f(v|w)}$ are unbounded as a function of v and strictly monotone increasing in v with $\frac{\partial}{\partial v} \hat{v}(v, w) > 0$ for all (w, v).

4.3 Implementable Policies

To characterize the revenue-maximizing scheme, we restrict attention, without loss of generality, to direct mechanisms where every agent, upon arrival, reports a type (w, v); the mechanism then specifies an allocation and a payment. In this section we characterize incentive compatibility for a class of allocation policies that necessarily contains the revenue-maximizing policy. The schemes we develop also have an obvious and immediate interpretation as indirect mechanisms, where the designer sets menus of per-unit prices depending on time and on the remaining capacity.

An allocation rule is called *deterministic* and *Markovian* if, at any period $t = 1, ..., T$ and for any possible type of agent arriving at t, it uses a nonrandom allocation rule that only depends on the arrival time t, on the declared type of the arriving agent, and on the still available capacity at period t, denoted by c. The restriction to these policies is innocuous as shown in section 4.4.

We can assume without loss of generality that a deterministic Markovian allocation rule for time t with remaining capacity c has the form α_t^c: $[0, +\infty)^2 \to \{1, 0\}$, where 1 (0) means that the reported capacity demand w is satisfied (not satisfied). Indeed it never makes sense to allocate an insufficient quantity $0 < w' < w$ because individually rational agents are not willing to pay for this. But allocating more capacity than the reported demand is useless as well: such allocations do not further increase agents' utility, and they may decrease continuation values for the designer. Let $q_t^c : [0, +\infty)^2 \to \mathbb{R}$ be the associated payment rule.

Proposition 5 *A deterministic, Markovian allocation rule* $\{\alpha_t^c\}_{t,c}$ *is implementable if and only if for every t and every c it satisfies the following two conditions:*

1. $\forall\,(w,v), v' \geq v,\ \alpha_t^c(w,v) = 1 \Rightarrow \alpha_t^c(w,v') = 1.$
2. *The function* $wp_t^c(w)$ *is nondecreasing in* w, *where*
   $p_t^c(w) = \inf\{v\,/\,\alpha_t^c(w,v) = 1\}.$[5]
   When the preceding two conditions are satisfied, the allocation rule $\{\alpha_t^c\}_{t,c}$
   together with the payment rule

$$q_t^c(w,v) = \begin{cases} wp_t^c(w) & \text{if } \alpha_t^c(w,v) = 1, \\ 0 & \text{if } \alpha_t^c(w,v) = 0, \end{cases}$$

   constitute an incentive compatible policy.

Proof   (1) So assume that conditions 1 and 2 are satisfied and define for any t, c,

$$q_t^c(w,v) = \begin{cases} wp_t^c(w) & \text{if } \alpha_t^c(w,v) = 1, \\ 0 & \text{if } \alpha_t^c(w,v) = 0. \end{cases}$$

Consider then an arrival of type (w, v) in period t with remaining capacity c. There are two cases:

Case 1. $\alpha_t^c(w,v) = 1$. In particular, $v \geq p_t^c(w)$. Then truth-telling yields utility $w(v - p_t^c(w)) \geq 0$. Assume the agent reports instead $(\widehat{w}, \widehat{v})$. If $\alpha_t^c(\widehat{w}, \widehat{v}) = 0$, further the agent's utility is zero and the deviation is not profitable. Assume further that $\alpha_t^c(\widehat{w}, \widehat{v}) = 1$. By the form of the utility function, a report of $\widehat{w} < w$ is never profitable. But, for $\widehat{w} \geq w$, the agent's utility is $wv - \widehat{w}p_t^c(\widehat{w}) \leq w(v - p_t^c(w))$, where we used condition 2. Therefore such a deviation is also not profitable.

Case 2. $\alpha_t^c(w,v) = 0$. In particular, $v \leq p_t^c(w)$. Truth-telling yields here a utility of zero. Assume that the agent reports instead $(\widehat{w}, \widehat{v})$. If $\alpha_t^c(\widehat{w}, \widehat{v}) = 0$, then the agent's utility remains zero, and the deviation is not profitable. Assume further that $\alpha_t^c(\widehat{w}, \widehat{v}) = 1$. By the form of the utility function, a report of $\widehat{w} < w$ is never profitable. Thus consider the case where $\widehat{w} \geq w$. In this case the agent's utility is $wv - \widehat{w}p_t^c(\widehat{w}) \leq w(v - p_t^c(w)) \leq 0$, where we used condition 2. Therefore such a deviation is also not profitable.

(2) Consider now an implementable, deterministic and Markovian allocation policy $\{\alpha_t^c\}_{t,c}$. Assume first, by contradiction, that condition 1 in the statement of the proposition is not satisfied. Then there exist (w, v) and (w, v')

such that $v' > v$, $\alpha_t^c(w, v) = 1$ and $\alpha_t^c(w, v') = 0$. We obtain the chain of inequalities $wv' - q_t^c(w, v) > wv - q_t^c(w, v) \geq -q_t^c(w, v')$, where the second inequality follows by incentive compatibility for type (w, v). This shows that a deviation to a report (w, v) is profitable for type (w, v'), a contradiction to implementability. Therefore condition 1 must hold.

In particular, note that for any two types who have the same weight request, (w, v) and (w, v'), if both are accepted, meaning $\alpha_t^c(w, v) = \alpha_t^c(w, v') = 1$, the payment must be the same (otherwise, the type which needs to make the higher payment would deviate and report the other type). Denote this payment by $r_t^c(w)$. Note also that any two types (w, v) and (w', v') such that $\alpha_t^c(w, v) = \alpha_t^c(w', v') = 0$ must also make the same payment (otherwise, the type that needs to make the higher payment would deviate and report the other type) and denote this payment by s.

Assume now, by contradiction, that condition 2 does not hold. Then there exist w and w' such that $w' > w$ but $w'p_t^c(w') < wp_t^c(w)$. In particular, $w'p_t^c(w') < \infty$, and therefore $p_t^c(w') < \infty$.

Assume first that $p_t^c(w) < \infty$. We have $w'p_t^c(w') - r_t^c(w') = wp_t^c(w) - r_t^c(w) = -s$ because, by incentive compatibility, both types $(w, p_t^c(w))$ and $(w', p_t^c(w'))$ must be indifferent between getting their request and not getting it. Since, by assumption, $w'p_t^c(w') < wp_t^c(w)$, we obtain that $r_t^c(w') < r_t^c(w)$. Consider now a type (w, v) for which $v > p_t^c(w)$. By reporting truthfully, this type gets utility $wv - r_t^c(w)$, while by deviating to (w', v), he gets utility $wv - r_t^c(w') > wv - r_t^c(w)$, a contradiction to incentive compatibility.

Assume now that $p_t^c(w)$ is infinite, and therefore that $wp_t^c(w)$ is infinite. Consider a type (w', v), where $v > p_t^c(w')$. The utility of this type is $w'v - r_t^c(w') > w'p_t^c(w') - r_t^c(w') = -s$. In particular, $r_t^c(w')$ must be finite. By reporting truthfully, a type (w, v) gets utility $-s$, while by deviating to a report of (w', v), he gets $wv - r_t^c(w')$. For v large enough, we obtain $wv - r_t^c(w') > -s$, a contradiction to implementability.

Thus condition 2 must hold, and in particular, the payment $r_t^c(w)$ is monotonic in w.   ∎

The threshold property embodied in condition 1 of the proposition above is standard, and it is a natural feature of welfare-maximizing rules under complete information. When there is incomplete information in the value dimension, this condition imposes limitations on the payments that can be extracted in equilibrium. Condition 2 is new: it reflects the limitations imposed in our model by the incomplete information in the weight dimension. The preceding simple result is based on a combination of three main factors: (1) due to our special utility function and to the pursued goal of revenue maximization, it is sufficient to consider only policies that allocate either the demanded weight to the agent or nothing; (2) the monotonicity requirement behind incentive compatibility boils down to the shown simple conditions above; and (3) the integrability condition is automatically satisfied by all monotone allocation rules in the considered class. In general, one has to consider more allocation functions, more implications of monotonicity, and possibly an integrability constraint.

4.4 Dynamic Revenue Maximization

We first demonstrate how the dynamic revenue maximization problem can be solved if w is observable, meaning the incentive constraints are relaxed. This is essentially the dynamic programming problem analyzed by Papastavrou, Rajagopalan, and Kleywegt (1996), translated from values to virtual values. Nevertheless, the logic of the derivation is somewhat involved, so we detail it below:

1. Without loss of generality, we can restrict attention to Markovian policies. The optimality of Markovian, possibly randomized, policies is standard for all models where, as is the case here, the per-period rewards and transition probabilities are history-independent—for example, see theorem 11.1.1 in Puterman (2005), which shows that for any history-dependent policy, there is a Markovian, possibly randomized, policy with the same payoff.

2. If there is incomplete information about v, but complete information about the weight requirement w, then Markovian, deterministic, and implementable policies are characterized for each t and c by the threshold property of condition 1 in proposition 5.

3. Naturally, in the given revenue-maximization problem with complete information about w we need to restrict attention to interim individually rational policies where no agent ever pays more than the utility obtained from her actual capacity allocation. It is easy to see that for any Markov, deterministic, and implementable allocation rule α_t^c, the maximal, individually rational payment function that supports it is given by

$$q_t^c(w, v) = \begin{cases} wp_t^c(w) & \text{if } \alpha_t^c(w, v) = 1, \\ 0 & \text{if } \alpha_t^c(w, v) = 0, \end{cases}$$

where $p_t^c(w) = \inf\{v \ / \ \alpha_t^c(w, v) = 1\}$ as defined in the previous section. Otherwise, the designer pays some positive subsidy to the agent, and this cannot be revenue maximizing.

4. At each period t, and for each remaining capacity c, the designer's problem under complete information about w is equivalent to a simpler,

one-dimensional static problem where a known capacity needs to be allocated to the arriving agent, and where the seller has a salvage value for each remaining capacity: the salvage values in the static problem correspond to the continuation values in the dynamic version. Analogously to the analysis of Myerson (1981), each static revenue-maximization problem has a monotone (in the sense of condition 1 in proposition 5), nonrandomized solution as long as, for any weight w, the agent's conditional virtual valuation $v - \frac{1-F(v|w)}{f(v|w)}$ is increasing in v.[6] If per-unit prices are set at $p_t^c(w)$ in period $t \leq T$ (so $T + 1 - t$ periods, including the current one, remain until the deadline) with remaining capacity c, and if the optimal Markovian policy is followed from time $t + 1$ onward, the expected revenue $R(c, T + 1 - t)$ can be written as

$$R(c, T+1-t) = \int_0^c w\, p_t^c(w)\,(1 - F(p_t^c(w)|w))\, \bar{f}_w(w)\, dw$$

$$+ \int_0^c [(1 - F(p_t^c(w)|w))R^*(c - w, T - t)$$

$$+ F(p_t^c(w)|w)R^*(c, T - t)]\, \bar{f}_w(w)\, dw,$$

where $\bar{f}_w$ denotes the marginal density in w and where R^* denotes optimal revenues, with $R^*(c, 0) = 0$ for all c. The first-order conditions for the revenue-maximizing unit prices $p_t^c(w)$ are given by[7]

$$w\left(p_t^c(w) - \frac{1 - F(p_t^c(w)|w)}{f(p_t^c(w)|w)}\right) = R^*(c, T - t) - R^*(c - w, T - t).$$

5. By backward induction, and by the reasoning above, the seller has a Markov, nonrandomized optimal policy in the dynamic problem with complete information about w. Note also that by a simple duplication argument, $R^*(c, T + 1 - t)$ must be monotone nondecreasing in c.

Points 1, 4, and 5 above imply that the restriction to deterministic and Markovian allocation policies is without loss of generality. If the preceding solution to the relaxed problem satisfies the incentive compatibility constraint in the weight dimension, namely if $w p_t^c(w)$ happens to be monotone as required by condition 2 of proposition 5, then the associated allocation where $\alpha_t^c(w, v) = 1$ if and only if $v \geq p_t^c(w)$ is also implementable in the original problem with incomplete information about both v and w. It then constitutes the revenue-maximizing scheme that we are after. The next example illustrates that condition 2 of proposition 5 can be binding.

Example 9 *Assume that $T = 1$. The distribution of the agents' types is given by the following stochastic process. First, the weight request w is realized according to an exponential distribution with parameter λ. Next, the per-unit value of the agent is sampled from the following distribution:*

$$F(v|w) = \begin{cases} 1 - e^{-\bar{\lambda}v} & \text{if } w > w^*, \\ 1 - e^{-\underline{\lambda}v} & \text{if } w \leq w^*, \end{cases}$$

where $\bar{\lambda} > \underline{\lambda}$ and $w^* \in (0, c)$.

In this case, for an observable weight request, the seller charges the take-it-or-leave-it offer of $\frac{1}{\underline{\lambda}}$ ($\frac{1}{\bar{\lambda}}$) per unit if the weight request is smaller (larger) than or equal to w^*. This implies that

$$wp_t^c(w) = \begin{cases} \frac{w}{\bar{\lambda}} & \text{if } w > w^*, \\ \frac{w}{\underline{\lambda}} & \text{if } w \leq w^*, \end{cases}$$

and therefore $wp_t^c(w)$ is not monotone.

4.4.1 The Hazard Rate Stochastic Ordering

A simple sufficient condition that guarantees implementability of the relaxed solution in the model where weights are unobservable is a stochastic ordering of the conditional distributions of per-unit values: the conditional distribution given a higher weight should be (weakly) statistically higher in the hazard rate order than the conditional distribution given a lower weight.

Theorem 15 *For each c, t, and w let $p_t^c(w)$ denote the solution to the revenue-maximizing problem under complete information about w, determined recursively by the Bellman equation*

$$w\left(p_t^c(w) - \frac{1 - F(p_t^c(w)|w)}{f(p_t^c(w)|w)}\right) = R^*(c, T - t) - R^*(c - w, T - t). \quad (4.1)$$

Assume that the following conditions hold:

1. For any w, the conditional hazard rate $\frac{f(v|w)}{1-F(v|w)}$ is nondecreasing in v.[8]

2. For any $w' \geq w$, and for any v, $\frac{f(v|w)}{1-F(v|w)} \geq \frac{f(v|w')}{1-F(v|w')}$.

Then $wp_t^c(w)$ is nondecreasing in w, and consequently the underlying allocation where $\alpha_t^c(w, v) = 1$ if and only if $v \geq p_t^c(w)$ is implementable. In particular, equation (4.1) characterizes the revenue-maximizing scheme under incomplete information about both values and weights.

Proof Let $w < w'$. We need to show that $wp_t^c(w) - w'p_t^c(w') \leq 0$. If $p_t^c(w) \leq p_t^c(w')$ the result is clear. Assume then that $p_t^c(w) > p_t^c(w')$. We obtain the following chain of inequalities:

$$w\left(\frac{1 - F(p_t^c(w)|w)}{f(p_t^c(w)|w)}\right) - w'\left(\frac{1 - F(p_t^c(w')|w')}{f(p_t^c(w')|w')}\right)$$

$$\leq w'\left(\frac{1 - F(p_t^c(w)|w)}{f(p_t^c(w)|w)} - \frac{1 - F(p_t^c(w')|w')}{f(p_t^c(w')|w')}\right)$$

$$\leq w'\left(\frac{1 - F(p_t^c(w')|w)}{f(p_t^c(w')|w)} - \frac{1 - F(p_t^c(w')|w')}{f(p_t^c(w')|w')}\right) \leq 0,$$

where the second inequality follows by the monotonicity of the hazard rate, and the third by the hazard rate ordering condition.

Since $R^*(c - w, T - t)$ is monotonically decreasing in w, we obtain

$$w\left(p_t^c(w) - \frac{1 - F(p_t^c(w)|w)}{f(p_t^c(w)|w)}\right) \leq w'\left(p_t^c(w') - \frac{1 - F(p_t^c(w')|w')}{f(p_t^c(w')|w')}\right) \Leftrightarrow$$

$$wp_t^c(w) - w'p_t^c(w') \leq w\left(\frac{1 - F(p_t^c(w)|w)}{f(p_t^c(w)|w)}\right)$$

$$- w'\left(\frac{1 - F(p_t^c(w')|w')}{f(p_t^c(w')|w')}\right) \leq 0,$$

where the last inequality follows by the derivation above. Hence $wp_t^c(w) - w'p_t^c(w') \leq 0$ as desired. ∎

An important special case for which the conditions of the theorem above hold is the one where the distribution of per-unit values is independent of the distribution of weights and has an increasing hazard rate.

4.4.2 The Role of Concavity

A major result for the case where capacity comes in discrete units, and where all weights are equal, is that optimal expected revenue is concave in capacity (see Gallego and Ryzin 1994 for a continuous time framework with Poisson arrivals and Bitran and Mondschein 1997 for a discrete time setting). This is an intuitive property because it says that additional capacity is more valuable to the designer when capacity itself is scarce. Due to the more complicated combinatorial nature of the knapsack problem with heterogeneous weights, concavity need not generally hold (see Papastavrou, Rajagopalan, and Kleywegt 1996 for examples where concavity of expected welfare in the framework with complete information fails). When concavity does hold, the optimal per-unit virtual value thresholds for the relaxed problem increase with weight, which facilitates implementation for the case of two-dimensional private information.

Our main result in this subsection identifies a condition on the distribution of types that, together with concavity of the expected revenue in the remaining capacity, ensures that, for each t and c, $wp_t^c(w)$ is increasing.

Theorem 16 *Assume that*

1. *The expected revenue $R^*(c, T+1-t)$ is a concave function of c for all periods t.*

2. *For any $w \le w'$, $v - \frac{1-F(v|w)}{f(v|w)} \ge \frac{vw}{w'} - \frac{1-F(\frac{vw}{w'}|w')}{f(\frac{vw}{w'}|w')}$.*

For each c, t, and w let $p_t^c(w)$ denote the solution to the revenue-maximizing problem under complete information about w, determined recursively by equation (4.1). Then $wp_t^c(w)$ is nondecreasing in w, and hence the underlying allocation where $\alpha_t^c(w,v) = 1$ if and only if $v \ge p_t^c(w)$ is implementable. In particular, equation (4.1) characterizes the revenue-maximizing scheme under incomplete information about both values and weights.

Proof For any concave function ϕ, and for any $x < y < z$ in its domain, the well known "three chord lemma" asserts that

$$\frac{\phi(y) - \phi(x)}{y - x} \ge \frac{\phi(z) - \phi(x)}{z - x} \ge \frac{\phi(z) - \phi(y)}{z - y}$$

Consider then $w < w'$, and let $x = c - w' < y = c - w < z = c$. For the case of a concave revenue, the lemma yields then

$$\frac{R^*(c-w, T-t) - R^*(c-w', T-t)}{w' - w} \ge \frac{R^*(c, T-t) - R^*(c-w', T-t)}{w'}$$

$$\ge \frac{R^*(c, T-t) - R^*(c-w, T-t)}{w}.$$

We obtain the price per unit of weight

$$p_t^c(w') - \frac{1 - F(p_t^c(w')|w')}{f(p_t^c(w')|w')} = \frac{R^*(c, T-t) - R^*(c-w', T-t)}{w'}$$

$$\ge \frac{R^*(c, T-t) - R^*(c-w, T-t)}{w} = p_t^c(w) - \frac{1 - F(p_t^c(w)|w)}{f(p_t^c(w)|w)},$$

which yields

$$p_t^c(w') - \frac{1 - F(p_t^c(w')|w')}{f(p_t^c(w')|w')} \ge p_t^c(w) - \frac{1 - F(p_t^c(w)|w)}{f(p_t^c(w)|w)}$$

$$\ge \frac{w}{w'}p_t^c(w) - \frac{1 - F(\frac{w}{w'}p_t^c(w)|w')}{f(\frac{w}{w'}p_t^c(w)|w')},$$

where the last inequality follows by the condition in the statement of the theorem. Since virtual values are increasing, this yields $p_t^c(w') \geq \frac{w}{w'} p_t^c(w) \Leftrightarrow w' p_t^c(w') \geq w p_t^c(w)$ as desired. ∎

Remark 3 *The sufficient conditions for implementability used in theorem 15 are, taken together, stronger than condition 2 in theorem 16. To see this, assume that, for any w, the conditional hazard rate $\frac{f(v|w)}{1-F(v|w)}$ is increasing in v, and that for any $w' \geq w$ and for all v, $\frac{f(v|w)}{1-F(v|w)} \geq \frac{f(v|w')}{1-F(v|w')}$. This yields*

$$v - \frac{1 - F(v|w)}{f(v|w)} \geq \frac{vw}{w'} - \frac{1 - F(\frac{vw}{w'}|w)}{f(\frac{vw}{w'}|w)} \geq \frac{vw}{w'} - \frac{1 - F(\frac{vw}{w'}|w')}{f(\frac{vw}{w'}|w')},$$

where the first inequality follows by the monotonicity of the hazard rate, and the second by the stochastic order assumption. Note also that condition 2 of theorem 16 can be formulated as requiring that the functions $\alpha v - \frac{1-F(\alpha v|\frac{w}{\alpha})}{f(\alpha v|\frac{w}{\alpha})}$ are nondecreasing in α. Finally, note that this condition will play an important role for implementability of the asymptotically optimal policy that we construct in section 4.5 below.

We next modify a result of Papastavrou, Rajagopalan, and Kleywegt (1996) in order to identify conditions on the joint distribution $F(w, v)$ that imply concavity of expected revenue with respect to c for all periods, as required by the preceding theorem. It is convenient to introduce the joint distribution of weight and total valuation $u = vw$, which we denote by $G(w, u)$ with density $g(w, u)$. By means of a transformation of variables, the densities f and g are related by $w g(w, wv) = f(w, v)$. In particular, marginal densities in w coincide:

$$\bar{f}_w(w) = \int_0^\infty f(w, v) \, dv = \int_0^\infty g(w, u) \, du = \bar{g}_w(w).$$

An increasing virtual value implies that the virtual total value is increasing in u with strictly positive derivative for any given w:

$$\hat{u}(u, w) := u - \frac{1 - G(u|w)}{g(u|w)} = wv - \frac{1 - F(v|w)}{f(v|w)/w} = w\hat{v}(v, w)$$

We write $\hat{u}^{-1}(\hat{u}, w)$ for the inverse of $\hat{u}(u, w)$ with respect to u and define a distribution $\hat{G}(\hat{u}, w)$ by both $\hat{G}(\hat{u}|w) := G(\hat{u}^{-1}(\hat{u}, w)|w)$ for all w and $\bar{\hat{g}}_w(w) := \bar{g}_w(w)$. On the level of $\hat{v}$, this corresponds to $\hat{F}(\hat{v}|w) = F(\hat{v}^{-1}(\hat{v}, w)|w)$ and $\bar{\hat{f}}_w(w) = \bar{f}_w(w)$.

For the proof of theorem 17, we first need a lemma on maximization of expected welfare under complete information. The result appears (without proof) in Papastavrou, Rajagopalan, and Kleywegt (1996).

Lemma 3 *Assume that the total value u has finite mean, and that both $g(w|u)$ and $\frac{d}{dw}g(w|u)$ are bounded and continuous. Consider the allocation policy that maximizes expected welfare under complete information (i.e., upon arrival the agent's type is revealed to the designer). If $G(w|u)$ is concave in w for all u, then the optimal expected welfare, denoted U_t^c is twice continuously differentiable and concave in the remaining capacity c for all periods $t \leq T$.*

Proof Note that for notational convenience throughout this proof, we index optimal expected welfare by the current time **t** and not by periods remaining to deadline. By standard arguments, the optimal policy for this unconstrained dynamic optimization problem is deterministic and Markovian, and U_t^c is nondecreasing in remaining capacity c by a simple strategy duplication argument. Moreover the optimal policy can be characterized by weight thresholds $w_t^c(u) \leq c$: If c remains at time t and a request whose acceptance would generate value u arrives, then it is accepted if and only if $w \leq w_t^c(u)$. If $U_{t+1}^c \geq u$, then the weight threshold must satisfy the indifference condition

$$u = U_{t+1}^c - U_{t+1}^{c-w_t^c(u)}. \tag{4.2}$$

Otherwise, we have $w_t^c(u) = c$.

We now prove the lemma by backward induction. At time $t = T$, that is, in the deadline period, it holds that

$$U_T^c = \int_0^\infty G(c|u)u\,\bar{g}_u(u)\,du.$$

This is concave in c because all $G(c|u)$ are concave by assumption, because $u\,\bar{g}_u(u)$ is positive, and because the distribution of u has a finite mean. Since both $g(w|u)$ and $\frac{d}{dw}g(w|u)$ are bounded and continuous, U_T^c is also twice continuously differentiable.

Suppose now that the lemma has been proven down to time $t + 1$. The optimal expected welfare at t provided that capacity c remains may be written as

$$U_t^c = \int_0^\infty \left[uG(w_t^c(u)|u) + \int_0^{w_t^c(u)} U_{t+1}^{c-w}g(w|u)\,dw \right. \tag{4.3}$$

$$\left. + (1 - G(w_t^c(u)|u))U_{t+1}^c \right] \bar{g}_u(u)\,du.$$

We proceed to show concavity with respect to c of the term in brackets, for all u. This in turn implies concavity of U_t^c and hence, with a short additional argument for differentiability, is sufficient to conclude the induction step. We distinguish the cases $u > U_{t+1}^c$ for which the indifference condition (4.2) does not hold, and $u \leq U_{t+1}^c$ for which it does. For both cases we demonstrate that the second derivative (one-sided if necessary) of the bracket term with respect to c is nonpositive, and thus we establish global concavity.

Case 1. $u > U_{t+1}^c$. The bracket term in (4.3) becomes $uG(c|u) + \int_0^c U_{t+1}^{c-w} g(w|u) \, dw + (1 - G(c|u))U_{t+1}^c$. By continuity of U_{t+1}^c, this representation also holds in a small interval around c. We find that

$$
\frac{d}{dc} \left[uG(c|u) + \int_0^c U_{t+1}^{c-w} g(w|u) \, dw + (1 - G(c|u))U_{t+1}^c \right]
$$

$$
= ug(c|u) + \int_0^c \frac{d}{dc} U_{t+1}^{c-w} g(w|u) \, dw + U_{t+1}^0 g(c|u)
$$

$$
- g(c|u) U_{t+1}^c + (1 - G(c|u))\frac{d}{dc} U_{t+1}^c
$$

$$
= (u - U_{t+1}^c)g(c|u) + \int_0^c \frac{d}{dc} U_{t+1}^{c-w} g(w|u) \, dw
$$

$$
+ (1 - G(c|u))\frac{d}{dc} U_{t+1}^c
$$

and

$$
\frac{d^2}{dc^2} \left[uG(c|u) + \int_0^c U_{t+1}^{c-w} g(w|u) \, dw + (1 - G(c|u))U_{t+1}^c \right]
$$

$$
= (u - U_{t+1}^c)g'(c|u) - g(c|u)\frac{d}{dc} U_{t+1}^c + \int_0^c \frac{d^2}{dc^2} U_{t+1}^{c-w} g(w|u) \, dw
$$

$$
+ \frac{d}{dw} U_{t+1}^w \big|_{w=0} g(c|u) - g(c|u)\frac{d}{dc} U_{t+1}^c
$$

$$
+ (1 - G(c|u))\frac{d^2}{dc^2} U_{t+1}^c. \tag{4.4}
$$

The last term is nonpositive by the concavity of U_{t+1}^c, the first term is nonpositive because $u > U_{t+1}^c$ and because $G(c|u)$ has a nonincreasing density by assumption. Moreover $g(c|u)\frac{d}{dc}U_{t+1}^c$ is nonnegative, and hence (4.4) is bounded from above by

$$\int_0^c \frac{d^2}{dc^2}U_{t+1}^{c-w}g(w|u)\,dw + g(c|u)\left(\frac{d}{dw}U_{t+1}^w\Big|_{w=0} - \frac{d}{dc}U_{t+1}^c\right).$$

But $\int_0^c \frac{d^2}{dc^2}U_{t+1}^{c-w}g(w|u)\,dw$ may be bounded from above by $g(c|u)\int_0^c \frac{d^2}{dc^2}U_{t+1}^{c-w}\,dw$ because of the decreasing density and because $\frac{d^2}{dc^2}U_{t+1}^{c-w} \leq 0$. Thus

$$\frac{d^2}{dc^2}\left[uG(c|u) + \int_0^c U_{t+1}^{c-w}g(w|u)\,dw + (1 - G(c|u))U_{t+1}^c\right]$$

$$\leq g(c|u)\left[\int_0^c \frac{d^2}{dc^2}U_{t+1}^{c-w}\,dw + \frac{d}{dw}U_{t+1}^w\Big|_{w=0} - \frac{d}{dc}U_{t+1}^c\right]$$

$$= g(c|u)\left[\int_0^c \frac{d^2}{dw^2}U_{t+1}^{c-w}\,dw + \frac{d}{dw}U_{t+1}^w\Big|_{w=0} - \frac{d}{dc}U_{t+1}^c\right] = 0.$$

$$(4.5)$$

Case 2. $u \leq U_{t+1}^c$. Here $u = U_{t+1}^c - U_{t+1}^{c-w_t^c(u)}$. Consequently the bracket term in (4.3) becomes

$$U_{t+1}^c - U_{t+1}^{c-w_t^c(u)}G(w_t^c(u)|u) + \int_0^{w_t^c(u)} U_{t+1}^{c-w}g(w|u)\,dw. \qquad (4.6)$$

Before computing its first and second derivatives, we differentiate the identity $u = U_{t+1}^c - U_{t+1}^{c-w_t^c(u)}$ to obtain an expression for $\frac{d}{dc}w_t^c(u)$ (derivative from the right if $u = U_{t+1}^c$):

$$0 = \frac{d}{dc}U_{t+1}^c - \frac{d}{dw}U_{t+1}^w\Big|_{w=c-w_t^c(u)}\left(1 - \frac{d}{dc}w_t^c(u)\right).$$

Since indeed $\frac{d}{dw}U_{t+1}^w > 0$ in our setup with strictly positive densities, this implies that

$$\frac{d}{dc}w_t^c(u) = \frac{\frac{d}{dw}U_{t+1}^w\big|_{w=c-w_t^c(u)} - \frac{d}{dc}U_{t+1}^c}{\frac{d}{dw}U_{t+1}^w\big|_{w=c-w_t^c(u)}}. \qquad (4.7)$$

By concavity of U_{t+1}^c, its derivative is nonincreasing and hence the identity (4.7) yields in particular $\frac{d}{dc} w_t^c(u) \geq 0$. We now compute the derivatives of (4.6):

$$\frac{d}{dc} \left[U_{t+1}^c - U_{t+1}^{c-w_t^c(u)} G(w_t^c(u)|u) + \int_0^{w_t^c(u)} U_{t+1}^{c-w} g(w|u)\, dw \right]$$

$$= \frac{d}{dc} U_{t+1}^c - \frac{d}{dw} U_{t+1}^w \Big|_{w=c-w_t^c(u)} \left(1 - \frac{d}{dc} w_t^c(u) \right) G(w_t^c(u)|u)$$

$$- U_{t+1}^{c-w_t^c(u)} g(w_t^c(u)|u) \frac{d}{dc} w_t^c(u)$$

$$+ U_{t+1}^{c-w_t^c(u)} g(w_t^c(u)|u) \frac{d}{dc} w_t^c(u) + \int_0^{w_t^c(u)} \frac{d}{dc} U_{t+1}^{c-w} g(w|u)\, dw$$

$$\overset{(4.7)}{=} \frac{d}{dc} U_{t+1}^c - \frac{d}{dc} U_{t+1}^c G(w_t^c(u)|u) + \int_0^{w_t^c(u)} \frac{d}{dc} U_{t+1}^{c-w} g(w|u)\, dw$$

$$= \frac{d}{dc} U_{t+1}^c (1 - G(w_t^c(u)|u)) + \int_0^{w_t^c(u)} \frac{d}{dc} U_{t+1}^{c-w} g(w|u)\, dw.$$

Thus

$$\frac{d^2}{dc^2} \left[U_{t+1}^c - U_{t+1}^{c-w_t^c(u)} G(w_t^c(u)|u) + \int_0^{w_t^c(u)} U_{t+1}^{c-w} g(w|u)\, dw \right]$$

$$= \frac{d^2}{dc^2} U_{t+1}^c (1 - G(w_t^c(u)|u)) - \frac{d}{dc} U_{t+1}^c g(w_t^c(u)|u) \frac{d}{dc} w_t^c(u)$$

$$+ \frac{d}{dw} U_{t+1}^w \Big|_{w=c-w_t^c(u)} g(w_t^c(u)|u) \frac{d}{dc} w_t^c(u)$$

$$+ \int_0^{w_t^c(u)} \frac{d^2}{dc^2} U_{t+1}^{c-w} g(w|u)\, dw$$

$$\leq g(w_t^c(u)|u) \frac{d}{dc} w_t^c(u) \left(\frac{d}{dw} U_{t+1}^w \Big|_{w=c-w_t^c(u)} - \frac{d}{dc} U_{t+1}^c \right)$$

$$+ \int_0^{w_t^c(u)} \frac{d^2}{dw^2} U_{t+1}^{c-w} g(w|u)\, dw.$$

For the final inequality we used concavity of U_{t+1}^c, as well as $\frac{d^2}{dc^2}U_{t+1}^{c-w} = \frac{d^2}{dw^2}U_{t+1}^{c-w}$. Noting that (4.7) implies that $\frac{d}{dc}w_t^c(u) \le 1$ and once more using concavity of U_{t+1}^c, we may bound the first term from above. Since $g(w|u)$ is nonincreasing in w, we can also bound the second term to obtain

$$\frac{d^2}{dc^2}\left[U_{t+1}^c - U_{t+1}^{c-w_t^c(u)}G(w_t^c(u)|u) + \int_0^{w_t^c(u)} U_{t+1}^{c-w}g(w|u)\,dw \right] \quad (4.8)$$

$$\le g(w_t^c(u)|u)\left(\frac{d}{dw}U_{t+1}^w\big|_{w=c-w_t^c(u)} - \frac{d}{dc}U_{t+1}^c \right.$$

$$\left. + \int_0^{w_t^c(u)} \frac{d^2}{dw^2}U_{t+1}^{c-w}\,dw \right) = 0.$$

Taken together, (4.5) and (4.8) establish concavity of the integrand in (4.3) with respect to c. This implies that U_t^c is concave. Having a second look at the computations just done reveals that the integrand in (4.3) has a kink in the second derivative at $u = U_{t+1}^c$. However, this event has measure zero for any given c, so that we also get that U_t^c is twice continuously differentiable. This completes the induction step.   ∎

Theorem 17 *Assume that the conditional distribution $\hat{G}(w|\hat{u})$ is concave in w for all $\hat{u}$, that both $\hat{g}(w|\hat{u})$ and $\frac{d}{dw}\hat{g}(w|\hat{u})$ are bounded, and that the total virtual value $\hat{u}$ has a finite mean. Then, in the revenue maximization problem where the designer has complete information about w, the expected revenue $R^*(c, T+1-t)$ is concave as a function of c for all times t.*

Proof The main idea of the proof is to translate the problem of setting revenue-maximizing prices when w is observable into the problem of maximizing welfare with respect to virtual values (rather than the values themselves), and then to use lemma 3.

   To begin, note that there is a dual way to describe the policy that maximizes expected welfare under complete information. In the proof of lemma 3 we characterized it by optimal weight thresholds $w_t^c(u)$. Alternatively, given any requested quantity w (not greater than the remaining c), we may set a valuation per unit threshold $v_t^c(w)$. Requests above this valuation are accepted; those below are not. Optimal such thresholds are characterized by the Bellman-type condition:

$$w\, v_t^c(w) = U_{t+1}^c - U_{t+1}^{c-w}. \tag{4.9}$$

Thus one way of writing the optimal expected welfare under complete information is

$$U_t^c = \int_0^c w \int_{v_t^c(w)}^\infty v f(v|w)\, dv\, \bar{f}_w(w)\, dw$$

$$+ \int_0^c \left[(1 - F(v_t^c(w)|w)) U_{t+1}^{c-w} + F(v_t^c(w)|w) U_{t+1}^c \right] \bar{f}_w(w)\, dw. \tag{4.10}$$

In contrast, the optimal expected revenue with complete information about w but incomplete information about v satisfies

$$R^*(c, T+1-t) = \int_0^c w\, p_t^c(w)\, (1 - F(p_t^c(w)|w))\, \bar{f}_w(w)\, dw \tag{4.11}$$

$$+ \int_0^c \left[(1 - F(p_t^c(w)|w)) R^*(c - w, T - t) \right.$$

$$\left. + F(p_t^c(w)|w) R^*(c, T - t) \right] \bar{f}_w(w)\, dw,$$

where $p_t^c(w)$ are the per-unit prices from (4.1). We rephrase this in terms of $\hat{F}$, whose definition required monotonicity of virtual values. Setting $\hat{v}_t^c(w) := \hat{v}(p_t^c(w), w)$ we have, on the one hand,

$$F(p_t^c(w)|w) = \hat{F}(\hat{v}_t^c(w)|w).$$

On the other hand,

$$p_t^c(w)\, (1 - F(p_t^c(w)|w)) = \int_{p_t^c(w)}^\infty [v f(v|w) - (1 - F(v|w))]\, dv$$

$$= \int_{p_t^c(w)}^\infty \hat{v}(v, w)\, \hat{f}(\hat{v}(v, w)|w) \frac{d}{dv} \hat{v}(v, w)\, dv$$

$$= \int_{\hat{v}_t^c(w)}^\infty \hat{v}\, \hat{f}(\hat{v}|w)\, d\hat{v}.$$

Plugging this and the identities for the marginal densities in w into (4.11), we obtain

$$R^*(c, T+1-t) = \int\limits_0^\infty w \int\limits_{\hat{v}_t^c(w)}^\infty \hat{v}\hat{f}(\hat{v}|w)\, d\hat{v}\, \bar{\hat{f}}_w(w)\, dw$$

$$+ \int\limits_0^\infty \Big[(1 - \hat{F}(\hat{v}_t^c(w)|w))R^*(c-w, T-t)$$

$$+ \hat{F}(\hat{v}_t^c(w)|w)R^*(c, T-t)\Big]\, \bar{\hat{f}}_w(w)\, dw.$$

Comparing this with (4.10), we find that maximizing expected revenue when w is observable is equivalent to maximizing expected welfare with respect to the distribution of weight and conditional virtual valuation (note the identical zero boundary values at $T+1$). Invoking lemma 3 applied to $\hat{G}$, we see that $R^*(c, T+1-t)$ is concave with respect to c for all t (note that the fact that the support of virtual valuations contains also negative numbers does not matter for the argument of lemma 3).   ■

Example 10 *A simple setting where the conditions of theorem 16 are satisfied while those of theorem 15 are violated is obtained as follows. Assume that $G(w, u)$ is such that u and w are independent, the hazard rate $\frac{g_u(u)}{1 - G_u(u)}$ is nondecreasing, and G_w is concave[9]. Then condition 1 of theorem 16 is satisfied according to theorem 17 because the $\hat{G}(w|\hat{u})$ is concave. Consider then $w < w'$.*

By independence of u and w, we have $w'\hat{v}(\frac{vw}{w'}, w') = \hat{u}(vw, w') = \hat{u}(vw, w) = w\hat{v}(v, w)$ and hence $\hat{v}(v, w) = \frac{w'}{w}\hat{v}(\frac{vw}{w'}, w')$. As $\frac{w'}{w} > 1$. This result implies condition 2 of theorem 16 in the relevant domain where virtual values are nonnegative. However, as we show now, condition 2 of theorem 15, which is the hazard rate ordering, is violated. Indeed the equation we have just derived implies also that $\frac{f(v|w)}{1-F(v|w)} = \frac{w}{w'}\frac{f(\frac{vw}{w'}|w')}{1-F(\frac{vw}{w'}|w')}$. But the conditional hazard rates of F are nondecreasing (because $\hat{G}_u$ has nondecreasing hazard rate) and $\frac{w}{w'} < 1$, so that $\frac{f(v|w)}{1-F(v|w)} = \frac{w}{w'}\frac{f(\frac{vw}{w'}|w')}{1-F(\frac{vw}{w'}|w')} < \frac{f(v|w')}{1-F(v|w')}$, which contradicts the hazard rate ordering of theorem 15.

4.5 Asymptotically Optimal and Time-Independent Pricing

The optimal policy identified above requires price adjustments in every period, and for any quantity request w. These dynamics are arguably too complicated to be applied in practice. Gallego and Ryzin (1994) use an asymptotic argument to show that the theoretical gain from optimal dynamic pricing compared to a suitably chosen, time-independent policy is usually small in the setting with unit demands. Our main theorem in this section extends their result to the dynamic knapsack problem with general distribution of types. We construct a static nonlinear price schedule that uses the existing correlations between w and v, and show that it is asymptotically optimal if both capacity and time horizon go to infinity.

While the basic strategy of the proof follows the suggestion made by Gallego and van Ryzin, there are several major differences. Moreover, in section 5 of their paper, these authors consider the case of heterogeneous capacity demands. However, they assume that weights and values are independent, and most important, their optimality benchmark does not even allow per-unit prices to depend on weight requests. But, as we have seen above, such weight dependency is a general property of the dynamically optimal solution, even if w and v are independent. We therefore take our solution of the relaxed problem as the optimality benchmark, and we also consider general type distributions F.

As above, we start by focusing on the case of observable weights. We then show that condition 2 of theorem 16 is a sufficient condition for implementability for the case with two-dimensional private information.

Like Gallego and van Ryzin, we first solve a simpler, suitably chosen deterministic maximization problem. The revenue obtained in the solution to that problem provides an upper bound for the optimal expected revenue of the stochastic problem, and the solution itself suggests the use of per-unit prices that depend on weight requests but that are constant in time. We next show that the derived policy is asymptotically optimal also in the original stochastic problem where both capacity and time go to infinity: the ratio of expected revenue from following the considered policy over expected revenue from the optimal Markovian policy converges to one. Moreover there are various ways to quantify this ratio for moderately large capacities and time horizons.

Let us first recall some assumptions and introduce further notation. The marginal density $\bar{f}_w(w)$ and the conditional densities $f(v|w)$ pin down the distribution of (independent) arriving types $(w_t, v_t)_{t=1}^T$. Given w, the demanded per-unit price p and the probability λ^w of a request being accepted are related by $\lambda^w(p) = 1 - F(p|w)$. Let $p^w(\lambda)$ be the inverse of λ, and note that this is well defined on $(0, 1]$. Because of monotonicity of conditional virtual values, the instantaneous (expected) per-unit revenue functions $r^w(\lambda) := \lambda p^w(\lambda)$ are strictly concave, and each one attains a unique interior maximum. Indeed

$p^w(\lambda) = F(\cdot|w)^{-1}(1-\lambda)$ and hence

$$\frac{d}{d\lambda}r^w(\lambda) = p^w(\lambda) - \lambda\frac{1}{f(p^w(\lambda)|w)} = p^w(\lambda)$$

$$-\frac{1 - F(p^w(\lambda)|w)}{f(p^w(\lambda)|w)} = \hat{v}(p^w(\lambda), w);$$

$$\frac{d^2}{d\lambda^2}r^w(\lambda) = -\left(\frac{\partial}{\partial v}\hat{v}\right)(p^w(\lambda), w)\frac{1}{f(p^w(\lambda)|w)} < 0.$$

Consequently r^w is strictly concave, strictly increasing up to the $\lambda^{w,*}$ that satisfies $\hat{v}(p^w(\lambda^{w,*}), w) = 0$, and strictly decreasing from there on.

4.5.1 The Deterministic Problem

We now formulate an auxiliary deterministic problem that closely resembles the relaxed stochastic problem. Let $\text{Cap} : (0,\infty) \to (0,\infty), w \mapsto \text{Cap}(w)$ be a measurable function. Consider the problem

$$\max_{\text{Cap}(\cdot)} \int_0^\infty \max_{(\lambda_t^w)_{t=1,\dots,T}} \left(\sum_{t=1}^T r^w(\lambda_t^w)\right) w\bar{f}_w(w)\, dw, \tag{4.12}$$

subject to

$$\sum_{t=1}^T \lambda_t^w\, w\bar{f}_w(w) \le \text{Cap}(w) \text{ a.s.} \quad \text{and} \quad \int_0^\infty \text{Cap}(w)\, dw \le C. \tag{4.13}$$

In words, we analyze a problem where:

1. The capacity C needs to be divided into capacities $\text{Cap}(w)$, one for each w.

2. In each w subproblem, a deterministic quantity request of $w\bar{f}_w(w)$ arrives in each period, and λ_t^w determines a share (not a probability!) of this request that is accepted and sold at per-unit price $p^w(\lambda_t^w)$.

3. In each subproblem, the allocated capacity over time cannot exceed $\text{Cap}(w)$, and total allocated capacity in all subproblems $\int_0^\infty \text{Cap}(w)\, dw$, cannot exceed C.

4. The designer's goal is to maximize total revenue. We call the revenue at the solution $R^d(C, T)$.

As r^w is strictly concave and increasing up to $\lambda^{w,*}$, it is straightforward to verify that, given a choice $\text{Cap}(w)$, the solution to the w subproblem,

$$\max_{(\lambda_t^w)_{t=1,\dots,T}} \left(\sum_{t=1}^T r^w(\lambda_t^w)\right) w\bar{f}_w(w) \text{ such that } \sum_{t=1}^T \lambda_t^w\, w\bar{f}_w(w) \le \text{Cap}(w),$$

is given by

$$
\lambda_t^w \equiv \lambda^{w,d} := \begin{cases} \lambda^{w,*} & \text{if } \lambda^{w,*} \leq \frac{\text{Cap}(w)}{Tw \bar{f}_w(w)}, \\ \frac{\text{Cap}(w)}{Tw \bar{f}_w(w)} & \text{else.} \end{cases} \tag{4.14}
$$

Accordingly, the revenue in the w subproblem is $r^w(\lambda^{w,d}) Tw \bar{f}_w(w)$.

Proposition 6 *The solution to the deterministic problem given by (4.12) and (4.13) is characterized by*

1. $\hat{v}(p^w(\lambda^{w,d}), w) = \beta(C, T) = const.,$
2. $\lambda_t^w = \lambda^{w,d} = \frac{\text{Cap}(w)}{Tw \bar{f}_w(w)},$
3. $\int_0^\infty \text{Cap}(w)\, dw = \min(C, T \int_0^\infty \lambda^{w,*} w \bar{f}_w(w) dw).$

Proof The proposition is an immediate consequence of the characterization (4.14) of optimal solutions for the w subproblems given $\text{Cap}(w)$, and of a straightforward variational argument ensuring that marginal revenues from marginal increase of $\text{Cap}(w)$ must be constant almost surely in w. ∎

To get an intuition for the above result, observe that the marginal increase of the optimal revenue for the w-subproblem from marginally increasing $\text{Cap}(w)$ is

$$
\left(\frac{d}{d\lambda} r^w\right)\left(\frac{\text{Cap}(w)}{Tw \bar{f}_w(w)}\right) = \hat{v}(p^w(\lambda^{w,d}), w) \qquad \text{if } \lambda^{w,*} > \frac{\text{Cap}(w)}{Tw \bar{f}_w(w)},
$$

and 0 else.

Proposition 6 says that, optimally, the capacity should be split in such a way that the marginal revenue from increasing $\text{Cap}(w)$ is the same for all w. Actually solving the problem amounts to the simple static exercise of determining the constant $\beta(C, T)$ in accordance with the integral feasibility constraint.

The preceding construction is justified by the following two-step argument. On the one hand, as we show in theorem 18 below, the optimal revenue in the deterministic problem, $R^d(C, T)$, bounds from above the optimal revenue in the original stochastic case. On the other hand, as we show in section 4.5.2, the optimal solution of the deterministic problem serves to define a simple time-independent policy that in the stochastic problem captures revenues $R^{TI}(C, T)$ such that $\frac{R^{TI}(C,T)}{R^d(C,T)}$ converges to one as C and T go to infinity. Combining these two points yields the kind of asymptotic optimality result we want to establish.

Since we assume here that weights are observable, a Markovian policy α for the original stochastic problem is characterized by the acceptance probabilities

$\lambda_t^{w_t}[c_t]$ contingent on current time t, remaining capacity c_t, and weight request w_t. Expected revenue from policy α at the beginning of period t (i.e., when there are $T - t + 1$ periods left) with remaining capacity c_t is given by

$$R_\alpha(c_t, T - t + 1) = E_\alpha\left[\sum_{s=t}^T w_s\, p^{w_s}(\lambda_s^{w_s}[c_s]) I_{\{v_s \geq p^{w_s}(\lambda_s^{w_s}[c_s])\}}\right]$$

subject to $\displaystyle\sum_{s=t}^T w_s\, I_{\{v_s \geq p^{w_s}(\lambda_s^{w_s}[c_s])\}} \leq c_t$.

Here the constraint must hold almost surely when following α. As before, we write $R^*(c_t, T - t + 1)$ for the optimal revenue, that is, the supremum of expected revenues taken over all feasible Markovian policies α.

Theorem 18 *For any capacity C and deadline T, it holds that $R^*(C, T) \leq R^d(C, T)$.*

Proof We need to distinguish two cases:

Case 1. Assume that $C > T \int_0^\infty \lambda^{w,*} w \bar{f}_w(w)\, dw$. In this case we know that $\beta(C, T) = 0$ and $R^d(C, T) = T \int_0^\infty r^w(\lambda^{w,*}) w \bar{f}_w(w)\, dw$. We also know that $R^*(C, T) \leq R^*(+\infty, T)$, where $R^*(+\infty, T)$ denotes the optimal expected revenue from a stochastic problem without any capacity constraint. But, for such a problem, the optimal Markovian policy maximizes at each period the instantaneous expected revenue upon observing w_t, $w_t\, r^{w_t}(\lambda)$. That is, the optimal policy sets $\lambda_t^{w_t}[+\infty] = \lambda^{w,*}$. Thus

$$R^*(C, T) \leq R^*(+\infty, T) = T \int_0^\infty w\, r^w(\lambda^{w,*}) \bar{f}_w(w)\, dw = R^d(C, T).$$

Case 2. Assume now that $C \leq T \int_0^\infty \lambda^{w,*} w \bar{f}_w(w)\, dw$. For $\mu \geq 0$, consider the unconstrained maximization problem

$$\max_{\text{Cap}(\cdot)} \left[\int_0^\infty r^w\left(\frac{\text{Cap}(w)}{Tw\bar{f}_w(w)}\right) Tw\bar{f}_w(w)\, dw \right.$$

$$\left. + \mu\left(C - \int_0^\infty \text{Cap}(w)\, dw\right)\right].$$

The Euler–Lagrange equation is $\left(\frac{d}{d\lambda}r^w\right)\left(\frac{\text{Cap}(w)}{Tw\bar{f}_w(w)}\right) = \mu$. Hence, if we write $R^d(C, T, \mu)$ for the optimal value of the problem above, and if we let $\mu = \beta(C, T)$, where $\beta(C, T)$ is the constant from proposition 6, then the solution equals the one of the constrained deterministic problem. In particular $\int_0^\infty \text{Cap}(w)\, dw = C$, and $R^d(C, T, \beta(C, T)) = R^d(C, T)$.

Recall that for the stochastic problem, and for any Markovian policy α, we have

$$R_\alpha(C, T) = E_\alpha\left[\sum_{t=1}^{T} w_t\, p^{w_t}\left(\lambda_t^{w_t}[c_t]\right) I_{\{v_t \geq p^{w_t}(\lambda_t^{w_t}[c_t])\}}\right],$$

and define

$$R_\alpha(C, T, \beta(C, T))$$

$$= R_\alpha(C, T) + \beta(C, T)\left(C - E_\alpha\left[\sum_{t=1}^{T} w_t\, I_{\{v_t \geq p^{w_t}(\lambda_t^{w_t}[c_t])\}}\right]\right).$$

Since for any policy α that is admissible in the original problem, it holds that

$$\sum_{t=1}^{T} w_t\, I_{\{v_t \geq p^{w_t}(\lambda_t^{w_t}[c_t])\}} \leq C \quad a.s.,$$

we have $R_\alpha(C, T) \leq R_\alpha(C, T, \beta(C, T))$. We will show below that for arbitrary α (which satisfies the capacity constraint or not), it holds that

$$R_\alpha(C, T, \beta(C, T)) \leq R^d(C, T, \beta(C, T)). \tag{4.15}$$

This yields for any α that is admissible in the original problem,

$$R_\alpha(C, T) \leq R_\alpha(C, T, \beta(C, T)) \leq R^d(C, T, \beta(C, T)) = R^d(C, T).$$

Taking the supremum over α concludes then the proof for the second case.

It remains to prove (4.15). The argument uses the filtration $\{\mathcal{F}_t\}_{t=1}^T$ of σ algebras containing information prior to time t (in particular, the value of c_t) and in addition the currently observed w_t:

$$R_\alpha(C, T, \beta(C, T))$$

$$= E_\alpha \left[\sum_{t=1}^T w_t \left(p^{w_t}(\lambda_t^{w_t}[c_t]) \right) - \beta(C, T) \right.$$

$$\left. \times I_{\{v_t \geq p^{w_t}(\lambda_t^{w_t}[c_t])\}} \right] + \beta(C, T) C$$

$$= E_\alpha \left[\sum_{t=1}^T E_\alpha \left[w_t \left(p^{w_t}(\lambda_t^{w_t}[c_t]) \right) - \beta(C, T) \right. \right.$$

$$\left. \left. \times I_{\{v_t \geq p^{w_t}(\lambda_t^{w_t}[c_t])\}} | \mathcal{F}_t \right] \right] + \beta(C, T) C$$

$$= E_\alpha \left[\sum_{t=1}^T w_t \left(p^{w_t}(\lambda_t^{w_t}[c_t]) \right) - \beta(C, T) \right.$$

$$\left. \times E_\alpha \left[I_{\{v_t \geq p^{w_t}(\lambda_t^{w_t}[c_t])\}} | \mathcal{F}_t \right] \right] + \beta(C, T) C$$

$$= E_\alpha \left[\sum_{t=1}^T w_t \left(r^{w_t}(\lambda_t^{w_t}[c_t]) - \beta(C, T) \lambda_t^{w_t}[c_t] \right) \right] + \beta(C, T) C$$

$$\leq E_\alpha \left[\sum_{t=1}^T w_t \left(r^{w_t}(\lambda^{w_t, d}) - \beta(C, T) \lambda^{w_t, d} \right) \right] + \beta(C, T) C$$

$$= E_{(w_t)_{t=1}^T} \left[\sum_{t=1}^T w_t \left(r^{w_t}(\lambda^{w_t, d}) - \beta(C, T) \lambda^{w_t, d} \right) \right] + \beta(C, T) C$$

$$= T \int_0^\infty (r^w(\lambda^{w, d}) - \beta(C, T) \lambda^{w, d}) w \bar{f}_w(w) \, dw + \beta(C, T) C$$

$$= R^d(C, T, \beta(C, T)).$$

For the inequality, we have used that $\lambda^{w, d}$ maximizes $r^w(\lambda) - \beta(C, T)\lambda$. ∎

4.5.2 A Simple Policy for the Stochastic Problem

Having established the upper bound of theorem 18, we now proceed with the second part of our two-step argument outlined in the preceding section. We use the optimal solution of the deterministic problem in order to define a w-contingent yet time-independent policy α_{TI} for the stochastic case as follows:

1. Given C and T, solve the deterministic problem to obtain $\beta(C,T)$, $\lambda^{w,d}$ and thus $p^{w,d} := p^w(\lambda^{w,d}) = \hat{v}^{-1}(\beta(C,T), w)$.

2. In the stochastic problem charge these weight-contingent prices $p^{w,d}$ for the entire time horizon, provided that the quantity request does not exceed the remaining capacity. Else, charge a price equal to $+\infty$ (i.e., reject the request).

Remark 4 *Note that under condition 2 of theorem 16, the time-independent policy α_{TI} is implementable also if weights are not observable! Indeed setting all virtual valuation thresholds equal to a constant is like setting them optimally for linear, and hence concave, salvage values.*

We now determine how well the time-independent policy constructed above performs compared to the optimal Markovian policy. Recall that we do this by comparing its expected revenue, $R^{TI}(C,T)$, with the optimal revenue in the deterministic problem, $R^d(C,T)$, which, as we know by theorem 18, provides an upper bound for the optimal revenue in the stochastic problem, $R^*(C,T)$.

For the proof of theorem 19, we first need a lemma:

Lemma 4 *Let $R^{TI}(C,T)$ be the revenue obtained from the stationary policy α_{TI}. Let $(\widetilde{w}_t, \widetilde{v}_t)_{t=1}^T$ be an independent copy of the process $(w_t, v_t)_{t=1}^T$. It holds that*

1.
$$
R^{TI}(C,T) = E_{(w_t)_{t=1}^T}\left[\sum_{t=1}^T r^{w_t}(\lambda^{w_t,d}) w_t \right.
$$
$$
\left. \times \left(1 - P\left[\sum_{s=1}^{t-1} \widetilde{w}_s I_{\{\widetilde{v}_s \geq p^{\widetilde{w}_s,d}\}} > C - w_t\right]\right)\right], \qquad (4.16)
$$

2.
$$
\frac{R^{TI}(C,T)}{R^d(C,T)} \geq 1 \qquad (4.17)
$$
$$
-\frac{\sum_{t=1}^T \int_0^\infty r^w(\lambda^{w,d}) w \left(\min\left(1, \dfrac{(t-1)\sigma_d^2}{((T-t+1)\mu_d - w)^2}\right) I_{\{w \leq (T-t+1)\mu_d\}} + I_{\{w > (T-t+1)\mu_d\}}\right) \bar{f}_w(w)\, dw}{T \int_0^\infty r^w(\lambda^{w,d}) w \bar{f}_w(w)\, dw},
$$

where

$$\mu_d := \frac{\min(C, T \int_0^\infty \lambda^{w,*} w \bar{f}_w(w)\, dw)}{T},$$

and where

$$\sigma_d^2 := E[w^2 I_{\{v \geq p^{w,d}\}}] - \mu_d^2 = \int_0^\infty w^2 \lambda^{w,d} \bar{f}_w(w)\, dw - \mu_d^2.$$

Proof (1) $R^{TI}(C,T)$ may be written as

$$R^{TI}(C,T)$$

$$= E_{(w_t,v_t)_{t=1}^T} \left[\sum_{t=1}^T p^{w_t,d} w_t I_{\{v_t \geq p^{w_t,d}\}} I_{\{\sum_{s=1}^{t-1} w_s I_{\{v_s \geq p^{w_s,d}\}} \leq C - w_t\}} \right]$$

$$= E_{(w_t)_{t=1}^T} \left[\sum_{t=1}^T r^{w_t}(\lambda^{w_t,d}) w_t \right]$$

$$- E_{(w_t,v_t)_{t=1}^T} \left[\sum_{t=1}^T p^{w_t,d} w_t I_{\{v_t \geq p^{w_t,d}\}} I_{\{\sum_{s=1}^{t-1} w_s I_{\{v_s \geq p^{w_s,d}\}} > C - w_t\}} \right].$$

In order to simplify the second term, we use the fact that v_t and $(w_s, v_s)_{s=1}^{t-1}$ are independent conditional on w_t:

$$E_{(w_t,v_t)_{t=1}^T} \left[\sum_{t=1}^T p^{w_t,d} w_t I_{\{v_t \geq p^{w_t,d}\}} I_{\{\sum_{s=1}^{t-1} w_s I_{\{v_s \geq p^{w_s,d}\}} > C - w_t\}} \right]$$

$$= E_{(w_t,v_t)_{t=1}^T} \left[\sum_{t=1}^T E \left[p^{w_t,d} w_t I_{\{v_t \geq p^{w_t,d}\}} \right. \right.$$

$$\times I_{\{\sum_{s=1}^{t-1} w_s I_{\{v_s \geq p^{w_s,d}\}} > C - w_t\}} \big| w_t \Big] \Big]$$

$$= E_{(w_t,v_t)_{t=1}^T} \left[\sum_{t=1}^T p^{w_t,d} w_t E \left[I_{\{v_t \geq p^{w_t,d}\}} | w_t \right] \right.$$

$$\times E \left[I_{\{\sum_{s=1}^{t-1} w_s I_{\{v_s \geq p^{w_s,d}\}} > C - w_t\}} | w_t \right] \Big]$$

$$= E_{(w_t, v_t)_{t=1}^T} \left[\sum_{t=1}^T p^{w_t, d} w_t \, \lambda^{w_t, d} \, P \left[\sum_{s=1}^{t-1} \widetilde{w}_s \, I_{\{\widetilde{v}_s \geq p^{\widetilde{w}_s, d}\}} > C - w_t \right] \right]$$

$$= E_{(w_t)_{t=1}^T} \left[\sum_{t=1}^T r^{w_t} (\lambda^{w_t, d}) \, w_t \, P \left[\sum_{s=1}^{t-1} \widetilde{w}_s \, I_{\{\widetilde{v}_s \geq p^{\widetilde{w}_s, d}\}} > C - w_t \right] \right].$$

This establishes equation (4.16).

(2) Recall that $R^d(C, T) = T \int_0^\infty r^w(\lambda^{w,d}) w \bar{f}_w(w) \, dw$. Observe further that $\lambda^{w,d}$ depends on C and T only through the ratio C^{eff}/T, where $C^{\text{eff}} = \min(C, T \int_0^\infty \lambda^{w,*} w \bar{f}_w(w) \, dw)$, via $E[w I_{\{v \geq p^{w,d}\}}] = \int_0^\infty w \lambda^{w,d} \bar{f}_w(w) \, dw = \frac{C^{\text{eff}}}{T} = \mu_d$. Observe first that

$$P \left[\sum_{s=1}^{t-1} \widetilde{w}_s \, I_{\{\widetilde{v}_s \geq p^{\widetilde{w}_s, d}\}} > C - w_t \right] \leq P \left[\sum_{s=1}^{t-1} \widetilde{w}_s \, I_{\{\widetilde{v}_s \geq p^{\widetilde{w}_s, d}\}} > T \mu_d - w_t \right]$$

$$= P \left[\sum_{s=1}^{t-1} \widetilde{w}_s \, I_{\{\widetilde{v}_s \geq p^{\widetilde{w}_s, d}\}} - (t-1)\mu_d > (T - t + 1)\mu_d - w_t \right].$$

We trivially bound the last expression by 1 if $(T - t + 1)\mu_d - w_t \leq 0$, and otherwise use Chebychev's inequality to deduce

$$P \left[\sum_{s=1}^{t-1} \widetilde{w}_s \, I_{\{\widetilde{v}_s \geq p^{\widetilde{w}_s, d}\}} - (t-1)\mu_d > (T - t + 1)\mu_d - w_t \right]$$

$$\leq P \left[\left(\sum_{s=1}^{t-1} \widetilde{w}_s \, I_{\{\widetilde{v}_s \geq p^{\widetilde{w}_s, d}\}} - (t-1)\mu_d \right)^2 > ((T - t + 1)\mu_d - w_t)^2 \right]$$

$$\leq \frac{E \left[\left(\sum_{s=1}^{t-1} \widetilde{w}_s \, I_{\{\widetilde{v}_s \geq p^{\widetilde{w}_s, d}\}} - (t-1)\mu_d \right)^2 \right]}{((T - t + 1)\mu_d - w_t)^2} = \frac{(t-1)\sigma_d^2}{((T - t + 1)\mu_d - w_t)^2}.$$

As we are bounding a probability, we can replace this estimate by the trivial bound 1 again whenever this is better, that is, if w_t is smaller than but close to $(T - t + 1)\mu_d$. Let $A_w \equiv \min \left(1, \frac{(t-1)\sigma_d^2}{((T-t+1)\mu_d - w)^2} \right)$.

Thus

$$E_{(w_t,v_t)_{t=1}^T} \left[\sum_{t=1}^T p^{w_t,d} \, w_t \, I_{\{v_t \geq p^{w_t,d}\}} \, I_{\{\sum_{s=1}^{t-1} w_s \, I_{\{v_s \geq p^{w_s,d}\}} > C - w_t\}} \right]$$

$$\leq \sum_{t=1}^T \int_0^\infty r^w(\lambda^{w,d}) \, w(A_w) \, I_{\{w \leq (T-t+1)\mu_d\}}$$

$$+ I_{\{w > (T-t+1)\mu_d\}} \big) \bar{f}_w(w) \, dw.$$

Finally, dividing by $R^d(C,T)$ yields the desired estimate. ∎

Theorem 19

1. For any joint distribution of values and weights,

$$\lim_{C,T \to \infty, \frac{C}{T} = const} \frac{R^{TI}(C,T)}{R^d(C,T)} = 1.$$

2. Assume that w and v are independent. Then

$$\frac{R^{TI}(C,T)}{R^d(C,T)} \geq \left(1 - \frac{\sqrt{E[w^2]/E[w]}}{2\sqrt{\min(C, \lambda^* E[w]T)}} \right).$$

In particular, $\lim_{\min(C,T) \to \infty} \frac{R^{TI}(C,T)}{R^d(C,T)} = 1.$

Proof (1) The starting point is the estimate from (4.17). Note that $r^w(\lambda^{w,d}) w \bar{f}_w(w)$ is an integrable upper bound for

$$r^w(\lambda^{w,d}) \, w \left(A_w \, I_{\{w \leq (T-t+1)\mu_d\}} + I_{\{w > (T-t+1)\mu_d\}} \right) \bar{f}_w(w).$$

Moreover, for fixed w, for arbitrary $\eta \in (0,1)$, and for $t \leq \eta T$ we have $w < (1-\eta)T\mu_d$ eventually as $T, C \to \infty$, $C/T = $ const. Moreover

$$\frac{(t-1)\sigma_d^2}{((T-t+1)\mu_d - w)^2} \leq \frac{\eta T \sigma_d^2}{((1-\eta)T\mu_d - w)^2} \to 0, \qquad \text{as } T \to \infty.$$

The dominated convergence theorem implies then that

$$\int_0^\infty r^w(\lambda^{w,d}) \, w \left(A_w \, I_{\{w \leq (T-t+1)\mu_d\}} + I_{\{w > (T-t+1)\mu_d\}} \right) \bar{f}_w(w) \, dw \to 0,$$

in the considered limit, for arbitrary $\eta \in (0,1)$ and for $t \leq \eta T$. Consequently also the term that is subtracted in the estimate (4.17) converges to zero.

(2) A straightforward application of the proof by Gallego and van Ryzin is possible for this last part. For completeness, we spell it out. If w and v are

independent, all the $\lambda^{w,d}$ for different w coincide, as do the $\lambda^{w,*}$. Call them λ^d and λ^*, respectively. We have then

$$
R^{TI}(C,T) = p(\lambda^d)E\left[\min\left(C, \sum_{t=1}^{T} w_t\, I_{\{v_t \geq p(\lambda^d)\}}\right)\right]
$$

$$
= p(\lambda^d)E\left[\sum_{t=1}^{T} w_t\, I_{\{v_t \geq p(\lambda^d)\}} - \left(\sum_{t=1}^{T} w_t\, I_{\{v_t \geq p(\lambda^d)\}} - C\right)^+\right].
$$

We use now the following estimate for $E[(X-k)^+]$, where X is a random variable with mean m and variance σ^2 and where k is a constant:

$$
E[(X-k)^+] \leq \frac{\sqrt{\sigma^2 + (k-m)^2} - (k-m)}{2}.
$$

Note that by independence

$$
E\left[\sum_{t=1}^{T} w_t\, I_{\{v_t \geq p(\lambda^d)\}}\right] = E[w]T\lambda^d;
$$

$$
\mathrm{Var}\left[\sum_{t=1}^{T} w_t\, I_{\{v_t \geq p(\lambda^d)\}}\right] = T\left(E[(w\, I_{\{v \geq p(\lambda^d)\}})^2] - E[w]^2(\lambda^d)^2\right)
$$

$$
= T\left(E[w^2]\lambda^d - E[w]^2(\lambda^d)^2\right)
$$

If $\lambda^*TE[w] > C$ and hence if $\lambda^d = C/TE[w]$ this yields

$$
R^{CP}(C,T)
$$

$$
\geq R^d(C,T) - p(\lambda^d)\frac{\sqrt{TE[w^2]\lambda^d}}{2} = R^d(C,T)\left(1 - \frac{\sqrt{E[w^2]/E[w]}}{2\sqrt{C}}\right).
$$

If $\lambda^*TE[w] \leq C$ and hence if $\lambda^d = \lambda^*$, then $C \geq E\left[\sum_{t=1}^{T} w_t\, I_{\{v_t \geq p(\lambda^d)\}}\right]$, so that $E\left[\left(\sum_{t=1}^{T} w_t\, I_{\{v_t \geq p(\lambda^d)\}} - C\right)^+\right] \leq \sqrt{\sigma^2}/2$. Thus

$$
R^{TI}(C,T)
$$

$$
\geq R^d(C,T) - p(\lambda^*)\frac{\sqrt{\lambda^*TE(w^2)}}{2} = R^d(C,T)\left(1 - \frac{\sqrt{E[w^2]/E[w]}}{2\sqrt{\lambda^*E(w)T}}\right).
$$

Hence we can conclude that

$$
\frac{R^{TI}(C,T)}{R^d(C,T)} \geq \left(1 - \frac{\sqrt{E[w^2]/E[w]}}{2\sqrt{\min(C,T\lambda^*E[w]))}}\right).
$$

∎

We have chosen to focus on these two general limit results, but various other quantitative ones can be proved by similar techniques at the expense of slightly more technical effort, and possibly some further assumptions on the distribution F. Since $R^d(C,T) \geq R^*(C,T) \geq R^{TI}(C,T)$ (the first inequality is theorem 4, and the second follows by optimality), our estimate in theorem 19-2 immediately extends to $\frac{R^*(C,T)}{R^d(C,T)}$, or to $\frac{R^{TI}(C,T)}{R^*(C,T)}$. Note that since policy α_{TI} is stationary, it does not generate incentives to postpone arrivals even in a more complex model where buyers are patient and can choose their arrival time.

Remark 5 *In a complete information knapsack model, Lin, Lu, and Yao (2008) study policies that start by accepting only high-value requests, and then switch over to accepting also lower values as time goes by. They establish asymptotic optimality of such policies (with carefully chosen switch over times) as available capacity and time go to infinity. In other words, their prices are time-dependent but do not condition on the weight request. It is easy to show that in our incomplete information model such policies are, in general, suboptimal. Consider first a one-period example where the seller has capacity 2, and where the arriving agent has either a weight request of 1 or 2 (equally likely). If the weight request is 1(2), the agent's per-unit value distributes uniformly between 0 and 1 (between 1 and 2). The optimal mechanism in this case is as follows: if the buyer requests one unit, the seller sells it for a price of 0.5, and if the buyer requests two units, the seller sells each unit at a price of 2. Note that this policy is implementable since the requested per-unit price is monotonically increasing in the weight request. The expected revenue is 9/8. If, however, the seller is forced to sell all units at the same per-unit price without conditioning on the weight request, he will charge the price of 1 for each unit, yielding an expected revenue of 1, and thus lose 1/8 versus the optimal policy. Replicate now this problem so that there are T periods and capacity $C = 2T$. Then the expected revenue from the optimal mechanism is 9/8T, while the expected revenue from the constrained mechanism is only T. Obviously the constrained mechanism is not asymptotically optimal.*

4.6 Related Literature

The dynamic and stochastic knapsack problem with complete information about values and requests has been analyzed by Papastavrou, Rajagopalan, and Kleywegt (1996) and by Kleywegt and Papastavrou (2001). These authors have characterized optimal policies in terms of weight-dependent value thresholds. Kincaid and Darling (1963), and Gallego and Ryzin (1994) looked at a model that can be reinterpreted as having (one-dimensional) incomplete information about values, but in their frameworks all requests have the same known weight. In particular, Gallego and van Ryzin show that optimal revenue is concave in capacity in the case of equal weights. Kleywegt and Papastavrou have examples showing that total value is not necessarily globally concave in capacity if the weight requests are heterogeneous, and provide a sufficient condition for this structural property to hold.

Gallego and Ryzin (1994) also showed that the optimal policy of their model, which exhibits complicated time dynamics, can often be replaced by a simple time-independent policy without much loss: this simpler policy is asymptotically optimal as the number of periods and the units to be sold go to infinity.

The theory of multidimensional mechanism design is relatively complex: the main problem is that incentive compatibility—which in the one-dimensional case often reduces to a monotonicity constraint—imposes, besides a monotonicity requirement, an integrability constraint that is not easily included in maximization problems (see examples in Rochet 1985; Armstrong 1996; Jehiel, Moldovanu, and Stacchetti 1999; and the survey of Rochet and Stole 2003). Other multidimensional mechanism design problems with restricted deviations in one or more dimensions have been studied by Blackorby and Szalay (2007), Che and Gale (2000), Iyengar and Kumar (2008), Kittsteiner and Moldovanu (2005), and Pai and Vohra (2013). These papers display related sufficient conditions for implementation in frameworks with restricted deviations.

Notes

1. Our results are easily extended to the setting where arrivals are stochastic and/or time is continuous.

2. It is an easy extension to assume that the arrival probability per period is given by $p < 1$.

3. The results below apply with the obvious modifications also if types in different periods are independent, but not necessarily drawn from identical distributions.

4. Alternatively, we can assume that each agent observes the entire history of the previous allocations. These assumptions are innocuous in the following sense: when we analyze revenue maximization in section 4.4, we first solve for the optimal policy in the relaxed problem with observable weight types w. We then provide conditions for when this relaxed solution is implementable. Since in the case of observable weight requests, the seller cannot gain by hiding the available capacity, the seller cannot increase expected revenue by hiding the remaining capacity also in the original problem.

5. We set $p_t^c(w) = \infty$ if the set $\{v/\alpha_t^c(w,v) = 1\}$ is empty.

6. Note that the optimal policy continues to be deterministic even if virtual valuations are not monotonic. This follows by a similar argument to the one given by Riley and Zeckhauser (1983). We nevertheless keep the monotonicity assumption for simplicity, and because we need related conditions for some of the results below.

7. By our assumption of unbounded conditional virtual values (which is a mild assumption on distributions with unbounded support), these first-order conditions always admit a solution and must therefore be satisfied at the optimum.

8. Note that this condition already implies the needed monotonicity in v of the conditional virtual value for all w.

9. We also assume that the other mild technical conditions of theorem 17 are satisfied.

5 Learning and Dynamic Efficiency

5.1 Introduction

The allocation model studied here is again based on the classical model due to Derman, Lieberman, and Ross (1972).[1] Learning in the complete-information DLR model has been first analyzed by Albright (1977).

When learning about the environment takes place, the information revealed by a strategic agent affects both the current and the option values attached by the designer to various allocations. Since option values for the future serve as proxies for the values of allocating resources to other (future) agents, the private values model with learning indirectly generates informational externalities.

In our model a necessary condition for extracting truthful information about values is the monotonicity of the (possible random) allocation rule; that is, agents with higher values should not be worse off than contemporaneous agents with lower values. Intuitively, monotonicity will be satisfied if the increased optimism about the future distribution of values associated with higher current observation is not too drastic. A drastic optimism may be detrimental for an agent whose revealed information induces it—leading to a failure of truthful revelation—if the designer decides in response to deny present resources in order to keep them for the "sunnier" future.

Efficient implementation is possible only if the efficient allocation satisfies a monotonicity condition, and monotonicity holds if the impact of currently revealed information on today's values is higher than the impact on option values. This observation translates to the dynamic framework with learning the single-crossing idea appearing in the theory of static efficient implementation with interdependent values.

We first derive direct conditions on the exogenous parameters of the allocation-cum-learning environment (e.g., conditions on the initial beliefs about the environment and on the learning protocol) that allow the implementation of the first best. Here we deal with both Bayesian and two adaptive, non-Bayesian learning models. The latter turn out to be much more permissible in terms of implementation.

For Bayesian learning we offer two sets of sufficient conditions under which the second-best policy coincides with the first-best (i.e., we offer conditions under which the complete information dynamically efficient policy characterized by Albright is incentive compatible). A common requirement is a stochastic dominance condition: higher current observations should lead to more optimistic beliefs about the distribution of future values. The other requirement puts a bound on the allowed optimism associated to higher observations in each period of search. The two obtained bounds differ in their response to an increase in the number of objects (or search periods): in the first result the bound becomes tighter in early search stages, whereas in the second the bound becomes tighter in later periods.

We next analyze the same model as above, but do not assume Bayesian learning. We show that some simple, but not trivial non-Bayesian updating procedures (that were used in the classical search literature) lead to very permissive implementation results, contrasting the rather restrictive results that have been obtained for Bayesian learning. This highlights the role of the learning procedure in dynamic mechanism design problems, and adds a new dimension that is mostly lacking both in the classical (static) mechanism design theory, and in the more recent literature on dynamic mechanism design.

We study two adaptive non-Bayesian learning processes that have been used for the classical, complete-information one-object search framework (see Rothschild 1974) by Bickhchandani and Sharma (1996) and by Chou and Talmain (1993), respectively. The first learning process constructs a posterior that is a convex combination of a prior and the empirical distribution, with more and more weight given to the empirical distribution. The second process starts with a maximum entropy prior and constructs a quantile preserving posterior based on the observations made so far. Both processes are consistent in the sense that they uniformly converge to the true distribution as the number of observations goes to infinity. In both cases this is a consequence of the well-known Glivenko–Cantelli theorem.

For both processes we prove that the efficient allocation is always implementable because new information is incorporated in option values at a slow rate, so the impact of new information on present values is always higher. As in the case of standard Bayesian learning, the efficient allocation maximizes at each decision period the sum of the expected utilities of all agents, given all the available information. The only difference to the Bayesian approach is in the inference made from new information.

A word of caution is needed here: Our results do not imply that the considered non-Bayesian procedures are "better" than Bayesian updating for the purposes of efficient implementation! Because expectations about the future also depend on the learning process, a non-Bayesian designer will generally prefer a different policy than a Bayesian one. Thus our results just say that the complete-information efficient allocation—whose calculation proceeds given an assumed learning procedure—can always be implemented for the particular adaptive processes studied here. An example will illustrate this issue.

Finally, we characterize—for the Bayesian setting—the optimal policy respecting the incentive constraints (second-best). We are able to offer here a complete characterization by using several concepts that were developed in the context of *majorization* theory. The crucial insight is that the second-best policy is deterministic, meaning it allocates to each type of agent, at each point in time, a well-defined available quality instead of a lottery over several feasible qualities.

Our analysis of the preceding questions reveals and exploits close, formal relations between the problem of ensuring monotone—and hence implementable—allocation rules in our dynamic allocation problems with incomplete information and learning, and between the older, classical problem of obtaining optimal stopping policies for search that are characterized by a *reservation price property*. In particular, and letting aside for a while the mechanism design/dynamic efficiency interpretation, our results about first-best implementation can also be seen as offering conditions ensuring that the optimal search policy without recall for highest prices for several (possibly heterogeneous) objects exhibits the relevant generalization of the reservation price property.[2]

It is important to note that in the classical search model, price quotations are nonstrategic and the monotonicity requirement behind the reservation price property is only a convenient, intuitive feature, facilitating the use of structural empirical methods in applied studies. In contrast, implementability is, of course, a "non–plus-ultra" requirement in our strategic, incomplete information model. In particular, our characterization of the second-best mechanism has no counterpart in the classical search literature.

We conclude this part by noting that if all payments can be delayed until a time in the future when no new arrivals occur (offline mechanisms), the efficient allocation can always be implemented because payments can be then conditioned on the actual allocation in each instance. But such uncoupling of the physical and monetary parts is not always realistic in applications, and we will abstract from it here. In yet another interpretation, our results can be then seen as delineating the loss entailed by requiring "online" payments in dynamic allocation problems.

5.2 The Model

We consider again the Derman–Lieberman–Ross model of chapter 2 with m objects having qualities $0 \leq q_m \leq q_{m-1} \leq \ldots \leq q_1$. Let period n denote the first period, period $n-1$ denote the second period, ..., period 1 denote the last period. We can assume without loss of generality that $m = n$.

The agents' types are assumed to be independent and identically distributed random variables X_i on $[0, +\infty)$ with common cumulative distribution function F.

In contrast to our treatment in the previous parts, we now assume that there are one or more unknown parameters of the distribution F from which agents' types are sampled. The beliefs about these parameters are originally given by a prior distribution, which is then sequentially updated via Bayes's rule as additional information is observed. Denote by Φ_n the designer's prior over possible distribution functions, and by $\Phi_k(x_n, \ldots, x_{k+1})$ his beliefs about the distribution function F after observing types $x_n, \ldots, x_{k+1}$. Given such beliefs, let $\widetilde{F}_k(x|x_n, \ldots, x_{k+1})$ denote the distribution of the next type x_k, conditional on observing $x_n, \ldots, x_{k+1}$, while $\widetilde{f}_k(x|x_n, \ldots, x_{k+1})$ denote the corresponding density. We assume that the distribution $\widetilde{F}_k(x|x_n, \ldots, x_{k+1})$ is symmetric with respect to observed signals—a feature satisfied by both the standard Bayesian learning model and the non-Bayesian updating schemes analyzed below. Finally, we assume that upon arrival, each agent observes the whole history of the previous play.

5.3 Learning under Complete Information

We start by characterizing the dynamically efficient allocation under complete information; that is, the agent's type is revealed to the designer upon the agent's arrival (but there is still uncertainty about the types of future agents). The efficient allocation maximizes at each decision period the sum of the expected utilities of all agents, given all the information available at that period.

Let the history at period k, H_k, be the ordered set of all signals reported by the agents that arrived at periods $n, \ldots, k+1$, and of allocations to those agents.[3] Let $\mathcal{H}_k$ be the set of all histories at period k. Denote by χ_k the ordered set of signals reported by the agents that arrived at periods $n, \ldots, k+1$. Finally, denote by Π_k the set of available objects at k (which has cardinality k by our convention that equates the number of objects with the number of periods). Note that an initial inventory Π_n and a history H_k completely determine the set Π_k.

Albright (1977) derived the efficient dynamic policy under complete information, namely when the agent's type is revealed to the designer upon the agent's arrival. The efficient allocation maximizes, at each decision period, the sum of the expected utilities of all agents, given all the information available at that period. In other words, the designer solves the following recursive maximization problem: if at period k the set of objects still available for allocation is Π_k, the designer solves

$$\max_{q_i \in \Pi_k} [q_i \cdot x_k + V_{k-1}(\Pi_k \setminus \{q_i\} \mid x_n, ..., x_k)], \tag{5.1}$$

where $V_{k-1}(\Pi_k \setminus \{q_i\} \mid x_n, ..., x_k)$ denotes the expected utility from the optimal future allocation of the remaining inventory $\Pi_k \setminus \{q_i\}$ given that the designer has already observed types $x_n, ..., x_k$.

It is important to note that due to the presence of learning about the uncertain environment, the expectation V_{k-1} is determined by the prior beliefs, by the agents' types observed so far, and by the belief-updating process.

The result below characterizes, at each period, the dynamically efficient policy in terms of cutoffs determined by the history of observed signals. This policy can be seen as the dynamic version of the assortative matching policy that is optimal in the static case where all agents arrive simultaneously (see Becker 1973).

Theorem 20 *(Albright 1977)*

1. *Assume that types $x_n, .., x_{k+1}$ have been observed, and consider the arrival of an agent with type x_k in period $k \geq 1$. There exist functions $0 = a_{k,k}(\chi_k, x_k) \leq a_{k-1,k}(\chi_k, x_k) \leq \cdots \leq a_{1,k}(\chi_k, x_k) \leq a_{0,k}(\chi_k, x_k) = \infty$ such that the efficient dynamic policy—which maximizes the expected value of the total reward—assigns the item with the i-highest type if $x_k \in (a_{i,k}(\chi_k, x_k), a_{i-1,k}(\chi_k, x_k)]$. The functions $a_{i,k}(\chi_k, x_k)$ do not depend on the q's.*

2. *These functions are related to each other by the following recursive formulas:*

$$a_{i,k+1}(\chi_{k+1}, x_{k+1}) = \int_{A_{i,k}} x_k d\widetilde{F}_k(x_k \mid \chi_{k+1}, x_{k+1})$$

$$+ \int_{\underline{A}_{i,k}} a_{i,k}(\chi_k, x_k) d\widetilde{F}_k(x_k \mid \chi_{k+1}, x_{k+1})$$

$$+ \int_{\overline{A}_{i,k}} a_{i-1,k}(\chi_k, x_k) d\widetilde{F}_k(x_k \mid \chi_{k+1}, x_{k+1}) \tag{5.2}$$

where[4]

$$\underline{A}_{i,k} = \{x_k : x_k \le a_{i,k}(\chi_k, x_k)\},$$
$$A_{i,k} = \{x_k : a_{i,k}(\chi_k, x_k) < x_k \le a_{i-1,k}(\chi_k, x_k)\},$$
$$\overline{A}_{i,k} = \{x_k : x_k > a_{i-1,k}(\chi_k, x_k)\}.$$

The cutoffs above have a natural interpretation: for each object i and period k the cutoff $a_{i,k}(\chi_k, x_k)$ equals the expected value of the agent's type to which the item with i-highest type is assigned in a problem with $k - 1$ periods before the period $k - 1$ signal is observed.[5]

5.4 Learning and Incomplete Information

We now focus on the additional constraints imposed by incentive compatibility in the model with incomplete information and learning. We therefore assume below that the agents' types x_i are private information. Without loss of generality, we can restrict attention to direct mechanisms where every agent, upon arrival, reports his type and where the mechanism specifies which item the agent gets (if any), and a payment.[6]

We first characterize incentive compatible allocations in our model: an allocation policy (which may be random) is implementable under incomplete information if and only if, in each period and for every history of events at preceding periods, the expected quality allocated to the current agent is nondecreasing in the agent's reported type.

Proposition 7 *For a fixed allocation policy, denote by $\mathbb{Q}_k(H_k, x)$ the expected quality allocated to an agent arriving at period k after history H_k and reporting signal x. An allocation policy is implementable if and only if for any k and for any H_k the expected quality $\mathbb{Q}_k(H_k, x)$ is nondecreasing in x.*

Proof For a given implementable allocation policy, assume, by contradiction, that there exist a period k, a history H_k, and two signals of the current agent $x' > x''$ such that $Q_k(H_k, x') < Q_k(H_k, x'')$. Denote by $P_k(H_k, x)$ the expected payment of the agent that arrives at period k after history H_k and reports x. The incentive constraint for type x'' implies that

$$x'' Q_k(H_k, x'') - P_k(H_k, x'') \ge x'' Q_k(H_k, x') - P_k(H_k, x').$$

Since, by assumption, $x' > x''$ and $Q_k(H_k, x') < Q_k(H_k, x'')$, the inequality above implies that

$$x'(Q_k(H_k, x'') - Q_k(H_k, x')) > x''(Q_k(H_k, x'') - Q_k(H_k, x'))$$
$$\ge P_k(H_k, x'') - P_k(H_k, x''),$$

which further implies that

$$x' \left(Q_k \left(H_k, x'' \right) - Q_k \left(H_k, x' \right) \right) > P_k \left(H_k, x'' \right) - P_k \left(H_k, x' \right)$$

The inequality above contradicts the incentive compatibility constraint for type x'.

We prove this part by constructing a payment scheme that implements a given monotonic allocation. Consider the following payment scheme:

$$P_k \left(H_k, x \right) = x Q_k \left(H_k, x \right) - \int_0^x Q_k \left(H_k, y \right) dy.$$

The expected utility of an agent with type x that arrives at period k after history H_k and reports truthfully is given by $\int_0^x Q_k \left(H_k, y \right) dy$. If he reports $x' \neq x$, his expected utility is given by

$$\left(x - x' \right) Q_k \left(H_k, x' \right) + \int_0^{x'} Q_k \left(H_k, y \right) dy.$$

We need to show that for any k, H_k, x, x' we have

$$\left(x - x' \right) Q_k \left(H_k, x' \right) + \int_0^{x'} Q_k \left(H_k, y \right) dy \leq \int_0^x Q_k \left(H_k, y \right) dy.$$

The last inequality can be written as

$$\left(x - x' \right) Q_k \left(H_k, x' \right) \leq \int_{x'}^x Q_k \left(H_k, y \right) dy,$$

which is true by the monotonicity of $Q_k \left(H_k, x \right)$. ∎

The next result displays an implicit sufficient condition on the cutoffs of the efficient, complete-information allocation, characterized in theorem 20 above.

Proposition 8

1. *Consider the first-best policy, characterized in theorem 20. This policy is implementable if and only if for any k, $i \leq k$, and χ_k the set of types that is matched with a given quality q_i,*

   $$A_{i,k} = \{ x_k : a_{i-1,k}(\chi_k, x_k) > x_k \geq a_{i,k}(\chi_k, x_k) \},$$

   is convex (i.e., it is an interval).

2. *Assume that for any k, χ_k, $i \in \{0, \ldots, k\}$, the cutoff $a_{i,k}(\chi_k, x_k)$ is a Lipschitz function of x_k with constant 1. Then the efficient dynamic policy is implementable under incomplete information.*

Proof   By theorem 20, the current agent k gets the object with quality q_i if and only if his type belongs to

$$A_{i,k} = \{x_k : a_{i-1,k}(\chi_k, x_k)) > x_k \geq a_{i,k}(\chi_k, x_k)\}.$$

The first claim follows then immediately from proposition 7: by theorem 20, if the sets $A_{i,k}$ are convex for any i, then for any $m, l \in \{1, ..., k\}$ with $m > l$ it must hold that

$$\inf\{x_k : x \in A_{m,k}\} \geq \sup\{x_k : x \in A_{l,k}\}.$$

In other words, the intervals $A_{i,k}$ are ordered

For the second claim, note that theorem 20 states that for any k, $i \leq k$, x, and χ_k we have $a_{i-1,k}(\chi_k, x_k) \geq a_{i,k}(\chi_k, x_k)$. Therefore it is sufficient to show that if there exist k, χ_k and $i \in \{0, ..., k\}$, and a signal x_k with $a_{i,k}(\chi_k, x_k) < x_k$, then there is no $x'_k > x_k$ such that $a_{i,k}(\chi_k, x'_k) > x'_k$. Assume by contradiction that such x'_k exists. Since $a_{i,k}$ is, by assumption, Lipschitz with constant 1, $a_{i,k}(\chi_k, x'_k) \leq x'_k - x_k + a_{i,k}(\chi_k, x_k)$. Since $a_{i,k}(\chi_k, x_k) < x_k$, we obtain $a_{i,k}(\chi_k, x'_k) < x'_l$, which yields a contradiction.   ∎

Recall that in the limiting case of no learning—where we know that the efficient allocation is implementable—we have $\frac{\partial}{\partial x_k} a_{i,k}(\chi_k, x_k) = 0$.

Examples where the resulting sets $A_{i,k}$ are convex include: (1) agents' types that are uniformly distributed on the interval $[0, W]$, and the designers' prior about W that is a Pareto distribution $P(\alpha, R)$ with $\alpha > 1$; 2. Agents' types distribute according to a gamma distribution $Gamma(\alpha, \beta)$ with unknown rate parameter β, and the designer's beliefs about β are given by another gamma distribution $Gamma(\gamma, \delta)$.

Due to the learning process, the current information affects both the current value of allocating some object to the arriving agent and the option value of keeping that object and allocating it in the future. The previous result requires the effect of the current information on the current value to be stronger than the effect on the option value, similarly to the well known *single-crossing* condition that appears in the theory of efficient design with interdependent valuations.[7]

5.4.1   An Illustration

In this subsection we illustrate the preceding insights in a simple example where the designer is uncertain about a shape parameter affecting the distribution of values.

Example 11   *There is one object of quality $q = 1$, and two periods (this corresponds to the general case of $q_1 = 1$ and $q_2 = 0$). The agents' valuations* *distribute on* $[0, 1]$*: with probability* α*, the distribution is* $F(x) = x$*, and with probability* $1 - \alpha$*, the distribution is* $F(x) = x^\theta$*, where* $\theta > 0$*.*

After observing the type of the agent who arrives at period 2 (the first period!) the designer's belief about the next period's type given the current observation is expressed as

$$\tilde{f}_1(x|x_2) = \frac{\alpha + (1 - \alpha) \, \theta^2 x_2^{\theta-1} x^{\theta-1}}{\alpha + (1 - \alpha) \, \theta x_2^{\theta-1}}.$$

Therefore the expected type at the next period is given by

$$E_{x|x_2}(x) = \frac{\frac{\alpha}{2} + (1 - \alpha) \, \frac{\theta^2}{\theta+1} x_2^{\theta-1}}{\alpha + (1 - \alpha) \, \theta x_2^{\theta-1}}.$$

Figure 5.1 shows the function $E_{x|x_2}(x)$ *for values* $\alpha = 0.2$ *and* $\theta = 12$. *The designer would like to allocate the object in period 2 if and only if his value exceeds the expected value of the agent that arrives at the next period. Therefore the designer wants to allocate the object at period 2 if and only if* $x_2 \in (x_{2a}, x_{2b}] \cup (x_{2c}, 1]$*, where* $x_{2a} \approx 0.513$*,* $x_{2b} \approx 0.691$*, and* $x_{2c} \approx 0.895$*.*

The efficient (first-best) allocation is not monotone, and hence, by proposition 7, it is not implementable. The reason for this nonmonotonicity is the following: when x_2 *is relatively low, the designer is almost certain that the*

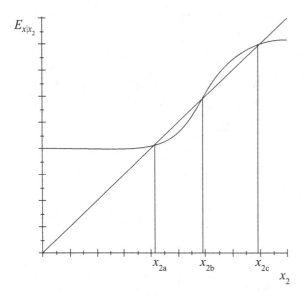

Figure 5.1
Efficient allocation that is not monotone

distribution is uniform (since the density of the second distribution is very low at the bottom of the type distribution). But, at some point, the density of the second distribution becomes very steep, and for low α, this causes the designer to adjust his beliefs also very steeply: he becomes more and more optimistic about the future, which is detrimental to a current agent with relatively high values.

5.4.2   Sufficient Conditions for Efficient Implementation

We now look for sufficient conditions on the model's primitives under which the first-best, complete-information policy is implementable. Before proving the main results about the implementability of the complete-information efficient allocation (first best), we prove two useful structural results about the efficient cutoffs.

First, we show that the average of all but the extreme cutoffs equals the expectation about the next type. Note that by theorem 20, we can write

$$a_{i,k+1}(\chi_{k+1}, x_{k+1}) = E_{x_k|x_{k+1}}(G_{i,k}(x_k, x_{k+1}, \chi_{k+1})), \tag{5.3}$$

where the function $G_{i,k}(x_k, x_{k+1}, \chi_{k+1})$ is given by

$$\begin{cases} a_{i,k}(\chi_{k+1}, x_{k+1}, x_k) & \text{if } x_k \leq a_{i,k}(\chi_{k+1}, x_{k+1}, x_k), \\ x_k & \text{if } a_{i,k}(\chi_{k+1}, x_{k+1}, x_k) < x_k \\ & \quad \leq a_{i-1,k}(\chi_{k+1}, x_{k+1}, x_k), \\ a_{i-1,k}(\chi_{k+1}, x_{k+1}, x_k) & \text{if } x_k > a_{i-1,k}(\chi_{k+1}, x_{k+1}, x_k). \end{cases} \tag{5.4}$$

In other words $G_{i,k}(x_k, x_{k+1}, \chi_{k+1})$ is the second highest order statistic out of the set $\{a_{i,k}(\chi_{k+1}, x_{k+1}, x_k),\ x_k\ ,\ a_{i-1,k}(\chi_{k+1}, x_{k+1}, x_k)\}$.

Lemma 5 *For any $k \leq n$, it holds that*

$$\sum_{i=1}^{k-1} a_{i,k}(\chi_k, x_k) = (k-1)\, E_{x_k|\chi_k}(x_k).$$

Proof We prove the claim by induction. For $k = 2$, $a_{1,2}(\chi_2, x_2) = \int_0^\infty x_1 d\widetilde{F}_1(x_1|\chi_1, x_2) = E_{x_1|\chi_2, x_2} x_1$. Theorem 20 implies that for any fixed x_k,

$$\sum_{i=1}^{k} \left[a_{i-1,k}(\chi_k, x_k) \mathbf{1}_{\overline{A}_{i,k}} + a_{i,k}(\chi_k, x_k) \mathbf{1}_{\underline{A}_{i,k}} \right] = \sum_{i=1}^{k-1} a_{i,k}(\chi_{k+1}, x_{k+1}, x_k),$$

$$\tag{5.5}$$

where 1_s is an index function. Using (5.2) and the previous expression, we obtain for period $k + 1$ that

$$\sum_{i=1}^{k} a_{i,k+1}(\chi_{k+1}, x_{k+1}) = \int_0^{\infty} x d\widetilde{F}_k(x|\chi_{k+1}, x_{k+1})$$

$$+ \sum_{i=1}^{k-1} E_{x_k|\chi_{k+1}, x_{k+1}} a_{i,k}(\chi_{k+1}, x_{k+1}, x_k)$$

$$= k E_{x_k|\chi_{k+1}, x_{k+1}} x_k$$

where the first equality follows from (5.5), and where the last equality follows from the induction argument. ∎

Next we derive monotonicity properties of the cutoffs that holds whenever higher observations induce more optimistic beliefs about the distribution of values:

Lemma 6 *Assume that for any k, and for any pair of ordered lists of reports $\chi_k \geq \chi'_k$ that differ only in one coordinate, $\widetilde{F}_k(x|\chi_k) \succsim_{FOSD} \widetilde{F}_k(x|\chi'_k)$. Then for any $i \in \{1, ..., k-1\}$ the cutoff $a_{i,k}(\chi_k, x_k)$ is nondecreasing in x_k.*

Proof The proof is by induction on the number of remaining periods. For $k = 2$ we have

$$a_{0,2}(\chi_2, x_2) = \infty,$$

$$a_{1,2}(\chi_2, x_2) = \int_0^{\infty} x_1 d\widetilde{F}_1(x_1|\chi_2, x_2),$$

$$a_{2,2}(\chi_2, x_2) = 0.$$

Stochastic dominance immediately implies that the cutoffs are nondecreasing in x_2. We now apply the induction argument, and assume that, for any χ_k and for any $i, a_{i,k}(\chi_k, x_k)$ is nondecreasing in x_k. This implies that the function $G_{i,k}(x_k, x_{k+1}, \chi_{k+1})$ is nondecreasing in x_k and that for any $i, x'_{k+1} \geq x_k$,

$$a_{i,k}(\chi_{k+1}, x_{k+1}, x_k) = a_{i,k}(\chi_{k+1}, x_k, x_{k+1}) \geq$$
$$a_{i,k}(\chi_{k+1}, x_k, x'_{k+1}) = a_{i,k}(\chi_{k+1}, x'_{k+1}, x_k),$$

where both equalities follow from the assumption of symmetry and switching the order of the observations does not affect the final beliefs. Therefore we obtain $G_{i,k}(x_k, x_{k+1}, \chi_{k+1}) \geq G_{i,k}(x_k, x'_{k+1}, \chi_{k+1})$ for any x_k. Moreover we have that

$$a_{i,k+1}(\chi_{k+1}, x_{k+1}) = E_{x_k|x_{k+1}} G_{i,k}(x_k, x_{k+1}, \chi_{k+1})$$
$$\geq E_{x_k|x_{k+1}} G_{i,k}(x_k, x'_{k+1}, \chi_{k+1})$$
$$\geq E_{x_k|x'_{k+1}} G_{i,k}(x_k, x'_{k+1}, \chi_{k+1}) = a_{i,k+1}(\chi_{k+1}, x'_{k+1}),$$

where the second inequality follows from the assumed stochastic dominance, and from the fact that by the induction argument, $G_k(x_k, x'_{k+1}, \chi_{k+1})$ is nondecreasing in x_k.   ∎

Theorem 21 *Assume that for any k, and for any pair of ordered lists of reports $\chi_k \geq \chi'_k$ that differ only in one coordinate, the following conditions hold:*

suff1 $\widetilde{F}_k(x|\chi_k) \succsim_{FOSD} \widetilde{F}_k(x|\chi'_k)$.

suff2 $E(x|\chi_k) - E(x|\chi'_k) \leq \frac{\Delta}{k-1}$, *where Δ is size of the difference between χ_k and χ'_k.*
           Then the efficient dynamic policy can be implemented also under incomplete information.

Proof   Lemma 5 and the second condition in the theorem's statement imply that

$$\sum_{i=1}^{k-1} \left(a_{i,k}(\chi_k, x_k) - a_{i,k}(\chi_k, x'_k) \right)$$
$$= (k-1) \left(E_{x_{k-1}|\chi_k, x_k} x_{k-1} - E_{x_{k-1}|\chi_k, x'_k} x_{k-1} \right)$$
$$\leq \frac{k-1}{k-1} (x_k - x'_k). \tag{5.6}$$

In other words, the sum of cutoffs $\sum_{i=1}^{k-1} a_{i,k}(\chi_k, x_k)$ is a Lipschitz function with constant 1 of x_k. By lemma 6 and the stochastic dominance condition, we know that the cutoff $a_{i,k}(\chi_k, x_k)$ is a nondecreasing function of x_k. Therefore inequality (5.6) implies that for any i, the function $a_{i,k}(\chi_k, x_k)$ must also be a Lipschitz function with constant 1 of x_k. By proposition 8, the efficient dynamic policy is then implementable.   ∎

The first condition (stochastic dominance) above says that higher observations should lead to optimism about future observations,[8] and the second condition puts a bound on this optimism. The result is simple, but its disadvantage is that as the number of objects (or search periods) grows, the second condition gets tighter (i.e., the bound on the optimism associated to higher observation gradually decreases) in the early search periods.

Learning models typically have a relatively high gradient in early learning periods, implying that our second condition is likely to be violated if there are many search periods. The next example illustrates this phenomenon.

Example 12 *Assume that with probability p the arriving agent's type x is distributed on the interval $[0,1]$ with density $f_1(x) = 1 - \frac{b_1}{2} + b_1 x$, and with probability $1 - p$ it is distributed on $[0,1]$ with density $f_2(x) = 1 - \frac{b_2}{2} + b_2 x$, where $b_1, b_2 \in [-2, 2)$. Note that*

$$E[F_i] = \frac{1}{2} + \frac{b_i}{12} \quad and$$

$$E(x|\chi_k) = \Pr(b_i = b_1|x_n, ..., x_{k+1}) E[F_1] + \Pr(b_i = b_2|x_n, ..., x_{k+1}) E[F_2].$$

Using Bayesian updating, we get

$$\Pr(b_i = b_1|x_n, ..., x_{k+1}) = \left(1 + \frac{1-p}{p} \prod_{j=k+1}^{n} \frac{1 - \frac{b_2}{2} + b_2 x_j}{1 - \frac{b_1}{2} + b_1 x_j}\right)^{-1}.$$

Therefore

$$E(x|\chi_k) - E(x|\chi'_k) = \frac{b_1 - b_2}{12} \left[\Pr(b_i = b_1|\chi_k) - \Pr(b_i = b_1|\chi'_k)\right].$$

Let χ_k and χ'_k be two sequences of observed signals that differ only in one coordinate, with $\chi_k \geq \chi'_k$. Then by simple calculations we obtain

$$E(x|\chi_k) - E(x|\chi'_k) < \frac{(b_1 - b_2)^2}{12} \frac{(x_i - x'_i)}{\left(1 - \frac{b_2}{2} + b_2 x_i\right)\left(1 - \frac{b_1}{2} + b_1 x'_i\right)}$$

$$\leq \frac{(b_1 - b_2)^2}{3(2 - b_2)(2 - b_1)} (x_i - x'_i).$$

Finally, if

$$\frac{(b_1 - b_2)^2}{3(2 - b_2)(2 - b_1)} \leq \frac{1}{n-1},$$

we obtain that

$$E(x|\chi_k) - E(x|\chi'_k) \leq \frac{(x_i - x'_i)}{n-1} \leq \frac{(x_i - x'_i)}{k-1}.$$

as desired. To see that the second condition of theorem 21 will not hold for sufficiently high number of periods, note that at the first period

$$E(x|\chi_{n-1}) - E(x|\chi'_{n-1}) = \frac{b_1 - b_2}{12} \left[\Pr(b_i = b_1|x_n) - \Pr(b_i = b_1|x'_n)\right]$$

is independent of the number of future observations n. Therefore there exist number of periods n and observations x_n and x'_n such that

$$E\left(x|\chi_{n-1}\right) - E\left(x|\chi'_{n-1}\right) > \frac{x_n - x'_n}{n-2}.$$

In order to obtain sufficient conditions on the learning process that hold independently of the number of objects/periods, we focus now on bounds that, as the number of objects grows, get tighter in late, rather than in early periods. Such conditions are, in principle, easier to satisfy, since in many learning models (in particular, in those where beliefs converge, e.g., to the true distribution) the impact of later observations is significantly lower than that of early observations. Thus a tighter bound on the allowed optimism associated with higher observations is less likely to be binding in late periods. For mathematical convenience, we make a mild differentiability assumption that allows us to work with bounds on derivatives rather than with the Lipschitz condition of proposition 8.

Theorem 22 *Assume that for all k, all x, and all $n - k \geq i \geq 1$, the conditional distribution function $\widetilde{F}_k\left(x|x_n,..,x_{k+1}\right)$ and the density $\widetilde{f}_k\left(x|x_n,\cdots,x_{k+1}\right)$ are continuously differentiable with respect to x_{k+i}. If for all x, χ_k, and all $n - k \geq i \geq 1$, it holds that*

$$0 \geq \frac{\partial \widetilde{F}_k\left(x|\chi_k\right)}{\partial x_{k+i}} \geq -\frac{1}{n-k}\frac{\partial \widetilde{F}_k\left(x|\chi_k\right)}{\partial x}, \tag{5.7}$$

then the efficient dynamic policy can be implemented also under incomplete information.

Proof Note first that

$$\frac{\partial E\left(x|\chi_k\right)}{\partial x_{k+i}} = \frac{\partial}{\partial x_{k+i}}\int_0^\infty \left(1 - \widetilde{F}_k\left(x|\chi_k\right)\right) dx_k$$

$$\leq \frac{1}{n-k}\int_0^\infty \frac{\partial \widetilde{F}_k\left(x|\chi_k\right)}{\partial x} dx_k = \frac{1}{n-k}, \tag{5.8}$$

where the inequality follows from the condition of the theorem. By proposition 8, it is sufficient to show that for any k, any history of reports χ_k, and any $n - k \geq i \geq 1$, the cutoff $a_{i,k}(\chi_k, x_k)$ is differentiable and satisfies $\frac{\partial}{\partial x_k} a_{i,k}(\chi_k, x_k) \leq 1$. Since $a_{i,k}(\chi_k, x_k) = E_{x_{k-1}|\chi_k, x_k} G_{i,k-1}(x_{k-1}, x_k, \chi_k)$, we need to show that $\frac{\partial}{\partial x_k} E_{x_{k-1}|\chi_k, x_k} G_{i,k-1}(x_{k-1}, x_k, \chi_k)$ exists and that

$$\frac{\partial}{\partial x_k} E_{x_{k-1}|\chi_k, x_k} G_{i,k-1}(x_{k-1}, x_k, \chi_k) \leq 1.$$

We claim now that $E_{x_k|\chi_{k+1}, x_{k+1}} G_{i,k}(x_k, x_{k+1}, \chi_{k+1})$ is differentiable and that

$$\frac{\partial E_{x_k|\chi_{k+1}, x_{k+1}} G_{i,k}(x_k, x_{k+1}, \chi_{k+1})}{\partial x_{k+1}} \leq \frac{1}{n - k}.$$

This yields $\frac{\partial}{\partial x_{k+1}} a_{i,k+1}(\chi_{k+1}, x_{k+1}) \leq \frac{1}{n-k}$ for any history of signals χ_{k+1}, any pair of signals x_k, x_{k+1}, any period $k + 1 > 1$, and any item i.

We prove the claim by induction on the number of the remaining periods k. For $k = 1$, note that $a_{1,1}(\chi_2, x_2, x_1) = 0$ and $a_{0,1}(\chi_2, x_2, x_1) = \infty$. Hence we have $G_{1,1}(x_1, x_2, \chi_2) = x_1$. Therefore inequality (5.8) implies that

$$\frac{\partial}{\partial x_2} E_{x_1|\chi_2, x_2} G_{1,1}(x_1, x_2, \chi_2) \leq \frac{1}{n - 1} \quad \text{and}$$

$$\frac{\partial}{\partial x_2} a_{1,2}(\chi_2, x_2) \leq \frac{1}{n - 1}.$$

Note also that continuous differentiability of $\widetilde{f}_1(x|x_n, ..., x_2)$ implies continuous differentiability of $a_{1,2}(\chi_2, x_2)$. Assume now that $a_{i,k}(\chi_k, x_k)$ is continuously differentiable and that

$$\frac{\partial E_{x_{k-1}|\chi_k, x_k} G_{i,k-1}(x_{k-1}, x_k, \chi_k)}{\partial x_k} \leq \frac{1}{n - k + 1},$$

$$\frac{\partial a_{i,k}(\chi_k, x_k)}{\partial x_k} \leq \frac{1}{n - k + 1}$$

Since $a_{i,k}(\chi_k, x_k)$ is continuous, the induction hypothesis implies that for any $i \in \{1, ..., k - 1\}$, there exists at most one solution to the equation $a_{i,k}(\chi_k, x) = x$. Denote this solution by $a_{i,k}^*(\chi_k)$. If $a_{i,k}(\chi_k, x) > x$ for any x, define $a_{i,k}^*(\chi_k) = \infty$, and if $a_{i,k}(\chi_k, x) < x$ for any x, define $a_{i,k}^*(\chi_k) = 0$.

Recall that by induction, we can rewrite

$$E_{x_k|\chi_{k+1},x_{k+1}}G_{i,k}(x_k,x_{k+1},\chi_{k+1})$$

$$= \int\limits_{0}^{a_{i,k}^*(\chi_k)} a_{i,k}(\chi_{k+1},x_{k+1},x_k)f(x_k|\chi_{k+1},x_{k+1})\,dx_k$$

$$+ \int\limits_{a_{i,k}^*(\chi_k)}^{a_{i-1,k}^*(\chi_k)} x_k f(x_k|\chi_{k+1},x_{k+1})\,dx_k$$

$$+ \int\limits_{a_{i-1,k}^*(\chi_k)}^{\infty} a_{i-1,k}(\chi_{k+1},x_{k+1},x_k)f(x_k|\chi_{k+1},x_{k+1})\,dx_k.$$

Since $a_{i,k}(\chi_{k+1},x_{k+1},x_k)$ is continuously differentiable in x_{k+1} for any $i \in \{1,...,k-1\}$ by the induction argument, and since $\widetilde{f}_k(x_k|\chi_{k+1},x_{k+1})$ is continuously differentiable by assumption, we can invoke the implicit function theorem to deduce that the fixed point $a_{i,k}^*(\chi_k)$ is continuously differentiable in x_{k+1}. Thus we obtain that $E_{x_k|\chi_{k+1},x_{k+1}}G_{i,k}(x_k,x_{k+1},\chi_{k+1})$ is continuously differentiable in x_{k+1}.

We now show that $\frac{\partial}{\partial x_{k+1}}E_{x_k|\chi_{k+1},x_{k+1}}G_{i,k}(x_k,x_{k+1},\chi_{k+1}) \leq \frac{1}{n-k}$. We have

$$\frac{\partial}{\partial x_{k+1}}\int\limits_{0}^{\infty} G_{i,k}(x_k,x_{k+1},\chi_{k+1})\widetilde{f}_k(x_k|x_{k+1},\chi_{k+1})\,dx_k$$

$$= \int\limits_{0}^{\infty} \frac{\partial G_{i,k}(x_k,x_{k+1},\chi_{k+1})}{\partial x_{k+1}}\widetilde{f}_k(x_k|x_{k+1},\chi_{k+1})\,dx_k \qquad (5.9)$$

$$+ \int\limits_{0}^{\infty} \frac{\partial \widetilde{f}_k(x_k|x_{k+1},\chi_{k+1})}{\partial x_{k+1}}G_{i,k}(x_k,x_{k+1},\chi_{k+1})\,dx_k. \qquad (5.10)$$

Consider the first term in the sum above (5.9):

$$\int\limits_{0}^{\infty} \frac{\partial G_{i,k}(x_k,x_{k+1},\chi_{k+1})}{\partial x_{k+1}}\widetilde{f}_k(x_k|x_{k+1},\chi_{k+1})\,dx_k$$

$$= \int_0^{a_{i,k}^*(x_{k+1},\chi_{k+1})} \frac{\partial G_{i,k}(x_k,x_{k+1},\chi_{k+1})}{\partial x_{k+1}} \widetilde{f}_k(x_k|x_{k+1},\chi_{k+1}) \, dx_k$$

$$+ \int_{a_{i,k}^*(x_{k+1},\chi_{k+1})}^{a_{i-1,k}^*(x_{k+1},\chi_{k+1})} \frac{\partial G_{i,k}(x_k,x_{k+1},\chi_{k+1})}{\partial x_{k+1}} \widetilde{f}_k(x_k|x_{k+1},\chi_{k+1}) \, dx_k$$

$$+ \int_{a_{i-1,k}^*(x_{k+1},\chi_{k+1})}^{\infty} \frac{\partial G_{i,k}(x_k,x_{k+1},\chi_{k+1})}{\partial x_{k+1}} \widetilde{f}_k(x_k|x_{k+1},\chi_{k+1}) \, dx_k$$

$$\leq \frac{1}{n-k+1} - \frac{1}{n-k+1} \left[\widetilde{F}_k \left(a_{i-1,k}^*(x_{k+1},\chi_{k+1})|x_{k+1},\chi_{k+1}\right) \right.$$

$$\left. - \widetilde{F}_k \left(a_{i,k}^*(x_{k+1},\chi_{k+1})|x_{k+1},\chi_{k+1}\right) \right],$$

where the existence of the fixed points $a_{i,k}^*(x_{k+1},\chi_{k+1})$ and $a_{i-1,k}^*$ (x_{k+1},χ_{k+1}) follows from the induction argument, while the inequality follows from the induction argument and from the fact that $\frac{\partial G_{i,k}(x_k,x_{k+1},\chi_{k+1})}{\partial x_{k+1}} = 0$ if $x_k \in \left[a_{i,k}^*(x_{k+1},\chi_{k+1}), a_{i-1,k}^*(x_{k+1},\chi_{k+1})\right]$.

Consider now the second term in the sum (5.10):

$$\int_0^{\infty} \frac{\partial \widetilde{f}_k(x_k|x_{k+1},\chi_{k+1})}{\partial x_{k+1}} G_{i,k}(x_k,x_{k+1},\chi_{k+1}) \, dx_k$$

$$= \left. \frac{\partial \widetilde{F}_k(x_k|x_{k+1},\chi_{k+1})}{\partial x_{k+1}} G_{i,k}(x_k,x_{k+1},\chi_{k+1}) \right|_{x_k=0}^{\infty}$$

$$- \int_0^{\infty} \frac{\partial \widetilde{F}_k(x_k|x_{k+1},\chi_{k+1})}{\partial x_{k+1}} \frac{\partial G_{i,k}(x_k,x_{k+1},\chi_{k+1})}{\partial x_k} \, dx_k$$

$$= - \int_0^{\infty} \frac{\partial \widetilde{F}_k(x_k|x_{k+1},\chi_{k+1})}{\partial x_{k+1}} \frac{\partial G_{i,k}(x_k,x_{k+1},\chi_{k+1})}{\partial x_k} \, dx_k$$

$$\leq \frac{1}{n-k+1} \int_0^{\infty} \frac{\partial \left[1 - \widetilde{F}_k(x_k|x_{k+1},\chi_{k+1})\right]}{\partial x_{k+1}} \, dx_k$$

$$-\frac{n-k}{n-k+1}\int_{a^*_{i,k}(x_{k+1},\chi_{k+1})}^{a^*_{i-1,k}(x_{k+1},\chi_{k+1})}\frac{\partial \widetilde{F}_k\left(x_k|x_{k+1},\chi_{k+1}\right)}{\partial x_{k+1}}dx_k$$

$$\leq \frac{1}{n-k+1}\frac{1}{n-k}-\frac{n-k}{n-k+1}\int_{a^*_{i,k}(x_{k+1},\chi_{k+1})}^{a^*_{i-1,k}(x_{k+1},\chi_{k+1})}\frac{\partial \widetilde{F}_k\left(x_k|x_{k+1},\chi_{k+1}\right)}{\partial x_{k+1}}dx_k,$$

where the first equality follows by integration by parts, and where the second equality follows because $\lim_{x\to\infty}\widetilde{F}_k\left(x|x_{k+1},\chi_{k+1}\right)=1$ and $\widetilde{F}_k\left(0|x_{k+1},\chi_{k+1}\right)=0$. The first inequality follows by the induction argument (which implies the existence of the fixed points $a^*_{i,k}\left(x_{k+1},\chi_{k+1}\right)$, $a^*_{i-1,k}\left(x_{k+1},\chi_{k+1}\right)$) and because

$$\frac{\partial G_{i,k}(x_k,x_{k+1},\chi_{k+1})}{\partial x_k}$$

$$=\begin{cases}1 & \text{if } x_k\in\left[a^*_{i,k}\left(x_{k+1},\chi_{k+1}\right),a^*_{i-1,k}\left(x_{k+1},\chi_{k+1}\right)\right],\\ \leq\frac{1}{n-k+1} & \text{if } x_k\notin\left[a^*_{i,k}\left(x_{k+1},\chi_{k+1}\right),a^*_{i-1,k}\left(x_{k+1},\chi_{k+1}\right)\right].\end{cases}$$

Combining now the two terms (5.9) and (5.10), we obtain

$$\frac{\partial}{\partial x_{k+1}}\int_0^\infty G_{i,k}(x_k,x_{k+1},\chi_{k+1})\widetilde{f}_k\left(x_k|x_{k+1},\chi_{k+1}\right)dx_k$$

$$\leq\frac{1}{n-k+1}-\frac{1}{n-k+1}\left[\widetilde{F}_k\left(a^*_{i-1,k}\left(x_{k+1},\chi_{k+1}\right)|x_{k+1},\chi_{k+1}\right)\right.$$

$$\left.-\widetilde{F}_k\left(a^*_{i,k}\left(x_{k+1},\chi_{k+1}\right)|x_{k+1},\chi_{k+1}\right)\right]$$

$$+\frac{1}{n-k+1}\frac{1}{n-k}-\frac{n-k}{n-k+1}\int_{a^*_{i,k}(x_{k+1},\chi_{k+1})}^{a^*_{i-1,k}(x_{k+1},\chi_{k+1})}\frac{\partial \widetilde{F}_k\left(x_k|x_{k+1},\chi_{k+1}\right)}{\partial x_{k+1}}dx_k.$$

$$(5.11)$$

Recall the miraculous relation

$$\frac{1}{n-k+1}\frac{1}{n-k}+\frac{1}{n-k+1}=\frac{1}{n-k}.$$

It is therefore sufficient to prove that

$$\frac{1}{n-k}\left[\widetilde{F}_k\left(a^*_{i-1,k}\left(x_{k+1},\chi_{k+1}\right)|x_{k+1},\chi_{k+1}\right)\right.$$

$$\left.-\widetilde{F}_k\left(a^*_{i,k}\left(x_{k+1},\chi_{k+1}\right)|x_{k+1},\chi_{k+1}\right)\right]$$

$$\geq -\int_{a^*_{i,k}(x_{k+1},\chi_{k+1})}^{a^*_{i-1,k}(x_{k+1},\chi_{k+1})} \frac{\partial \widetilde{F}_k\left(x_k|x_{k+1},\chi_{k+1}\right)}{\partial x_{k+1}} dx_k.$$

Integrating with respect to x both sides of the assumed inequality

$$-\frac{\partial \widetilde{F}_k\left(x|\chi_k\right)}{\partial x_{k+i}} \leq \frac{1}{n-k}\frac{\partial \widetilde{F}_k\left(x|\chi_k\right)}{\partial x}$$

between the fixed points $a^*_{i-1,k}\left(x_{k+1},\chi_{k+1}\right)$ and $a^*_{i,k}\left(x_{k+1},\chi_{k+1}\right)$ yields the desired result. ∎

Example 13 below further illustrates these conditions on a simple two-periods setting.

Example 13 *There are two periods. The agents' valuations distribute on* $[0,1]$: *with probability* α *the distribution is* $F(x) = x$, *while with probability* $1 - \alpha$ *the distribution is* $F(x) = x^\theta$, *where* $\theta > 0$. *Recall that the designer's belief about the next period's type given the current observation is given by*

$$\widetilde{f}_1\left(x|x_2\right) = \frac{\alpha + (1-\alpha)\theta^2 x_2^{\theta-1}x^{\theta-1}}{\alpha + (1-\alpha)\theta x_2^{\theta-1}}.$$

Condition (5.7) requires here that

$$0 \geq \frac{\partial \widetilde{F}_1\left(x|x_2\right)}{\partial x_2} \geq -\frac{\partial \widetilde{F}_1\left(x|x_2\right)}{\partial x} \iff$$

$$0 \geq \frac{\alpha(1-\alpha)\theta(\theta-1)x_2^{\theta-2}x\left(x^{\theta-1}-1\right)}{\left(\alpha + (1-\alpha)\theta x_2^{\theta-1}\right)} \geq -\alpha - (1-\alpha)\theta^2 x_2^{\theta-1}x^{\theta-1}.$$

The left-hand-side inequality—stochastic dominance—holds for any $\theta \geq 1$. *It is also easy to see that the right-hand-side inequality holds for any* α *whenever* θ *is close enough to 1. Hence the efficient allocation is implementable for any* α *if* θ *is relatively close to 1. This is intuitive, since in those cases the two possible distributions are very close to each other and hence, for any* x_2, *the designer's belief about the agent that arrives next will not be significantly updated. When*

θ is larger, the condition holds for a smaller range of values of the parameter
α, where the designer is relatively more confident that the uniform distribution
is the true one. For example, when θ = 2 the sufficient condition holds for any
α ≥ $\frac{1}{3}$.

As already mentioned above, our condition is not necessary for imple-
mentability. While it guarantees that for any $x_2 \in [0,1]$, $\frac{\partial E[x|x_2]}{\partial x_2} \leq 1$, a neces-
sary and sufficient condition for the monotonicity of the efficient allocation in
this example is that this inequality holds at the indifference points $E[x|x_2] =$
x_2. Figure 5.2, plotted for $\alpha = 0.8$ and $\theta = 18$, reveals that $\frac{\partial E[x|x_2]}{\partial x_2} > 1$ for
relatively high x_2. Nevertheless, the efficient allocation is here monotone and
hence implementable.

Remark 6 *While the left-hand inequality in condition (5.7) is just another*
way to express the stochastic dominance condition also employed in theorem
21, it is worth to deeper explore the right-hand side.

1. *Putting aside differentiability, this condition is equivalent to requiring that*
   the function $\widetilde{F}_k \left(x + \frac{z}{n-k} | x_{k+1}, ., x_{k+i} + z, x_{k+i+1}, ., x_n \right)$ is nondecreas-
   ing in z. In other words, after having made n − k observations, a small shift
   to the right—which moves the value of the distribution upward—is enough
   to compensate the downward effect on the distribution's value caused by an
   $(n − k)$ times larger upward shift in one of the past observations (recall that
   by stochastic dominance, higher observations move the entire distribution
   downward).

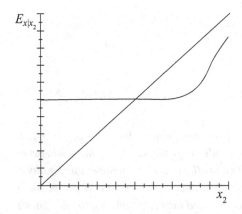

Figure 5.2
Sufficiency in condition (5.7)

2. *Alternatively, denote by $x^*(u)$ the uth percentile of next type's conditional distribution function $\widetilde{F}_k(x|\chi_k)$, that is, $\widetilde{F}_k(x^*(u)|\chi_k) = u$. Condition (5.7) implies that*

$$\frac{\partial x^*(u)}{\partial x_{k+i}} = -\left.\frac{\frac{\partial \widetilde{F}_k(x|\chi_k)}{\partial x_{k+i}}}{\frac{\partial \widetilde{F}_k(x|\chi_k)}{\partial x}}\right|_{x=x^*(u)} \leq \frac{1}{n-k}.$$

*In other words, the effect of an increase in a previous observation on **any** percentile of the distribution governing the next observation is bounded by $\frac{1}{n-k}$, where $n-k$ is the number of observations already made.*

3. *Note that our condition guarantees that $\forall i, k, n, \frac{\partial a_{i,k}(\chi_k, x_k)}{\partial x_k} \leq \frac{1}{n-k}$ although $\frac{\partial a_{i,k}(\chi_k, x_k)}{\partial x_k} \leq 1$ seems sufficient for the implementation of the efficient allocation. Nevertheless, the long-term effect of each nonterminal observation makes it impossible to obtain tighter conditions that apply generally. To see that, recall equation (5.3) which shows that each cutoff is given by the expectation of the second highest value among the type observed next period, and two adjacent next-period cutoffs. In particular, the current observation affects today's cutoffs via (1) an impact on next period cutoffs and (2) a shift of the relevant distribution of the second highest order statistic. The second effect is bounded by*

$$\frac{\partial E(x_{k-1}|x_k, \chi_k)}{\partial x_k} = \frac{\partial}{\partial x_k}\int_0^\infty \left(1 - \widetilde{F}_{k-1}(x|x_k, \chi_k)\right) \leq \frac{1}{n-k+1}.$$

With a bound of 1 instead of $1/n - k$, the first effect would be bounded by

$$1 - \left[\widetilde{F}_{k-1}(a_{i-1,k-1}|x_k, \chi_k) - \widetilde{F}_{k-1}(a_{i,k-1}|x_k, \chi_k)\right],$$

where $a_{i,k-1}$ are tomorrow's optimal cutoffs. Since for any period $k-1$ there exists an i such that $\widetilde{F}_{k-1}(a_{i-1,k-1}|x_k, \chi_k) - \widetilde{F}_{k-1}(a_{i,k-1}|x_k, \chi_k) \leq \frac{1}{k-1}$, we would obtain

$$1 - \left[\widetilde{F}_{k-1}(a_{i-1,k-1}|x_k, \chi_k) - \widetilde{F}_{k-1}(a_{i,k-1}|x_k, \chi_k)\right] \geq \frac{k-2}{k-1},$$

which is arbitrarily close to 1 if the number of the remaining objects is high. Thus the combined effect may be bigger than 1 for any $k \geq \frac{n}{2} + 1$, which would violate the single-crossing condition.

4. *Albright (1977) displays a list of families of distributions/conjugate priors for which, at each period, the sets of types that get assigned to various qualities form an ordered sequence of intervals (see theorem 20). In those cases, the efficient dynamic allocation (first best) is implementable. For example,*

consider a normal distribution of values $\tilde{x} \sim N(\mu, 1)$ with unknown mean μ, and prior beliefs about μ of the form $\tilde{\mu} \sim N(\mu_0, \frac{1}{\tau})$, where $\tau > 0$. We now show that the conditions of theorem 22 are indeed satisfied.

After observing $x_n, \ldots, x_{k+1}$, we write the posterior on $\tilde{\mu}$ as $N(\overline{\mu}, 1/(\tau + n - k))$, where

$$\overline{\mu} = \frac{\tau \mu_0 + \sum x_i}{\tau + (n - k)}.$$

This yields

$$\widetilde{F}_k(x | x_n, \ldots, x_{k+1}) = N(\overline{\mu}, 1 + 1/(\tau + n - k)).$$

Note that

$$\widetilde{F}_k\left(x + \frac{z}{\tau + (n - k)} \Big| x_n, \ldots, x_i + z, \ldots, x_{k+1}\right)$$
$$= \widetilde{F}_k(x | x_n, \ldots, x_i, \ldots, x_{k+1}), \tag{5.12}$$

so the stochastic dominance condition necessarily holds. By differentiating with respect to z both sides of the identity (5.12), and by letting z go to zero, we obtain

$$\frac{\partial \widetilde{F}_k(x | x_n, \ldots, x_{k+1})}{\partial x_{k+i}} = -\frac{1}{\tau + n - k} \widetilde{f}_k(x | x_n, \ldots, x_{k+1}) \Rightarrow$$

$$\frac{\partial \widetilde{F}_k(x | x_n, \ldots, x_{k+1})}{\partial x_{k+i}} \geq -\frac{1}{n - k} \widetilde{f}_k(x | x_n, \ldots, x_{k+1})$$

as desired.

5.5 Search for the Lowest Price and the Reservation Price Property

In a famous paper, Rothschild (1974) studied the problem of a buyer who obtains a sequence of price quotations from various sellers, and who must decide when to stop the (costly) search for a lower price. The buyer has only partial information about the price distribution, and she updates (in a Bayesian way) her beliefs after each observation. Under full information about the environment, the optimal stopping rule is characterized by a reservation price R such that the searcher accepts (or stops search) at any price less than or equal to R, and rejects (or continues to search) any price higher than R. One of the appealing features of this policy (see Rothschild's paper for the others) is that if all buyers follow it, a firm in the market will face a well-behaved demand function: expected sales are a nonincreasing function of the price it charges. Such regularity conditions are extensively used in theoretical and empirical studies, and thus it is of major interest to find out when they are validated by theory.

In the case studied by Rothschild, stopping prices necessarily change as information changes, and hence the optimal policy cannot be characterized by a single reservation price. But, in order to have expected sales decreasing in price, it is enough to assume that, for each information state, a searcher follows *a reservation price policy*; that is, for each information state s there exists a price $R(s)$ such that prices above are rejected and prices below are accepted. The optimal Bayesian search rule need not generally have this property (see Rothschild 1974 and Kohn and Shavell 1974 for examples). Rothschild showed that the reservation price property holds for a searcher equipped with a Dirichlet prior about the parameters of a multinomial distribution governing the price quotations.[9]

The conditions derived in our book are more stringent than those obtained in the search literature, mainly because of the presence of multiple objects: these induce a more complex structure of the optimal search policies, and more stringent conditions are needed in order to control it.[10]

The first general conditions ensuring that the optimal search policy in Rothschild's search model is characterized by a sequence of reservation prices appear in a subtle paper by Rosenfield and Shapiro (1981). In order to understand the relation between our results and theirs, recall first our condition from theorem 22: for all x, χ_k, and all $n - k \geq i \geq 1$,

$$0 \geq \frac{\partial \widetilde{F}_k(x|\chi_k)}{\partial x_{k+i}} \geq -\frac{1}{n-k} \frac{\partial \widetilde{F}_k(x|\chi_k)}{\partial x}. \tag{5.13}$$

The first requirement in the paper by Rosenfield and Shapiro is identical to our stochastic dominance condition (the left-hand side of condition 5.13), while their second condition—translated to the differentiable case and to the case of a searching seller instead of a searching buyer in order to facilitate comparison—reads: for all x, k, χ_k, and all $n - k \geq i \geq 1$,

$$\int_x^\infty \frac{\partial \widetilde{F}_k(y|\chi_k)\, dy}{\partial x_{k+i}} \geq -\frac{1}{n-k}(1 - \widetilde{F}_k(x|\chi_k)). \tag{5.14}$$

In other words, theirs is simply the "average" version of the right-hand side of our condition (5.13), and hence it is obviously implied by it.

Seiderstad (1992) offers another variant. Besides stochastic dominance, his condition reads (again in the differentiable case): for all x, k, and χ_k,

$$\sum_{i=1}^{n-k} \frac{\partial \widetilde{F}_k(x|\chi_k)}{\partial x_{k+i}} \geq -\widetilde{f}_k(x|\chi_k), \tag{5.15}$$

which is also clearly implied by our condition (5.13). The reason why we need stronger conditions than those of both Rosenfield and Shapiro and Seierstad is intimately related to the fact that we analyze a model with several objects: at each point in time we have several critical cutoffs to control, instead of only one. In particular, the reservation price property is connected in our model to the existence of several fixed points at each period, and we need to control the conditional distribution of future values between any two such fixed points (without a priori knowing where they will be). In contrast, in the one-object search problem there are only two fixed points to consider at each period, and one of them is trivially equal to either "minus infinity" (for a searching buyer) or "plus infinity" (for a searching seller). This fact allows Rosenfield and Shapiro to use an average bound, and Seierstad to use a bound that aggregates the effect of all past observations.

5.6   Non-Bayesian Learning and Dynamic Implementation

We now analyze the same model as above, but we do not assume Bayesian learning. We show that some simple non-Bayesian updating procedures that were used in the classical search literature lead here to very permissive implementation results, contrasting the rather restrictive results that have been obtained above for Bayesian learning.

5.6.1   Adaptive Learning Based on the Empirical Distribution

Assume that before stage n (the first stage), the designer's prior belief about the distribution of the first type x_n is given by a distribution B. Then, conditional on sequentially observing $x_n, x_{n-1}, ..., x_{k+1}$ at stages $n, n-1, ..., k+1$, the designer's belief about the distribution of the next type $x = x_k$ is given by

$$\widetilde{F}_k(x|x_n, ..., x_{k+1})$$

$$= (1 - \beta_k^n) B(x) + \beta_k^n \frac{1}{n-k} \sum_{i=k+1}^{n} 1_{[x_i, \infty)}(x), \qquad k = 1, 2, ..., n-1,$$

where $0 < \beta_k^n < 1$, and where $1_{[z,\infty)}(x)$ denotes the indicator function of the set $[z, \infty)$. Thus at each stage the posterior distribution is a convex combination of the prior distribution and of the empirical distribution. Since, by the Glivenko–Cantelli theorem, the empirical distribution uniformly converges to the true underlying distribution, the posterior distribution also converges to the true distribution if the weight on the empirical distribution satisfies: $\forall k$, $\lim_{n \to \infty} \beta_k^n = 1$.

For the proof of theorem 23 below we first need the following well-known lemma:

Lemma 7 *Let $u(x)$ be a function on the interval $[a,b]$ such that there exist a division of the interval $a = z_0 < z_1 \ldots, < z_n = b$ and values $c_1, \ldots, c_n$ with $u(x) = c_i$ for $z_i < x < z_{i+1}, i = 0, 1, \ldots, n-1$. Then, for any continuous function $v(x)$ on $[a,b]$, it holds that*

$$\int_a^b v(x) du(x) = \sum_{i=0}^n v(z_i)(c_{i+1} - c_i),$$

where $\int$ denotes here the Stieltjes integral.

The proofs of both theorem 23 and theorem 24 proceed by showing that the respective learning processes satisfy the implementability conditions of proposition 8.

Theorem 23 *Assume that the designer learns based on the empirical distribution. Then the efficient dynamic policy can always be implemented under incomplete information.*

Proof By theorem 20, we can write

$$a_{i,k+1}(\chi_{k+1}, x_{k+1}) = E_{x_k | x_{k+1}} G_{i,k}(x_k, x_{k+1}, \chi_{k+1}), \tag{5.16}$$

where the function $G_{i,k}(x_k, x_{k+1}, \chi_{k+1})$ is given by

$$\begin{cases} a_{i,k}(\chi_{k+1}, x_{k+1}, x_k) & \text{if} \quad x_k \leq a_{i,k}(\chi_{k+1}, x_{k+1}, x_k), \\ x_k & \text{if} \quad a_{i,k}(\chi_{k+1}, x_{k+1}, x_k) < x_k \\ & \qquad \leq a_{i-1,k}(\chi_{k+1}, x_{k+1}, x_k), \\ a_{i-1,k}(\chi_{k+1}, x_{k+1}, x_k) & \text{if} \quad x_k > a_{i-1,k}(\chi_{k+1}, x_{k+1}, x_k). \end{cases} \tag{5.17}$$

In words, $G_{i,k}(x_k, x_{k+1}, \chi_{k+1})$ is the second highest order statistic out of the set $\{a_{i,k}(\chi_{k+1}, x_{k+1}, x_k), x_k, a_{i-1,k}(\chi_{k+1}, x_{k+1}, x_k)\}$. Let $\mathbf{mx} = (x, x, \ldots x)$ denote an m-vector of x. We show by induction that $\forall m$, $m \leq n - k + 1$, the function $a_{i,k}(x_n, \ldots x_{k+m}, \mathbf{mx})$ is continuously differentiable in the observed signals with

$$\forall i, k, \quad \frac{\partial a_{i,k}(x_n, \ldots, x_{k+m}, \mathbf{mx})}{\partial x} < 1.$$

Since the conditional distribution $\widetilde{F}_k(x | x_n, \ldots, x_{k+1})$ does not have here a well-defined density, we use below the notion of *Stieltjes integral*. In the last but one period $k = 2$, the only relevant, nontrivial cutoff is

$$a_{1,2}(x_n, ..., x_2) = \int_0^\infty x_1 d\widetilde{F}_1(x_1|x_n, ..., x_2)$$

$$= (1 - \beta_2^n) \int_0^\infty x_1 dB(x_1)$$

$$+ \beta_2^n \frac{1}{n-1} \int_0^\infty x_1 d\left(\sum_{i=2}^n 1_{[x_i,\infty)}(x_1)\right)$$

$$= (1 - \beta_2^n)E(B) + \beta_2^n \frac{1}{n-1}\sum_{i=2}^n x_i.$$

The second equality follows by the additivity property of the Stieltjes integral. The third equality follows by lemma 7, since $\sum_{i=2}^n 1_{[x_i,\infty)}(x)$ is a step function. Thus, as required, we obtain that $a_{1,2}(x_n, ..., x_2)$ is continuously differentiable in the observed signals and that

$$\frac{\partial a_{1,2}(x_n, ..., x_{2+m}, \mathbf{mx})}{\partial x} \leq \frac{m\beta_2^n}{n-1} < 1, \qquad m = 1, 2, ..., n-1.$$

Assume now that the statement holds for all periods up to k (recall that period 1 is the last period, etc.), and let us look at period $k+1$, and at $m \leq n - k$. Since $a_{i,k}(x_n, ..., x_k)$ is continuous, the induction hypothesis implies that for any $i \in \{1, ..., k-1\}$ there exists at most one solution to the equation $a_{i,k}(x_n, ..., x_{k+1}, x) = x$. Denote this solution by $a_{i,k}^*(x_n, ..., x_{k+1})$. By the induction hypothesis, and by the implicit function theorem, we obtain that $a_{i,k}^*(x_n, ..., x_{k+1})$ is continuously differentiable in the observed signals. If $a_{i,k}(x_n, ..., x_{k+1}, x) > x$ for any x, define $a_{i,k}^*(x_n, ..., x_{k+1}, x) = \infty$, and if $a_{i,k}(x_n, ..., x_{k+1}, x) < x$ for any x define $a_{i,k}^*(x_n, ..., x_{k+1}, x) = 0$. Then we can write

$$a_{i,k+1}(x_n, ..., x_{k+1})$$

$$= \int_0^{a_{i,k}^*(\chi_k)} a_{i,k}(x_n, ..., x_{k+1}, x_k) d\widetilde{F}_k(x_k|x_n, ..., x_{k+1})$$

$$+ \int_{a_{i,k}^*(\chi_k)}^{a_{i-1,k}^*(\chi_k)} x_k d\widetilde{F}_k(x_k|x_n, ..., x_{k+1})$$

$$+ \int_{a_{i-1,k}^*(\chi_k)}^\infty a_{i-1,k}(x_n, ..., x_{k+1}, x_k) d\widetilde{F}_k(x_k|x_n, ..., x_{k+1}).$$

By the induction hypothesis, we obtain that $a_{i,k+1}(x_n, ..., x_{k+1})$ is continuously differentiable. We obtain moreover that

$$a_{i,k+1}(x_n, ..., x_{k+m+1}, \mathbf{mx})$$

$$= \int_0^\infty G_{i,k}(x_n, ..., x_{k+1+m}, \mathbf{mx}, x_k) d\widetilde{F}_k(x_k | (x_n, ..., x_{k+1+m}, \mathbf{mx}))$$

$$= (1 - \beta_{k+1}^n) \int_0^\infty G_{i,k}(x_n, ..., x_{k+1+m}, \mathbf{mx}, x_k) dB(x_k)$$

$$+ \frac{m\beta_{k+1}^n}{n-k} [G_{i,k}(x_n, ..., x_{k+m}, (\mathbf{m}+1)\mathbf{x})]$$

$$+ \frac{\beta_{k+1}^n}{n-k} \sum_{j=k+m}^n G_{i,k}(x_n, ..., x_{k+m}, \mathbf{mx}, x_j),$$

where the second equality follows from lemma 7. Hence, for any $m \leq n - k$, we obtain

$$\frac{\partial a_{i,k+1}((x_n, ..., x_{k+m+1}, \mathbf{mx})}{\partial x}$$

$$= (1 - \beta_{k+1}^n) \int_0^\infty \frac{\partial G_{i,k}(x_n, ..., x_{n-k-m}, \mathbf{mx}, x_k)}{\partial x} dB(x_k)$$

$$+ \frac{m\beta_{k+1}^n}{n-k} \frac{\partial G_{i,k}(x_n, ..., x_{k+1+m}, (\mathbf{m}+1)\mathbf{x})}{\partial x}$$

$$+ \frac{\beta_{k+1}^n}{n-k} \sum_{j=k+m}^n \frac{\partial G_{i,k}(x_n, ..., x_{k+m}, \mathbf{mx}, x_j)}{\partial x}$$

$$< (1 - \beta_{k+1}^n) + \beta_{k+1}^n \left(\frac{m}{n-k} + \frac{n-k-m}{n-k} \right) = 1,$$

where the inequality follows by the induction hypothesis. By setting $m = 1$, we now obtain

$$\forall i, k \quad \frac{\partial a_{i,k}(x_n, ..., x_{k+1})}{\partial x_{k+1}} < 1.$$

Together with proposition 8, this proves the result.   ∎

For special prior distributions, the process studied above does in fact coincide with the standard Bayesian learning. This is the case, for example, for a multinomial *Dirichlet* prior or for a *Dirichlet process* prior. Thus for such priors theorem 23 also asserts the implementability of the efficient dynamic allocation under Bayesian learning. Bickhchandani and Sharma (1996) showed that the above learning model induces optimal search with the reservation price property in Rothschild's one-object model with complete information (where implementation issues do not play any role). Our result can also be interpreted as saying that their insight continues to hold for the case with several hetero-geneous objects.

5.6.2   Maximum Entropy/Quantile Preserving Learning

We now assume that designer believes that types distribute continuously on a finite interval, which we normalize here to be the interval $[0, 1]$. It is well known that the *maximum entropy* distribution among all continuous distributions with support on an interval $[c, b]$ is the uniform distribution on this interval.[11] More generally, consider a sub-division $c = c_0 < c_1 < ... < c_m = b$ and probabilities $p_1, ..., p_m$ which add up to one, and consider the class of all continuous distributions supported on $[c, b]$ such that

$$\Pr\{c_{i-1} \leq X \leq c_i\} = p_i, \qquad i = 1, ..., m.$$

Then the density of the maximum entropy distribution for this class is constant on each of the intervals $[c_{j-1}, c_j)$. Guided by this principle, Chou and Talmain (1993) looked at the following *quantile preserving* updating procedure.[12] Prior to any observation, the designer estimates the unknown distribution by the uniform distribution. Suppose that m observations were observed, and order them in increasing order $\{x_{(1)}, ..., x_{(m)}\}$. Let $x_{(0)} = 0$ and $x_{(m+1)} = 1$. Then the type of the next arrival is estimated according to the density

$$f_k(x|x_n, ..., x_{n-m+1}) = \sum_{i=1}^{m+1} \frac{\mathbf{1}_{[x_{(i-1)}, x_{(i)})}(x)}{(m+1)\left(x_{(i)} - x_{(i-1)}\right)}.$$

In other words, each interval of the form $[x_{(i-1)}, x_{(i)})$ gets assigned a probability $p_i = 1/m + 1$, and the density within the interval is constant.[13] The rationale behind the equal weights of $1/m + 1$ for each interval becomes apparent by recalling that for m large,

$$E[X_{i,m}] \approx F^{-1}\left(\frac{i}{m+1}\right) \quad \text{and} \quad F(E[X_{i,m}]) - F(E[X_{i-1,m}]) \approx \frac{1}{m+1},$$

where the $X_{i,m}$ is the i-th highest order statistic, $i = 1, ..., m$, of a random variable X distributed according to distribution F.

Theorem 24 *Assume that the designer uses the maximum entropy/quantile preserving learning procedure. Then the efficient dynamic policy can always be implemented under incomplete information.*

Proof We can show that for any i, k, χ_k and x_k, the cutoff $a_{i,k}(\chi_k, x_k)$ is continuously differentiable in x_k with $\frac{\partial}{\partial x_k} a_{i,k}(\chi_k, x_k) \leq \frac{1}{n-k+2}$. We prove this result by induction on k, the number of remaining periods. Note first that lemma 6 is applicable here, since all the steps of its proof hold for the assumed updating process, and yields the monotonicity of $a_{i,k+1}(\chi_{k+1}, x_{k+1})$ in x_{k+1}.

We denote by $x_{(i)}$, the ith highest observation among the $n - k + 1$ observations made up to and including period k, with $x_{(0)} = 1$ and $x_{(n-k+2)} = 0$. For $k = 2$, we have

$$a_{1,2}(x_n, ..., x_2) = \sum_{i=1}^{n} \int_{x_{(i)}}^{x_{(i-1)}} \frac{x}{n\left(x_{(i-1)} - x_{(i)}\right)} dx$$

$$= \frac{1 + 2\sum_{i=1}^{n-1} x_{(i)}}{2n} = \frac{1 + 2\sum_{i=2}^{n} x_i}{2n} \Rightarrow$$

$$\frac{\partial a_{1,2}(x_n, ..., x_2)}{\partial x_2} = \frac{1}{n}.$$

Assume now that the statement holds for all periods up to k. This implies that there exists at most one solution to the equation $a_{i,k}(\chi_k, x_k) = x_k$, denoted by $a_{i,k}^*(\chi_k)$. Let $l = \max\left\{j : x_{(j)} \leq a_{i,k}^*(\chi_k)\right\}$ and $m = \max\left\{j : x_{(j)} \leq a_{i-1,k}^*(\chi_k)\right\}$, and assume, for simplicity, that $m > l$ (the case $m = l$ is analogous). Using the definition of $a_{i,k+1}(\chi_{k+1}, x_{k+1})$, we obtain

$$a_{i,k+1}(\chi_{k+1}, x_{k+1})$$

$$= \sum_{j=1}^{l} \frac{\int_{x_{(j)}}^{x_{(j-1)}} a_{i,k}(\chi_k, x_k) dx_k}{(n-k+1)\left(x_{(j-1)} - x_{(j)}\right)} + \frac{\int_{x_{(l)}}^{a_{i,k}^*(\chi_k)} a_{i,k}(\chi_k, x_k) dx_k}{(n-k+1)\left(x_{(l)} - x_{(l+1)}\right)}$$

$$+ \frac{\int_{a_{i,k}^*(\chi_k)}^{x_{(l+1)}} x_k dx_k}{(n-k+1)\left(x_{(l)} - x_{(l+1)}\right)} + \sum_{j=l+2}^{m} \frac{\int_{x_{(j)}}^{x_{(j-1)}} x_k dx_k}{(n-k+1)\left(x_{(j-1)} - x_{(j)}\right)}$$

$$+ \frac{\int_{x_{(m)}}^{a_{i-1,k}^*(\chi_k)} x_k dx_k}{(n-k+1)\left(x_{(m)} - x_{(m+1)}\right)} + \frac{\int_{a_{i-1,k}^*(\chi_k)}^{x_{(m+1)}} a_{i-1,k}(\chi_k, x_k) dx_k}{(n-k+1)\left(x_{(m)} - x_{(m+1)}\right)}$$

$$+ \sum_{j=m+1}^{n-k+1} \frac{\int_{x_{(j)}}^{x_{(j-1)}} a_{i-1,k}(\chi_k, x_k) dx_k}{(n-k+1)\left(x_{(j-1)} - x_{(j)}\right)}.$$

Let j be the index satisfying $x_{(j)} = x_{k+1}$. There are three different cases:

1. $x_{k+1} \leq x_{(m)}$,
2. $x_{(m)} < x_{k+1} \leq x_{(l)}$,
3. $x_{k+1} > x_{(l)}$.

We prove the result for the first case; the proofs of the other two cases are very similar, and we omit them here. We obtain

$$
\frac{\partial a_{i,k+1}(\chi_{k+1}, x_{k+1})}{\partial x_{k+1}}
$$

$$
= \frac{a_{i,k}(\chi_k, x_{(j)})}{(n-k+1)\left(x_{(j)} - x_{(j+1)}\right)} - \frac{a_{i,k}(\chi_k, x_{(j)})}{(n-k+1)\left(x_{(j-1)} - x_{(j)}\right)}
$$

$$
+ \sum_{s=1}^{l} \frac{\int_{x_{(s)}}^{x_{(s-1)}} \frac{\partial a_{i,k}(\chi_k, x_k)}{\partial x_{k+1}} dx_k}{(n-k+1)\left(x_{(s-1)} - x_{(s)}\right)} + \frac{\int_{x_{(l)}}^{a_{i,k}^*(\chi_k)} \frac{\partial a_{i,k}(\chi_k, x_k)}{\partial x_{k+1}} dx_k}{(n-k+1)\left(x_{(l)} - x_{(l+1)}\right)}
$$

$$
+ \frac{\int_{a_{i-1,k}^*(\chi_k)}^{x_{(m+1)}} \frac{\partial a_{i-1,k}(\chi_k, x_k)}{\partial x_{k+1}} dx_k}{(n-k+1)\left(x_{(m)} - x_{(m+1)}\right)} + \sum_{s=m+1}^{n-k+1} \frac{\int_{x_{(s)}}^{x_{(s-1)}} \frac{\partial a_{i-1,k}(\chi_k, x_k)}{\partial x_{k+1}} dx_k}{(n-k+1)\left(x_{(s-1)} - x_{(s)}\right)}
$$

$$
- \frac{\int_{x_{(j)}}^{x_{(j-1)}} a_{i,k}(\chi_k, x_k) dx_k}{(n-k+1)\left(x_{(j-1)} - x_{(j)}\right)^2} + \frac{\int_{x_{(j+1)}}^{x_{(j)}} a_{i,k}(\chi_k, x_k) dx_k}{(n-k+1)\left(x_{(j)} - x_{(j+1)}\right)^2}.
$$

Note that

$$
\sum_{s=1}^{l} \frac{\int_{x_{(s)}}^{x_{(s-1)}} \frac{\partial a_{i,k}(\chi_k, x_k)}{\partial x_{k+1}} dx_k}{(n-k+1)\left(x_{(s-1)} - x_{(s)}\right)} + \frac{\int_{x_{(l)}}^{a_{i,k}^*(\chi_k)} \frac{\partial a_{i,k}(\chi_k, x_k)}{\partial x_{k+1}} dx_k}{(n-k+1)\left(x_{(l)} - x_{(l+1)}\right)} \tag{5.18}
$$

$$
+ \frac{\int_{a_{i-1,k}^*(\chi_k)}^{x_{(m+1)}} \frac{\partial a_{i-1,k}(\chi_k, x_k)}{\partial x_{k+1}} dx_k}{(n-k+1)\left(x_{(m)} - x_{(m+1)}\right)} + \sum_{s=m+1}^{n-k+1} \frac{\int_{x_{(s)}}^{x_{(s-1)}} \frac{\partial a_{i-1,k}(\chi_k, x_k)}{\partial x_{k+1}} dx_k}{(n-k+1)\left(x_{(s-1)} - x_{(s)}\right)}
$$

$$
\leq \frac{1}{(n-k+1)} \frac{n-k-m+l+1}{n-k+2} \leq \frac{1}{(n-k+1)} \frac{n-k}{n-k+2},
$$

where the first inequality follows from the inductive assumption $\left(\frac{\partial a_{i-1,k}(\chi_k, x_k)}{\partial x_{k+1}} \leq \frac{1}{n-k+2} \right)$ while the second inequality follows because $m > l$.

In addition

$$\frac{a_{i,k}(\chi_k, x_{(j)})}{(n-k+1)\left(x_{(j)} - x_{(j+1)}\right)} - \frac{a_{i,k}(\chi_k, x_{(j)})}{(n-k+1)\left(x_{(j-1)} - x_{(j)}\right)} \tag{5.19}$$

$$+ \frac{\int_{x_{(j)}}^{x_{(j-1)}} a_{i,k}(\chi_k, x_k)dx_k}{(n-k+1)\left(x_{(j-1)} - x_{(j)}\right)^2} - \frac{\int_{x_{(j+1)}}^{x_{(j)}} a_{i,k}(\chi_k, x_k)dx_k}{(n-k+1)\left(x_{(j)} - x_{(j+1)}\right)^2}$$

$$\leq \frac{a_{i,k}(\chi_k, x_{(j)})}{(n-k+1)\left(x_{(j)} - x_{(j+1)}\right)} - \frac{a_{i,k}(\chi_k, x_{(j)})}{(n-k+1)\left(x_{(j-1)} - x_{(j)}\right)}$$

$$+ \frac{a_{i,k}(\chi_k, x_{(j-1)})}{(n-k+1)\left(x_{(j-1)} - x_{(j)}\right)} - \frac{a_{i,k}(\chi_k, x_{(j+1)})}{(n-k+1)\left(x_{(j)} - x_{(j+1)}\right)}$$

$$= \frac{a_{i,k}(\chi_k, x_{(j-1)}) - a_{i,k}(\chi_k, x_{(j)})}{(n-k+1)\left(x_{(j-1)} - x_{(j)}\right)} + \frac{a_{i,k}(\chi_k, x_{(j)}) - a_{i,k}(\chi_k, x_{(j+1)})}{(n-k+1)\left(x_{(j)} - x_{(j+1)}\right)}$$

$$= \frac{1}{n-k+1}\left[\frac{\partial}{\partial x_{k+1}}a_{i-1,k}(\chi_k, x_k') + \frac{\partial}{\partial x_{k+1}}a_{i-1,k}(\chi_k, x_k'')\right]$$

$$\leq \frac{1}{n-k+1}\frac{2}{n-k+2},$$

where $x_k' \in \left[x_{(j-1)}, x_{(j)}\right]$ and $x_k'' \in \left[x_{(j)}, x_{(j+1)}\right]$. The first inequality follows from the monotonicity of $a_{i-1,k}(\chi_k, x_k)$, and the last inequality follows from the induction argument. Combining (5.18) and (5.19), we obtain

$$\frac{\partial a_{i,k+1}(\chi_{k+1}, x_{k+1})}{\partial x_{k+1}} \leq \frac{1}{n-k+1},$$

as desired.   ∎

It is now illustrative to compare Bayesian and non-Bayesian learning in a simple example where the dynamically efficient allocation is not implementable under Bayesian learning.

Example 14

1. *There are two periods and one indivisible object. Before starting the allocation process, the designer believes that the distribution of values is uniform on the interval $[0, \frac{1}{2}]$ with probability $\frac{1}{2}$, while with probability $\frac{1}{2}$ he believes that it is uniform on $[\frac{1}{2}, 1]$. Under Bayesian learning, the posterior, after observing $x_2 < (>)\frac{1}{2}$, is that x_1 is uniformly distributed*

on $[0, \frac{1}{2}]$ ($[\frac{1}{2}, 1]$). This yields

$$a_{1,2}^B(x_2) = \begin{cases} \frac{1}{4} & \text{if } x_2 < \frac{1}{2}, \\ \frac{1}{2} & \text{if } x_2 = \frac{1}{2}, \\ \frac{3}{4} & \text{if } x_2 > \frac{1}{2}. \end{cases}$$

Thus the first arriving agent should efficiently get the object if $x_2 \in [\frac{1}{4}, \frac{1}{2}] \cup [\frac{3}{4}, 1]$. This policy is not monotone and hence cannot be implemented.

2. *Consider now the learning process based on the empirical distribution with weight $0 < \beta < 1$ on the empirical distribution, and with the same prior as above. Then, after having observed x_2, the beliefs of the designer are given by $F(x_1|x_2) = (1 - \beta)U([0, 1]) + \beta 1_{[x_2, 1]}$, which yields*

$$a_{1,2}^{ED}(x_2) = \frac{1}{2}(1 - \beta) + \beta x_2.$$

Thus the first arriving agent should get the object if and only if $x_2 \geq a_{1,2}^{ED}(x_2) \Leftrightarrow x_2 \geq \frac{1}{2}$, which can be implemented by a take-it-or-leave-it offer at a price of $\frac{1}{2}$. Note, however, that the implemented allocation differs here from the one that needs to be implemented under Bayesian learning.

3. *Finally consider the maximum entropy/quantile preserving procedure. Then, after having observed x_2, the beliefs of the designer are given by the density*

$$f_k(x_1|x_2) = \frac{1}{2}\left(\frac{1_{[0,x_2]}(x)}{x_2} + \frac{1_{[x_2,1]}(x)}{1 - x_2}\right),$$

which yields

$$a_{1,2}^{ME}(x_2) = \frac{1}{4} + \frac{1}{2}x_2.$$

Thus the first arriving agent should get the object if and only if $x_2 \geq a_{1,2}^{ME}(x_2) \Leftrightarrow x_2 \geq \frac{1}{2}$, which can again be implemented by a take-it-or-leave-it offer at a price of $\frac{1}{2}$.[14]

5.7 The Incentive Efficient (Second-Best) Policy

We characterize here the policy that maximizes expected welfare over the entire class of implementable compatible policies. This is particularly relevant for the case of Bayesian learning, where, as we saw above, the first best is implementable only under restrictive conditions.

The proof of the theorem below proceeds by backward induction, and the main mathematical idea used to prove that this policy is deterministic relies on an idea from majorization theory. The decision at the last period is trivial. At the last but one period there are at most two objects left, and the question is whether to allocate the higher quality to the current agent. We adapt a *no-haggling* argument due to Riley and Zeckhauser (1983) in order to show that the optimal mechanism uses a cutoff rule. This argument is also analogous to the well-known one showing that the revenue-maximizing mechanism for a seller facing one buyer—whose virtual value need not be increasing—is always a take-it-or-leave-it offer at a certain reserve price. The analogy follows because in all these cases the decision variable is binary.

The main challenge is then to prove that the optimal allocation is deterministic also at earlier periods, where several objects with different qualities are available. Assume then that the optimal mechanism is deterministic at all later stages k, $k - 1, ..., 1$, and consider stage $k + 1$.

Given the observed signals so far, let $b_{i,k+1}$ denote here the expected value of the agent's type to which the item with ith highest type is assigned in the future (from stage k on, before the period k signal is observed). Then, because the optimal mechanism from period k on is deterministic, and because cutoffs are chosen optimally, expected welfare is given by $\sum_{i=1}^{k} q_{(i)} b_{i,k+1}$, where $q_{(i)}$ denotes here ith highest quality among the items available for allocation at period k.

By monotonicity of implementable rules, by the definition of the terms $b_{i,k+1}$, and by theorem 2, expected welfare is a Schur-convex function of the available qualities at stage k. Since this function takes higher values for more dispersed vectors of qualities—in the sense of majorization—the designer prefers to leave for the future the most disperse set of feasible qualities (among all feasible and incentive compatible allocations that are welfare equivalent at period $k + 1$). Turning this argument on its head, the allocation at period $k + 1$ should be the least dispersed possible among all welfare equivalent and incentive compatible allocations. This implies that for any agent arriving at $k + 1$, the allocation either should be deterministic or should randomize among at most two neighboring qualities.[15]

Finally, randomization among two neighboring qualities cannot be optimal—this follows by the same argument used above for binary decisions.

For the proof of the theorem 25, we need first the following lemma:

Lemma 8 *Consider a set of m numbers $0 \leq q_m \leq q_{m-1} \leq ... \leq q_1$, and assume that q_j is deleted from the set with probability p_j ,where $0 \leq p_j \leq 1$ and $\sum_j p_j = 1$.[16] Let $Q = \sum_{j=1}^{m} p_j q_j$ denote the expectation of the deleted term. Denote by $\widetilde{q}_{(m-1)}$ the expectation of the lowest order statistic out of the $(m - 1)$ remaining terms, by $\widetilde{q}_{(m-2)}$ the second lowest order statistic, and so on, until $\widetilde{q}_{(1)}$.*

1. *If there exists i such that $Q = q_i$, then the $(m-1)$-dimensional vector $(\widetilde{q}_{(1)}, \widetilde{q}_{(2)}, ..., \widetilde{q}_{(m-1)})$ is majorized by the $(m-1)$-dimensional vector $(q_1, q_2, ..., q_{i-1}, q_{i+1}, ..., q_m)$ obtained by deleting q_i with probability 1.*

2. *If there exist no i such that $Q = q_i$, let l and $\alpha \in (0,1)$ be such that $Q = \sum_{j=1}^{m} p_j q_j = \alpha q_l + (1-\alpha) q_{l+1}$.[17] Delete q_l with probability α, and q_{l+1} with probability $(1-\alpha)$, and denote by $\widetilde{\widetilde{q}}_{(1)}, \widetilde{\widetilde{q}}_{(2)}, ..., \widetilde{\widetilde{q}}_{(m-1)}$ the expectations of the order statistics out of the $(m-1)$ remaining terms. Then the $(m-1)$-dimensional vector $(\widetilde{q}_{(1)}, \widetilde{q}_{(2)}, ..., \widetilde{q}_{(m-1)})$ is majorized by the $(m-1)$-dimensional vector $(\widetilde{\widetilde{q}}_{(1)}, \widetilde{\widetilde{q}}_{(2)}, ..., \widetilde{\widetilde{q}}_{(m-1)})$.*

Proof (1) If there exists j with $p_j = 1$, the claim is obvious. Assume therefore that at least two probabilities p_j are strictly positive (in particular this implies $q_m < Q < q_1$). We need to show that the following holds:

$$\sum_{l=1}^{m-1} \widetilde{q}_{(l)} = \sum_{l=1}^{m} q_l - q_i$$

$$\forall k = 1, .., m-1, \ \sum_{l=1}^{k-1} \widetilde{q}_{(l)} \leq q_1 + ... + q_{i+1} + q_{i-1} + ... + q_k.$$

The first equality is clear by the the definition of $\widetilde{q}_{(l)}$. Note also that for each $l = 1, ..., m-1$, we have $q_l \geq \widetilde{q}_{(l)} \geq q_{l+1}$. For the inequalities there are two cases:

Case 1. $k \geq i$. Then $q_l \geq \widetilde{q}_{(l)}$ implies that

$$\sum_{l=k}^{m-1} \widetilde{q}_{(l)} \geq \sum_{l=k}^{m-1} q_l \Leftrightarrow \sum_{l=1}^{m-1} \widetilde{q}_{(l)} - \sum_{l=k}^{m-1} \widetilde{q}_{(l)} \leq \left(\sum_{l=1}^{m} q_j - q_i\right) - \sum_{l=k}^{m-1} q_l$$

$$\Leftrightarrow \sum_{l=1}^{k-1} \widetilde{q}_{(l)} \leq q_1 + ... + q_{i+1} + q_{i-1} + ... + q_k.$$

Case 2. $k < i$. Then $\widetilde{q}_{(l)} \geq q_{l+1}$ implies that

$$\sum_{l=1}^{k-1} \widetilde{q}_{(l)} \leq \sum_{l=1}^{k-1} q_l.$$

(2) The proof is very similar to the above one, and is omitted here. ∎

Theorem 25

1. *At each period k, expected welfare (calculated before the arrival of the period k agent) is a Schur-convex, linear function of the available qualities at that period.*

2. *The incentive compatible, optimal mechanism (second-best) is deterministic. That is, for every history at period k, H_k, and for every type x of the
agent that arrives at that period, there exists a quality q that is allocated to
that agent with probability 1 .*

3. *At each period, the optimal mechanism partitions the type set of the arriving
agent into a collection of disjoint intervals such that all types in a given
interval obtain the same quality with probability 1, and such that higher
types obtain a higher quality.*

Proof 1. (Argument for the last but one period) Consider period $k = 2$,
and define $b_{1,2}(\chi_2, x_2) = \int_0^\infty x_1 d\widetilde{F}_1(x_1|\chi_2, x_2)$. This is the expectation of the
agent's type who arrives at period 1, as a function of the observed history.
Denote by $q_{(1:\Pi_2)} \geq q_{(2:\Pi_2)} \geq 0$ the two highest remaining qualities—only
these are relevant here for welfare-maximizing allocations—and by $p(x_2)$ the
probability that the period 2 agent gets the object with the higher quality. It is
easy to see that incentive compatibility is equivalent here to p being monotonically increasing. The designer's problem is given by

$$\max_p \int_0^\infty (p(x_2)[q_{(1:\Pi_2)} \; x_2 + q_{(2:\Pi_2)} \; b_{1,2}(\chi_2, x_2)]$$
$$+ (1 - p(x_2))[q_{(2:\Pi_2)} \; x_2 + q_{(1:\Pi_2)} \; b_{1,2}(\chi_2, x_2)])d\widetilde{F}_2(x_2|\chi_2)$$
over increasing functions p with range in $[0, 1]$.

After simple manipulations the problem above reduces to

$$\max_p \left(q_{(1:\Pi_2)} - q_{(2:\Pi_2)}\right) \int_0^\infty p(x_2)[x_2 - b_{1,2}(\chi_2, x_2)]d\widetilde{F}_2(x_2|\chi_2)$$
over increasing functions p with range in $[0, 1]$.

Note that the solution of the maximization problem above does not depend
on the values of $q_{(1:\Pi_2)} \geq q_{(2:\Pi_2)} \geq 0$. The problem is completely analogous
to the classical problem faced by a revenue-maximizing seller who wants to
allocate an indivisible object to a unique buyer whose virtual valuation (which
need not be increasing) is given by the function $x_2 - b_{1,2}(\chi_2, x_2)$. By an argument originally due to Riley and Zeckhauser (1984), the solution is deterministic and is given by

$$p(x_2) = \begin{cases} 1 & \text{for } x_2 \geq b^*_{1,2}(\chi_2), \\ 0 & \text{otherwise}, \end{cases}$$

where $b_{1,2}^*(\chi_2) = \arg\max_{x \in [0,\infty)} \int_x^\infty [x_2 - b_{1,2}(\chi_2, x_2)] d\widetilde{F}_2(x_2|\chi_2)$. In particular, note that in order to be a maximizer $b_{1,2}^*(\chi_2)$ must necessarily belong to the set

$$\beta_{1,2}(\chi_2)$$

$$= \left\{ \begin{array}{c} x : \exists \varepsilon > 0 \text{ such that } \forall y \in (x, x + \varepsilon) \text{ it holds that } b_{1,2}(\chi_2, y) \leq y \\ \text{and } \forall z \in (x - \varepsilon, x) \text{ it holds that } b_{1,2}(\chi_2, z) \geq z \end{array} \right\}$$

In other words, if $b_{1,2}(\chi_2, x_2)$ is continuous in x_2, then $b_{1,2}^*(\chi_2)$ is one of the solutions of $x_2 = b_{1,2}(\chi_2, x_2)$.

Finally, note that the expected welfare after the allocation of period 2 has been made, but before the period 1 agent arrives, is given by $q_{(1:\Pi_1)}b_{1,2}(\chi_2, x_2)$.

2. (Formula for expected welfare) Assume that the allocation at stages $1, 2, ..., k$ is deterministic and uses cutoffs $b_{i-1,j}^*(\chi_j)$, $j = 1, 2, ..., k$. Let $b_{1,2}(\chi_2, x_2) = \int_0^\infty x_1 d\widetilde{F}_1(x_1|\chi_2, x_2)$ and define inductively

$$b_{i,k+1}(\chi_{k+1}, x_{k+1}) = \int_{B_{i,k}} x_k d\widetilde{F}_k(x_k|\chi_{k+1}, x_{k+1})$$

$$+ \int_{\underline{B}_{i,k}} b_{i,k}(\chi_k, x_k) d\widetilde{F}_k(x_k|\chi_{k+1}, x_{k+1})$$

$$+ \int_{\overline{B}_{i,k}} b_{i-1,k}(\chi_k, x_k) d\widetilde{F}_k(x_k|\chi_{k+1}, x_{k+1}), \qquad (5.20)$$

where

$$\underline{B}_{i,k} = \left\{ x_k : x_k \leq b_{i,k}^*(\chi_k) \right\},$$
$$B_{i,k} = \left\{ x_k : b_{i,k}^*(\chi_k) < x_k \leq b_{i-1,k}^*(\chi_k) \right\},$$
$$\overline{B}_{i,k} = \left\{ x_k : x_k > b_{i-1,k}^*(\chi_k) \right\}.$$

That is, $b_{i,k+1}(\chi_{k+1}, x_{k+1})$ equals the expected value of the agent's type to which the item with ith highest type is assigned in a problem with k periods (before the period k signal is observed) in a nonrandom mechanism that uses cutoffs $b_{i,k}^*(\chi_k)$. Note that for any k, χ_k, x_k and i, we have $b_{i,k}(\chi_k, x_k) \leq b_{i-1,k}(\chi_k, x_k)$.

Denote by $q_{(i:\Pi_k)}$ the ith highest quality among the items available for allocation at period k, Π_k. We now show that the expected utility after the allocation at period $k + 1$ has been completed is given by

$$\sum_{i=1}^k q_{(i:\Pi_k)} b_{i,k+1}(\chi_{k+1}, x_{k+1}). \qquad (5.21)$$

By theorem 2, the function above is a Schur-convex function of the available qualities at stage k.

The statement holds for period 2 (see point 1 above). Now assume, by induction, that the expected utility from allocating the object of quality q in period k to an agent with type x_k is $qx_k + \sum_{i=1}^{k-1} q_{(i:\Pi_k \backslash q)} b_{i,k}(\chi_k, x_k)$, where $\Pi_k \backslash q$ is the set of the available objects after the allocation of the object of quality q at period k. Taking the expectation over x_k and using the inductive formulas (5.20), we obtain

$$\sum_{j=1}^{k} \int_{B_{j,k}} \left[q_{(j:\Pi_k)} x_k + \sum_{i=1}^{k-1} q_{(i:\Pi_k \backslash q_j)} b_{i,k}(\chi_k, x_k) \right] d\widetilde{F}_k(x_k | \chi_{k+1}, x_{k+1})$$

$$= \sum_{j=1}^{k} q_{(j:\Pi_k)} \int_{B_{j,k}} x_k d\widetilde{F}_k(x_k | \chi_{k+1}, x_{k+1})$$

$$+ \sum_{j=1}^{k} \sum_{i=1}^{k-1} q_{(i:\Pi_k \backslash q_j)} \int_{B_{j,k}} b_{i,k}(\chi_k, x_k) d\widetilde{F}_k(x_k | \chi_{k+1}, x_{k+1})$$

$$= \sum_{j=1}^{k} q_{(j:\Pi_k)} \int_{B_{j,k}} x_k d\widetilde{F}_k(x_k | \chi_{k+1}, x_{k+1})$$

$$+ \sum_{j=1}^{k} \sum_{i=1}^{j-1} q_{(i:\Pi_k)} \int_{B_{j,k}} b_{i,k}(\chi_k, x_k) d\widetilde{F}_k(x_k | \chi_{k+1}, x_{k+1})$$

$$+ \sum_{j=1}^{k} \sum_{i=j+1}^{k} q_{(i:\Pi_k)} \int_{B_{j,k}} b_{i-1,k}(\chi_k, x_k) d\widetilde{F}_k(x_k | \chi_{k+1}, x_{k+1})$$

$$= \sum_{j=1}^{k} q_{(j:\Pi_k)} \int_{B_{j,k}} x_k d\widetilde{F}_k(x_k | \chi_{k+1}, x_{k+1})$$

$$+ \sum_{i=1}^{k-1} q_{(i:\Pi_k)} \sum_{j=i+1}^{k} \int_{B_{j,k}} b_{i,k}(\chi_k, x_k) d\widetilde{F}_k(x_k | \chi_{k+1}, x_{k+1})$$

$$+ \sum_{i=2}^{k} q_{(i:\Pi_k)} \sum_{j=1}^{i-1} \int_{B_{j,k}} b_{i-1,k}(\chi_k, x_k) d\widetilde{F}_k(x_k | \chi_{k+1}, x_{k+1})$$

$$= \sum_{j=1}^{k} q_{(j:\Pi_k)} \int_{B_{j,k}} x_k d\widetilde{F}_k(x_k | \chi_{k+1}, x_{k+1})$$

$$+ \sum_{i=1}^{k-1} q_{(i:\Pi_k)} \int_{\underline{B}_{i,k}} b_{i,k}(\chi_k, x_k) d\widetilde{F}_k(x_k | \chi_{k+1}, x_{k+1})$$

$$+ \sum_{i=2}^{k} q_{(i:\Pi_k)} \int_{\overline{B}_{i,k}} b_{i-1,k}(\chi_k, x_k) d\widetilde{F}_k(x_k | \chi_{k+1}, x_{k+1})$$

$$= \sum_{j=1}^{k} q_{(j:\Pi_k)} b_{j,k+1}(\chi_{k+1}, x_{k+1}).$$

The the third equality is obtained by changing the order of summation, and the fourth equality follows from the definition of sets $\overline{B}_{j,k}$ and $\underline{B}_{j,k}$.

3. (Optimal mechanism is deterministic) We now show that the optimal allocation at period $k + 1$ is nonrandom. Take any incentive compatible mechanism such that the expected quality assigned to type x after history H_{k+1} is given by $Q_{k+1}(H_{k+1}, x)$. Recall that expected utility from stage k on is a Schur-convex function of the remaining qualities. In particular, this function is monotonically increasing in the majorization order. Apply now lemma 8 to Π_{k+1}, the set of items available for allocation at period $k + 1$, with "deletion of quality q_j" taken to mean "allocate quality q_j at period $k + 1$." This application yields another incentive compatible mechanism that generates at least the same welfare as the original one, and that uses for any history H_{k+1} and arriving type x at stage $k + 1$ either a nonrandom allocation rule, or a random rule that assigns positive probability only to two neighboring qualities.[18]

Together with the necessary monotonicity of the expected quality, the argument above implies that without loss of generality, we can restrict attention to allocation rules that divide the type space of the arriving agent into intervals $[0, \underline{x}^{k+1}), [\underline{x}^{k+1}, \overline{x}^{k+1}), [\overline{x}^{k+1}, \underline{x}^{k}), [\underline{x}^{k}, \overline{x}^{k}), \ldots, [\overline{x}^{2}, \underline{x}^{1}), [\underline{x}^{1}, \infty)$, where $[\underline{x}^{l}, \overline{x}^{l})$ is the interval of the types that get assigned to object $q_{(l:\Pi_{k+1})}$ with probability 1, while $[\overline{x}^{l}, \underline{x}^{l-1})$ is the interval of randomization between $q_{(l-1:\Pi_{k+1})}$ and $q_{(l:\Pi_{k+1})}$ (where on interval $[0, \underline{x}^{k})$ the randomization is between allocating object $q_{(k+1:\Pi_{k+1})}$ and getting no object). To complete the proof, we need to show that for each potential interval of randomization $[\overline{x}^{l}, \underline{x}^{l-1}]$ there exists a cutoff $x_{*}^{l-1} \in [\overline{x}^{l}, \underline{x}^{l-1}]$ such that the designer can increase expected welfare by using (instead of randomization) a deterministic policy that allocates the object of quality q_l if $x \in [\overline{x}^{l}, x_{*}^{l-1})$ and allocate the object of quality q_{l-1} if $x \in [x_{*}^{l-1}, \underline{x}^{l-1})$. Since this argument involves only two adjacent qualities, the proof is identical to the one used at point 1 above, and we omit it here.

4. (Determination of optimal cutoffs) We finally show that the optimal cutoffs at period $k + 1$, $b^*_{i,k+1}(\chi_{k+1})$ must belong to the set

$$
\begin{aligned}
&\beta_{i,k+1}(\chi_{k+1}) \\
&= \left\{ \begin{array}{l} x : \exists \varepsilon > 0 \text{ such that: } \forall y \in (x, x + \varepsilon) \text{ holds } b_{i,k+1}(\chi_{k+1}, y) \le y \\ \text{and } \forall z \in (x - \varepsilon, x) \text{ holds } b_{i,k+1}(\chi_{k+1}, z) \ge z \end{array} \right\}.
\end{aligned}
$$

(5.22)

If such set is empty, that is, if $b_{i,k+1}(\chi_{k+1}, x_{k+1}) > x_{k+1}$ for any x_{k+1}, object i is never allocated to agent that arrives at period k after history χ_{k+1}, and we set $b^*_{i,k+1}(\chi_{k+1}) = \infty$ in this case.

By the derivation at point 3 above, the expected welfare at period $k + 1$ if an object of quality q is allocated to the agent arriving at $k + 1$ and if future allocations are governed by the optimal policy is given by

$$
q x_{k+1} + \sum_{j=1}^{k} q_{(j : \Pi_{k+1 \setminus q})} b_{j,k+1}(\chi_{k+1}, x_{k+1}).
$$

(5.23)

Assume, by contradiction, that there exists a cutoff $x^*_i(\chi_{k+1})$ that is used for allocating an object with quality $q_{(i : \Pi_{k+1})}$ such that $x^*_i(\chi_{k+1}) \notin \beta_{i,k+1}(\chi_{k+1})$. Then either there exists $\varepsilon > 0$ such that for any $y \in (x^*_i(\chi_{k+1}), x^*_i(\chi_{k+1}) + \varepsilon)$ we have $b_{i,k+1}(\chi_{k+1}, y) > y$, or there exists $\varepsilon > 0$ such that for any $y \in (x^*_i(\chi_{k+1}) - \varepsilon, x^*_i(\chi_{k+1}))$ we have $b_{i,k+1}(\chi_{k+1}, y) < y$. Take the first case (the second is analogous), and change the cutoff from $x^*_i(\chi_{k+1})$ to $x^*_i(\chi_{k+1}) + \epsilon$ where $0 < \epsilon \le \varepsilon$. Such a change is possible only if the cutoff for the adjacent higher quality is above $x^*_i(\chi_{k+1}) + \epsilon$. Then the change increases expected welfare, since it has an impact only if $x_{k+1} \in (x^*_i(\chi_{k+1}), x^*_i(\chi_{k+1}) + \epsilon)$, in which case the current agent gets object $q_{(i+1 : \Pi_{k+1})}$ instead of $q_{(i : \Pi_{k+1})}$. The effect of the increase on (5.23) is given by

$$
(b_{i,k+1}(\chi_{k+1}, x_{k+1}) - x_{k+1})(q_{(i : \Pi_{k+1})} - q_{(i+1 : \Pi_{k+1})}) > 0.
$$

If the cutoff for the adjacent higher quality object $q_{(i-1 : \Pi_{k+1})}$ is also equal to $x^*_i(\chi_{k+1})$, then adjust both cutoffs upwards by ϵ. In this case the increase has an impact only if $x_{k+1} \in (x^*_i(\chi_{k+1}), x^*_i(\chi_{k+1}) + \epsilon)$, and the effect on welfare is

$$
(b_{i+1,k+1}(\chi_{k+1}, x_{k+1}) - x_{k+1})(q_{(i-1 : \Pi_{k+1})} - q_{(i+1 : \Pi_{k+1})}) > 0
$$

To complete the proof, we need to show that the selection of cutoffs from the set $\beta_{i,k+1}(\chi_{k+1})$ is independent of the qualities of the available objects.

This, however, follows from the linearity of expected welfare in the available qualities. ∎

Example 15 *Let us go back to example 11 where we had one object and two periods, and where the agents' valuations distribute on $[0,1]$: with probability α the distribution is $F(x) = x$, while with probability $1 - \alpha$ the distribution is $F(x) = x^\theta$ where $\theta > 0$. Under complete information, the designer wants to allocate the object at period 2 if and only if $x_2 \in (x_{2a}, x_{2b}] \cup (x_{2c}, 1]$ where $x_{2a} \approx 0.513$, $x_{2b} \approx 0.691$, and $x_{2c} \approx 0.895$. Since this allocation is not monotone, it cannot be implemented.*

As shown above, the second-best mechanism is characterized by a fixed cutoff above which the object is allocated in the current period, and below which the object is carried to the next period. When choosing this cutoff, the goal of the designer is to minimize the disutility from misallocating the object relative to the efficient allocation. For example, if the designer chooses a cutoff $b \in (x_{2a}, x_{2b})$, misallocation occurs if the signal of the first agent if $x_2 \in (x_{2a}, b] \cup (x_{2b}, x_{2c})$. It is straightforward to see that a cutoff at x_{2a} dominates such an allocation, since then the object will be misallocated only if $x_2 \in (x_{2b}, x_{2c})$. Moreover any cutoff below x_{2a} is dominated by the cutoff of x_{2a}. Similarly the cutoff of x_{2c} dominates the allocation induced by any cutoff in the interval $[x_{2b}, x_{2c})$, and by any cutoff above x_{2c}. Therefore the optimal cutoff is either x_{2a} or x_{2c}. In other words, the optimal cutoff is one of the types that makes the designer indifferent between allocating the object and keeping it.

Which of these two cutoffs is optimal? A cutoff at x_{2a} causes misallocation in case the signal of the first agent belongs to the interval (x_{2b}, x_{2c}), since then the efficient allocation prescribes to keep the object until the next period. The disutility from the misallocation is

$$\int_{x_{2b}}^{x_{2c}} \left(E\left[x|x_2\right] - x_2 \right) \tilde{f}_2(x_2) dx_2.$$

Setting the cutoff at x_{2c}, causes misallocation in case the signal of the first agent belongs to the interval (x_{2a}, x_{2b}), since then efficient allocation prescribes to allocate the object to that agent. The disutility from the misallocation is given by

$$\int_{x_{2a}}^{x_{2b}} \left(x_2 - E\left[x|x_2\right] \right) \tilde{f}_2(x_2) dx_2.$$

Because $\int_{x_{2a}}^{x_{2b}} (x_2 - E[x|x_2]) \tilde{f}_2(x_2)dx_2 < \int_{x_{2b}}^{x_{2c}} (E[x|x_2] - x_2) \tilde{f}_2(x_2)dx_2$, the cutoff x_{2c} is here optimal. Note how the density of next arrival's type, its expected value, and all types that make the designer indifferent between allocating today and tomorrow are involved in this calculation. Finally, note that backward induction can be used for cases with more periods in order to show that second-best mechanisms have a cutoff structure.

An interesting alternative approach for analyzing learning in our dynamic mechanism design environment is to restrict attention to some simple class of indirect mechanisms that may be appealing for applications, such as a menu of prices at each period. It is important though to point out that such mechanisms entail some suboptimality because the designer is not able then to elicit precise information about the agents' types. Thus she will learn less than in a direct mechanism, and each particular specification of prices also determines how much is being learned.

5.8 "Offline" Mechanisms

The preceding analysis has assumed that agents' types are independently distributed. Even if the distribution of types is known, qualitatively similar dynamic implementation problems occur if types are correlated. In a static environment with correlated types—where the efficient allocation can always be implemented—Cremer and McLean (1985), Cremer and McLean (1988) show how the designer can extract the entire surplus by using payments contingent on the information revealed by other agents.[19] As already shown in chapter 2, the ability to delay payments confers more flexibility precisely because it enables the use of contingent payments. This contrasts the insight for dynamic independent private values frameworks without learning where delaying payments does not improve the ability to achieve the dynamically efficient outcome (see Parkes and Singh 2003).

Assume then that the designer still needs to allocate the objects upon arrival, but that he is able to delay payments until the end of stage one, the last stage. Consider the following mechanism: upon arrival, agents report their types, and objects are assigned according to the first-best allocation policy described in theorem 20. If an agent gets an object he pays the relevant VCG price computed given the **revealed** types of all agents (which are all known at the end of stage one) rather than a VCG price based on **expected** externalities; It is easy to see that reporting truthfully is an equilibrium. Thus we obtain:[20]

Proposition 9 *If payments can be delayed until no more arrivals occur, it is always possible to implement the first-best allocation policy.*

Although theoretically appealing, a delayed scheme such as this scheme may be problematic in real-life situations where arrivals are separated by significant periods of time because (1) early agents may not even "exist" when later ones arrive; (2) it may be difficult to write contracts that cover numerous contingencies covering a distant, uncertain future, and to execute monetary payments based on events that lie in the distant past; and (3) the last agent's information has no effect on his own allocation (both physical and monetary), but it does influence the payments of all preceding agents. It is not clear what are the incentives of this agent to report truthfully.[21] Moreover this feature is conducive to collusive agreements, and more significantly so than in static frameworks where the colluders need to jointly solve both a physical and a monetary allocation problem under two-sided incomplete information.

5.9   Related Literature

Albright (1977) computed several cases of Bayesian learning with conjugate priors where a generalized reservation price property holds in his model with several objects. This requires then that sets of types to whom particular objects are allocated are convex and ordered, with better objects being allocated to higher types. An obvious open problem was to establish some more or less general, sufficient conditions under which optimal search policies have the reservation price property. For the one-object case studied by Rothschild, various answers to this problem were offered by Rosenfield and Shapiro (1981), Morgan (1985), Seiderstad (1992), and Bickhchandani and Sharma (1996).

Segal (2003) analyzed revenue maximization in a static environment with an unknown distribution of the agents' values, and also observed that agents have an informational effect on others. But, the type of problems highlighted in our present paper do not occur in Segal's static model since a standard VCG mechanism always leads there to the efficient outcome.

Chen and Wang (1999) study the learning process of a revenue-maximizing seller who employs posted prices in a related model with one object, infinite horizon, and time discounting. In their setting there are two possible true distributions of values. Assuming that these two distributions are ordered in the hazard rate order, and have an increasing hazard rate they show that after each rejection, more and more weight is put on the stochastically worse distribution, and therefore prices decline over time. These authors did not consider the optimal mechanism as would constitute the revenue analogue of what we do here.

Babaioff et al. (2011) offer several bounds on the ratio between the revenue that can be obtained by employing posted prices in models where the distribution is unknown and the revenue obtained when the distribution is known.

Finally, Dasgupta and Maskin (2000) and Jehiel and Moldovanu (2001) have analyzed efficient implementation in static models with direct informational externalities. Kittsteiner and Moldovanu (2005) used these insights in a dynamic model with direct externalities and without learning.

For independent types, the role of posterior information and contingent payments toward increasing revenue from sales has been pointed out by Hansen (1985). Mezzetti (2007) studies surplus extraction with interdependent values.

Notes

1. Our model can be easily generalized to allow for random arrival of agents (e.g., arrivals governed by a stochastic process). In such a framework an interesting extension is to also allow learning about arrival rates. See, for example, Mason and Välimäki (2011) and the discussion in chapter 6.

2. Our results can also be easily adapted for the version where a buyer who wants to buy several units searches for the lowest prices offered by sellers who each possess one unit.

3. Since we allow for random mechanisms, the history needs to include the results of the previous randomizations. But a mechanism that depends on these can be replicated by another mechanism that only depends on the result of the current randomization. For notational simplicity, we therefore exclude the results of the previous randomizations from the specification of histories.

4. We set $+\infty \cdot 0 = -\infty \cdot 0 = 0$.

5. Note also that if $\widetilde{F}_k(x_k | \chi_{k+1}, x_{k+1})$ is symmetric with respect to the observed signals, then $a_{i,k+1}(\chi_{k+1}, x_{k+1})$ is symmetric as well.

6. Since agents observe the history, they are better informed after directly observing types. Yet the argument holds because: (1) if a policy is implementable by a general mechanism, then, with private values, it is also implementable via an augmented mechanism where, in addition, agents report types, but the designer does not use this information; (2) this augmented mechanism can be replicated by a direct one.

7. Note that the first-best policy can be always implemented (using type-independent transfers) if the sequence of beliefs $\Phi = \Phi_n, \Phi_{n-1}, .., \Phi_1$ induces successive marginal distributions of types that form a sub(super)-martingale. Then the efficient policy is to allocate the items successively in ascending (descending) order of types.

8. The stochastic dominance condition is, for example, a simple consequence of a standard setting found in the literature (Milgrom 1981). Assume that values x are drawn according to a density $f(x|\theta)$, where $\theta \in \mathbb{R}$. Denote by $h(\theta)$ the density of θ, and by $H(\theta)$ the corresponding probability distribution—the prior belief which gets then updated after each observation. If $f(x|\theta)$ has the monotone likelihood ratio (MLR) property, then $\widetilde{F}_k(x|\chi_k) \succsim_{FOSD} \widetilde{F}_k(x|\chi_k')$.

9. The Dirichlet is the conjugate prior of the multinomial distribution, so the posterior is also Dirichlet in this case.

10. These more stringent conditions are needed even if all objects are homogeneous.

11. Similar exercises can be performed starting with other initial beliefs. For example, the maximum entropy distribution, given that a continuous random variable is known to have (normalized) zero mean and unit variance, is the standard normal distribution. See Jaynes (2003).

12. They studied search with recall and did not look at the reservation price property for search without recall.

13. As was noted above, the Glivenko–Cantelli theorem implies that the above-estimated distribution uniformly converges to the true distribution.

14. The fact that the efficient policies given the non-Bayesian procedures coincide here is a mere coincidence, due to the uniform prior assumed in this example for the learning based on the empirical distribution.

15. In other words, if the designer seeks to allocate the object of expected quality $\tilde{q}$ to the current agent, he may use different lotteries between the available qualities. However, different lotteries leave different vectors of the qualities available for the future allocations. The lottery that randomizes between two neighboring qualities leaves for future allocation the most dispersed vector of expected ordered qualities of the objects.

16. In our application below, the deleted element is the quality of the object allocated today while the remaining qualities stay for future allocation.

17. Note that such an l and α must exist and are unique.

18. The new mechanism is incentive compatible since, by the constructions used in lemma 1, each type gets the same expected quality as in the original mechanism.

19. Note though that in our framework with independent types, full surplus extraction is impossible even if payments are delayed.

20. An analogous result for a much more general model has been proven by Athey and Segal (2013)—see their proposition 1.

21. See also Mezzetti (2004).

6 Long-lived Agents

In this chapter we review several models that relax one of the main assumptions made so far, namely that agents are short lived, and thus they cannot manipulate the timing of their purchase. Relaxing this assumption is, of course, important for various practical applications. This relaxation often results in even more complex models that are less amenable to precise analysis. This is, we believe, an area where more research will prove especially fruitful. This chapter is different from the preceding chapters because we do not focus on a specific model and study it in depth, but rather we briefly survey a large set of models that allow for long-lived agents.

6.1 Long-lived Agents / Perishable Goods

The simplest framework with long-lived agents is the polar case to the case we have studied so far, where each object is short lived and can be allocated to agents during a single period of time only. Such a model is analyzed by Said (2012). He considers an infinite horizon, discrete-time environment where in each period a seller has several units of a homogeneous and indivisible good. The number of units available in each period is a random variable drawn independently across time. The objects are nonstorable, and objects that are not immediately sold cannot be carried over to the future periods. The number of arriving buyer's is also random, and drawn independently across time (and independently from the number of units). Buyers are long lived.[1] An important assumption is that buyers cannot conceal their presence. Each buyer wishes to obtain a single unit of the seller's good. Buyers are characterized by a privately known, fixed value for the unit. Each value is drawn independently of other values. Both seller and buyers discount the future with a common discount factor.

Under complete information, the dynamically efficient policy has a very simple form that does not involve any trade-off: since units immediately disappear, they must be immediately allocated to those present buyers that value them most. This allocation can be clearly implemented via the corresponding dynamic VCG mechanism, where each buyer who obtains a unit pays the externality he imposes on other buyers. It is important to note that this externality refers only to already present buyers (since the unit allocated today is not available in the future), and that, crucially, it also needs to take into account the possibility that an already present buyer who is not served immediately may be served in the future. Thus the externality depends on the expectations about future arrivals of units and buyers, and on the buyer's behavior.

Said (2012) is mainly interested in devising an indirect auction mechanism that implements the efficient allocation, and it seems, at first glance, that a sequence of uniform price auctions may do the trick. For example, Kittsteiner, Nikutta, and Winter (2004) have shown that a sequence of second-price auctions is indeed efficient in a dynamic setting where all buyers are present in the initial period, and where there is only one object arriving per period. But, when buyers arrive over time, this intuition is not correct, as explained in the following example.

Example 16 *Assume that a single new unit object is available in each of three periods, after which no further units arrive. Assume also that there are two buyers present at period one (the "incumbents"), two new buyers at period two (the "entrants"), and no further entry afterward. All values are independently drawn from the uniform distribution on* $[0, 1]$*. Consider a second-price sealed-bid auction conducted in each period. Since no units arrive after the third period, all buyers have a zero option value at the third period. Thus each buyer will bid her own value at the third-period auction, and the third-period unit will indeed be allocated efficiently. Now consider the second period, where the competitors are the two entrants and the incumbent who lost the auction previously conducted at the first period. While the incumbent perceives two symmetric competitors whose values are uniformly drawn from the interval* $[0, 1]$*, the entrants are aware that the incumbent has lost the previous auction and therefore, in an efficient equilibrium, must infer that her value is distributed as the minimum of two independent draws from the uniform distribution. Thus beliefs about competitors are asymmetric here. While such asymmetries do not play any role in a static second-price auction, they are important here because buyers do not bid their true values in the second period! Instead, they shade their bids downward because they need to take into account the positive option value of losing today while winning a unit at the next period. These option values depend on the expected price at the next period, and hence* *on the expected values of potential competitors. This means that the situation resembles a first-price auction where asymmetries in beliefs induce asymmetric bidding functions that destroy efficiency.*

Despite the fact that buyers have independent private values, repeated competition over time among asymmetric buyers who have arrived at different periods generate, via the effect on option values, asymmetric value interdependences. It is known that the second-price auction is no longer efficient in such settings, and hence one has to consider here some open-format auction at each period. Indeed, Said (2012) shows that a sequence of ascending price auctions (where a price clock rises continuously and where buyers publicly drop out of the auction at various points) has an efficient equilibrium. Similarly the revenue-maximizing mechanism can be implemented by a sequence of ascending clock auctions augmented by (individualized) reserve prices.

6.2   Long-lived Agents / Nonperishable Goods

We now turn to a review of several models where both agents and goods are long lived. Hence at each point in time there are both allocative trade-offs and new, possibly complex, types of strategic behavior.

6.2.1   Search with Recall: Discrete Time

Let us first go back to the basic one object version of the Derman–Lieberman–Ross problem (where the quality of the object is assumed to be $q = 1$), but let us now allow the recall of past offers. In order to deal with both the finite and infinite horizon cases, let us assume here that the designer discounts the future at rate $r(t) = \delta^t$. In this subsection we count periods in the usual, chronological order.

Consider first the finite horizon problem. That is, there is a deadline $T > 0$ after which the object perishes. In every period one agent arrives. The agent's information is two dimensional: the value v the agent gets if allocated the object and the time of the arrival t. If the agent with value v_i gets the object at period t and pays p at period t', the utility of this agent is $v_i \delta^t - p \delta^{t'}$. The agent's valuations are represented by IID random variables $\widetilde{v}_i$, distributed according to a function F, with density f on the support $[0, a]$. The designer's utility if the object is allocated to an agent with value v_i at period t is given by $v_i \delta^t$. Thus the goal is welfare maximization.

Complete-Information Case   Following the system of all previous chapters, we first describe a classical result from the theory of search with recall (i.e., where past offers can be retained) under complete information. Thus there are no incentive constraints to consider. The next well-known result characterizes the complete information solution to the problem above.

Theorem 26 (Bertsekas 2005)   *At all periods* $1, 2, ..., T - 1$ *the optimal policy is characterized by a constant cutoff* v^*: *the object is allocated to the first agent who arrives with value of at least* v^*. *The cutoff* v^* *is independent of* T *and solves the equation*

$$ v^* = \frac{\delta}{1 - \delta} \int_{v^*}^{1} (v - v^*) \, f(v) \, dv. $$

At the last period, if the object has not been sold before, it is allocated to the agent with the highest value.

The intuition for the result above is simple, and based on the so-called one-step look-ahead property. In the last period T, when there are T agents with values $v_1, ..., v_T$, the designer allocates the object to the agent with the highest value. It generates utility of $v_{(1:T)} \delta^T$, where $v_{(1:T)}$ is the highest value among $v_1, ..., v_T$. At the penultimate period $T - 1$, the expected utility of the designer from stopping and allocating the object to the agent with the highest value is given by $v_{(1:T-1)} \delta^{T-1}$, where $v_{(1:T-1)}$ is the highest value among $v_1, ..., v_{T-1}$. Therefore, at the penultimate period, the designer stops if and only if $v_{(1:T-1)} \geq v_{T-1}^*$, where v_{T-1}^* is a solution to

$$ v_{T-1}^* = \delta \left[v_{T-1}^* + \int_{v_{T-1}^*}^{1} (v - v_{T-1}^*) \, f(v) \, dv \right]. $$

The theorem states that in all previous periods, the cutoff is the same as in the penultimate period, v_{T-1}^*. Let us give a brief intuition for this result. First, recall that the designer stops at period $T - 1$ if and only if there is no continuation policy that generates utility higher than v_{T-1}^*. However, this policy is still available at period $T - 2$; therefore $v_{T-2}^* \geq v_{T-1}^*$. We now show that $v_{T-2}^* = v_{T-1}^*$. Assume that $v_{T-2}^* > v_{T-1}^*$, and that $v_{(1:T-1)} \in (v_{T-1}^*, v_{T-2}^*)$. Notice that in this case, the next period is the last period. Therefore the optimal stopping cutoff is v_{T-1}^*.

Remark 7

1. *Although recall is feasible, the analysis above implies that it is never used by the optimal policy before the last period!*

2. *In case of an infinite horizon, a similar argument implies that the designer always uses a fixed cutoff equal to* $v^* = v_{T-1}^* = v_{T-2}^*$.

3. *If in every period a (potentially random) number of agents arrives, the basic analysis does not change: the highest value among the agents that arrived at that period becomes the relevant value at each period.*

4. *If the designer seeks to allocate K objects, then at each period there is a cutoff for allocating a single unit at that period, another cutoff for allocating two units, and so on. The cutoff for allocating k units exceeds the cutoff for allocating $k - 1$ units. The allocation is based on the highest possible volume of trade at that period: that is, i objects are allocated if and only if the ith highest value of the agents that arrived until that period exceeds the cutoff for allocation of i units, but the $i + 1$ highest value is below the cutoff of $i + 1$ unit.*

Incomplete Information Let us assume now that the agent's two-dimensional information (value v and arrival time t) are private information. The above-described efficient allocation can be implemented by a sequence of posted prices complemented by a second price auction at the last period ("fire sale").

It is important to note that in contrast to the allocation cutoffs, these posted prices are not constant; rather they decrease over time: at each period, the posted price has to keep the cutoff type indifferent between buying upon arrival and waiting until the last period. The diminishing pattern of posted price obtains since the cutoff type that arrives at later periods has to wait less periods until the "fire sale" and runs a lower risk that the object will be sold to another.

Consider now the problem of a revenue-maximizing seller, a setting analyzed by Board and Skrzypacz (2010). A standard mechanism design exercise implies that if an agent with value v gets the object at period t, the expected discounted revenue is given by $\delta^t [v - (1 - F(v))/f(v)] = \delta^t J(v)$. Assuming that the virtual value function J is monotone, this observation allows to replicate the analysis above by computing the efficient allocation with respect to the function $J(v)$. Thus, in case of a single object, the revenue-maximizing allocation is given by a cutoff that is fixed in all but the last period! In the last period the standard static revenue-maximizing allocation is implemented (via an auction). When there are multiple objects, the cutoffs change between periods and decrease if no sales have occurred in the previous period.

In this model we assumed that agents arrive sequentially, and that time is discounted. McAfee and McMillan (1988) considered a seller (endowed with one object) that has per-buyer fixed costs, and showed that in the revenue-maximizing mechanism the seller chooses to sample buyers sequentially, as above. Thus their optimal mechanism coincides with the one given above.

6.2.2   Search with Recall: Continuous Time

Consider now the same problem as above, but assume that time is continuous. We assume that one unit is being allocated. The agents' arrivals are described by a counting process $\{\mathcal{N}(t), t \geq 0\}$, where $\mathcal{N}(t)$ is a random variable representing the number of arrivals up to time t.[2] The time horizon is potentially infinite, but the framework is rich enough to embed the finite horizon case by considering arrival process where after some time T no more arrivals occur, that is, where $\mathcal{N}(t)$ is constant for any $t \geq T$.[3] Since arrivals are described by general counting processes, the designer's beliefs about future arrivals may evolve over time and may depend on the number of past arrivals and their exact timing.

Each agent's information is two-dimensional: the arrival time $t \geq 0$ and the value $v \geq 0$ he gets if he is allocated the object. In other words, we assume that the designer does not observe agents' arrivals. If the agent arrives at time t, gets the object at time $\tau \geq t$, and pays p at time $\tau' \in [t, \tau]$, then her utility is given by $e^{-\delta\tau}v - e^{-\delta\tau'}p$, where $\delta \in (0, 1)$ is the discount factor. We implicitly assume here that all agents disappear after the allocation of the object, meaning (1) payments cannot be conditioned on information that arrives after the sale and (2) the item cannot be reallocated after an initial assignment.

The agents' values are assumed to be represented by IID random variables $\widetilde{v}_i$ on support $[0, a]$ where $a \leq \infty$, with common c.d.f. F, and with continuous density f. We assume that each $\widetilde{v}_i$ has a finite mean and a finite variance. We also assume that for each agent, his arrival time is independent of his value. This allows us to focus on the information revealed by manipulating arrivals, as opposed to information revealed by manipulating values.

If the object is allocated to the agent with type (t, v) at time $\tau \geq t$, the designer's utility is given by $e^{-\delta\tau}v$. The designer's goal is to implement the efficient allocation (that maximizes his discounted expected utility) in a Bayes–Nash equilibrium.

Complete Information   Let us briefly consider the benchmark case where the designer observes the agents' arrivals and their values for the object, so that agents have no private information. This is the standard continuous-time, infinite horizon search model with recall. Since the main focus here is on the implementation of the efficient dynamic allocation (or, equivalently, the implementation of the optimal stopping policy), we assume that an optimal stopping time in the complete information model exists, and is almost surely finite.

The optimal stopping policy is deterministic. If the planner allocates the object at some time T, then he will allocate it to the agent with the highest value that arrived until T. Denote by $X(T)$ the highest value observed until time T (if until T no agent arrived, we set $X(T) = 0$), and by $\mathbf{t}_{\mathcal{N}(T)} = \left(t_1, ..., t_{\mathcal{N}(T)}\right)$ the agents' arrival times until T. Since values are independent of arrival times, the state of the process at T—on which the stopping policy depends—can be taken to be $\{X(T), T, \mathbf{t}_{\mathcal{N}(T)}\}$.

Optimal policies in our framework have the following property. A stopping policy satisfies the *instant reservation price (IRP)* property if for any time T and for any history of arrivals $\mathbf{t}_{\mathcal{N}(T)}$, stopping at state $\{X(T), T, \mathbf{t}_{\mathcal{N}(T)}\}$ implies stopping also at all states $\{X'(T), T, \mathbf{t}_{\mathcal{N}(T)}\}$ with $X'(T) \geq X(T)$.

Proposition 10 *The optimal stopping policy in the complete information case satisfies the* IRP *property. In particular, for any time T and for any history of arrivals $\mathbf{t}_{\mathcal{N}(T)}$, there exists a cutoff $v_T^*(\mathbf{t}_{\mathcal{N}(T)})$ such that it is optimal to stop search as soon as the highest available value exceeds this cutoff.*

Proof Assume by contradiction that the optimal policy Υ does not satisfy *IRP*. Then there exist some period (time) T history of arrivals $\mathbf{t}_{\mathcal{N}(T)}$ and $X'(T) > X(T)$ such that Υ prescribes to continue search at state $\{X'(T), T, \mathbf{t}_{\mathcal{N}(T)}\}$, while it prescribes stopping (and accepting $X(T)$) at state $\{X(T), T, \mathbf{t}_{\mathcal{N}(T)}\}$.

The expected utility under Υ at state $\{X'(T), T, \mathbf{t}_{\mathcal{N}(T)}\}$ can be written as $X'(T)\alpha\left(T, \mathbf{t}_{\mathcal{N}(T)}, \Upsilon\right) + \beta\left(T, \mathbf{t}_{\mathcal{N}(T)}, \Upsilon\right)$, where $\alpha\left(T, \mathbf{t}_{\mathcal{N}(T)}, \Upsilon\right)$ is the discounted probability that the object will be allocated to the agent with value $X'(T)$ and where $\beta\left(T, \mathbf{t}_{\mathcal{N}(T)}, \Upsilon\right)$ is the discounted expected utility from all continuations where the object is not allocated to the agent with value $X'(T)$. The probability that the object will be allocated to the agent with value $X'(T)$ is less than one (otherwise, it would be optimal to stop at state $\{X'(T), T, \mathbf{t}_{\mathcal{N}(T)}\}$) and therefore $\alpha\left(T, \mathbf{t}_{\mathcal{N}(T)}, \Upsilon\right) < 1$. Since Υ prescribes to continue search at state $\{X'(T), T, \mathbf{t}_{\mathcal{N}(T)}\}$, it must be the case that

$$X'(T)\alpha\left(T, \mathbf{t}_{\mathcal{N}(T)}, \Upsilon\right) + \beta\left(T, \mathbf{t}_{\mathcal{N}(T)}, \Upsilon\right) \geq X'(T),$$

which implies that

$$\beta\left(T, \mathbf{t}_{\mathcal{N}(T)}, \Upsilon\right) \geq \left(1 - \alpha\left(T, \mathbf{t}_{\mathcal{N}(T)}, \Upsilon\right)\right) X'(T).$$

Change now policy Υ into Υ' where the only difference between the policies is at state $\{X(T), T, \mathbf{t}_{\mathcal{N}(T)}\}$. Policy Υ' continues search at time T and applies the same continuation policy at state $\{X(T), T, \mathbf{t}_{\mathcal{N}(T)}\}$ as Υ prescribed after the state $\{X'(T), T, \mathbf{t}_{\mathcal{N}(T)}\}$ (while allocating the object to the agent with value $X(T)$ if Υ prescribes to stop and to allocate the object to an agent with value $X'(T)$).

The expected utility generated by Υ' if state $\{X(T), T, \mathbf{t}_{\mathcal{N}(T)}\}$ was reached is $X(T)\alpha\left(T, \mathbf{t}_{\mathcal{N}(T)}, \Upsilon\right) + \beta\left(T, \mathbf{t}_{\mathcal{N}(T)}, \Upsilon\right)$. Since we know that $\beta\left(T, \mathbf{t}_{\mathcal{N}(T)}, \Upsilon\right) > \left(1 - \alpha\left(T, \mathbf{t}_{\mathcal{N}(T)}, \Upsilon\right)\right) X'(T)$, we obtain

$$X(T)\alpha\left(T, \mathbf{t}_{\mathcal{N}(T)}, \Upsilon\right) + \beta\left(T, \mathbf{t}_{\mathcal{N}(T)}, \Upsilon\right) \geq$$
$$X(T)\alpha\left(T, \mathbf{t}_{\mathcal{N}(T)}, \Upsilon\right) + \left(1 - \alpha\left(T, \mathbf{t}_{\mathcal{N}(T)}, \Upsilon\right)\right) X'(T) > X(T).$$

That is, there exists a continuation policy applied at state $\{X(T), T, \mathbf{t}_{\mathcal{N}(T)}\}$ that generates a higher expected utility than $X(T)$. This contradicts the optimality of stopping at $\{X(T), T, \mathbf{t}_{\mathcal{N}(T)}\}$.   ∎

Contrary to what one may expect from the above analyzed discrete case with deterministic arrivals, or from the Poisson process case (see Mortensen 1986 for the analysis of this case), the designer may not wish to allocate the object immediately upon arrival; that is, the recall option may be used by the optimal stopping policy. This implies that the optimal stopping policy may have a complicated structure.

For example, consider a process where times between consecutive arrivals can be either ε or Δ, where $\varepsilon \ll \Delta$. Assume that a buyer with a moderately high value arrives at t. Then, for not too low discount factors, it may be optimal to wait until $t + \varepsilon$, hoping for a new arrival with a higher value, but then immediately stop search at $t + \varepsilon$ while recalling the previous buyer if no arrival occurred (because now the next arrival is known to be at the much more distant $t + \Delta$).

In order to completely characterize the complete information, dynamically efficient policy in a special, but important setting (e.g., which covers the Poisson arrival process), we use a result by Zuckerman (1988) who assumed that the arrival process is a *renewal*; namely inter-arrival times are IID, random variables with known, common distribution G.[4] Note that although inter-arrival times are independently distributed random variables, arrival times are correlated in a renewal process. In particular, the planner's belief about the timing of the next arrival depends on the elapsed time since the last arrival.

Zuckerman identified a large class of inter-arrival distributions G for which the optimal policy never employs the recall option, and is therefore characterized by a reservation value such that the object is allocated to the first arrival whose value is above the reserve. Thus the efficient policy coincides with the one obtained for renewal processes without recall by Albright (1974); see chapter 2.

Recall that a nonnegative random variable W is called *NBU* (new better than used) if, for every $y > 0$, W is stochastically larger than the conditional random variable $(W - y|W \geq y)$. In particular $E[W] \geq E[(W - y|W \geq y)]$ for any $y \geq 0$.

Theorem 27 (Zuckerman 1988)   *Assume that the inter-arrival distribution G satisfies the NBU property, and let ϕ denote its Laplace transform. Then the optimal stopping policy allocates the object to the first arrival whose value is above v^*, where v^* is the unique solution to*

$$v^* = \frac{\phi(\delta)}{1 - \phi(\delta)} \int_{v^*}^{\infty} (v - v^*) dF(v).$$

In particular, recall is never used by the optimal policy, and all allocations occur upon arrival.

The intuition behind this elegant result is as follows: between arrivals the seller updates her belief about the timing of the next arrival, and about the option value of not allocating the object right now. If the inter-arrival time satisfies the NBU property, the seller is most pessimistic about the timing of the next arrival immediately following an arrival, but gets more and more optimistic about it as time passes without arrivals. Thus, if it is optimal not to allocate the object immediately following an arrival—because the current option value of waiting is higher—it will not be optimal to do so until the next arrival.

Incomplete Information   For arrivals governed by a renewal process, we now demonstrate that the efficient allocation is implementable even if each agent's information (arrival time $t \geq 0$ and value $v \geq 0$) is private.

Without loss of generality (see Myerson 1981)[5] we can restrict attention to mechanisms where the agents do not observe the history, and only know whether the object is still available or not.[6] Since arrivals are unobservable, without loss of generality, we can restrict attention to direct mechanisms where each agent reports his value and arrival time, and where the mechanism specifies a probability and a time of getting the object and a payment as a function of the reported value, reported arrival time and the time of the report. Moreover, without loss of generality, we can restrict attention to direct mechanisms where each agent reports his type upon arrival, namely the time of the report coincides with the arrival time.[7]

Since recall may be employed by the optimal policy, an allocation to an agent can be conditioned also on information that accrues between the arrival of that agent and the allocation time. We denote by $\eta(T)$ a history at time T: this is a list of reported arrivals and the reported values up to time T.

Then $\mathcal{H}_T = \prod_{\mathcal{N}(T)=0}^{\infty} [0,T]^{\mathcal{N}(T)} \times \mathbb{R}_+^{\mathcal{N}(T)}$ is the set of all possible histories at time T. We denote by h a history from the beginning of the game (time zero) until infinity, namely $h = \lim_{T \to \infty} \eta(T)$.

A direct mechanism specifies at every time t and for every agent that reported an arrival at $t' \le t$ the probability of getting the object and a payment. An incentive compatible mechanism is (ex post) individually rational if the utilities of all agents in the truth-telling equilibrium are nonnegative.

Since incentive compatibility considers possible deviations by only one agent, it will be helpful to introduce additional notation. Let h_{-i} be the history (from the beginning of game until infinity) formed by agents' reports other than i, and let $\eta_{-i}^h(t)$ denote the derived history up to time t formed by the reports of agents other than i. We denote by μ the measure on histories generated by the renewal process, and by $\mu(h_{-i}|t)$ the conditional measure given an arrival of agent i at time t.

Denote by $\tau_v(t, h_{-i})$ the optimal stopping time if agent i arrives at time t and reports value v while the other agents form history h_{-i}. Recall that by the standard definition of stopping times, if $\tau_v(t, h_{-i}) = T$, then $\tau_v(t, h'_{-i}) = T$ for any h'_{-i} that agrees with h_{-i} up to time T. In other words $\tau_v(t, h_{-i})$ depends on h_{-i} only via $\eta_{-i}^h(\tau)$.

Finally, denote by $V(t, v, \eta_{-i}(t'), t')$ the designer's expected utility at time t' when agent i arrives at time $t \le t'$ and has value v while the other agents' types form history η_{-i}, and when the designer uses the optimal stopping rule.

Denote by $\mathbb{T}$ the elapsed time since the arrival of the last agent. Recall that $X(T)$ denotes the highest value observed until time T, and note that in a renewal process the bivariate process $(X(T), \mathbb{T}(T))$ is Markov. Therefore the efficient cutoffs v_T^* can be characterized only in terms of $\mathbb{T}$, the time since the last arrival.

Proposition 11 *Assume that the arrival process is a renewal*

1. The payment scheme

$$
P(t, v, \eta_{-i}^h(T), T)
$$
$$
= \begin{cases} V(t, 0, \eta_{-i}^h(T), T) & \text{if } T = \tau_v(t, h_{-i}) \text{ and if } v_i = X(T), \\ 0 & \text{otherwise}, \end{cases}
$$

implements the dynamically efficient allocation.

2. Assume that the inter-arrival distribution G satisfies the NBU property, and let ϕ denote its Laplace transform. Then charging for the object *the constant price* $P(t, v, \eta_{-i}(T), T) = v^*$, *where* v^* *is the unique solution to*

$$v^* = \frac{\phi(\delta)}{1 - \phi(\delta)} \int\limits_{v^*}^{\infty} (v - v^*) dF(v)$$

implements the efficient allocation.

Proof (1) Assume for a moment that arrivals are observable. Then the payment scheme described above is a variant of the standard generalization of a dynamic Vickrey–Clarke–Groves mechanism (e.g., see Bergeman and Välimäki 2010), and hence implements the efficient allocation in case of observable arrivals. We now show that for renewals, the payment scheme also provides incentives to correctly report arrivals. Consider an agent with true type (v, t) who reports type (v', t'), where $t' > t$ and where v' is optimized given the reported arrival time t' and true type (v, t). Such a report is relevant only if the agent then gets the object with positive probability, and if his expected utility is positive.

Notice that the value function depends only on the highest value and the elapsed time since the last arrival. We claim that a report (v', t''), where $t \le t'' < t'$ leads to a higher expected utility than a report (v', t'). Indeed, if an agent with report (v', t') gets the object at some time T, then he should get the object with a report (v', t''), $t'' \le t'$ either at T or earlier. This is so because at the time of the allocation the elapsed time from the last arrival must be the same, independent of the reported arrival time of that agent. The price charged for the object depends on the elapsed time since the last arrival, and on the second highest value reported up to the time of the allocation. Moreover this price is monotonically increasing in the second highest reported value. Thus a later arrival may postpone the allocation, and this increases the probability of new arrivals, which in turn increases the second highest value and the charged price. Therefore a report (v', t'') with $t'' < t'$ leads to either a similar or an earlier allocation at either a similar or a lower price and is thus a more advantageous deviation than a report (v', t'). Adjusting the reported value to the earlier arrival further increases expected utility, which allows us to conclude that truthful report maximizes the agent's expected utility, as desired.

(2) The result follows immediately from point 1 above together with theorem 27. ∎

The payment scheme given above is based on an expected externality argument. Gershkov, Moldovanu, and Strack (2013) show that this payment scheme may alone not be sufficient for efficient implementation if arrivals are governed by other, more general, processes. Since in such environments arrivals may be correlated in complex ways, the expected externality may contain an informational component, and the implementation of the efficient policy generally requires a subsidy for early arrivals: this induces agents to internalize the positive informational externality they exert on the planner via his learning process. Interestingly, no subsidy must be paid if the counting process governing arrivals is Markov (e.g., which covers the ubiquitous model of learning about the parameter of a Poisson process).

Revenue Maximization with Deadlines   Let us briefly look at the infinite horizon variant of the above problem where the planner aims to maximize revenue (this was first studied in a discrete time, finite horizon and undiscounted model by Pai and Vohra 2013): each buyer i's private information is characterized by a triple (v_i, t_i, d_i), where v_i is the value for the object, t_i is the arrival time, and $d_i \geq t_i$ is the exit time.[8] We are able to completely solve this problem for our setting if arrivals are governed by an NBU renewal process. Assume that the virtual valuation $v - \frac{1-F(v)}{f(v)}$ is strictly increasing, and denote by H the implied distribution of virtual values. Then, for any $d_i \geq t_i$, the revenue-maximizing policy is to charge a constant price P, where P is the unique solution to the equation

$$p = \frac{\phi(\delta)}{1 - \phi(\delta)} \int\limits_{p}^{\infty} (z - p) dH(z).$$

The proof follows immediately from the proposition above, and from the standard exercise of replacing revenue maximization with welfare maximization with respect to virtual values. Since in this case no recall occurs in the revenue-optimizing policy, the solution coincides with the one found by Gallien (2006) for the case $d_i = \infty$ (perfect recall) and by Gershkov and Moldovanu (2009a) for the case $d_i = t_i$ (no recall; see chapter 2). Gallien's analysis is relatively involved since he derived the above result without using Zuckerman's (1988) insight on the continuos-time search problem for NBU renewals.[9] More results about revenue maximization in the Markov case can be found in Gershkov, Moldovanu, and Strack (2013)—but they require a more delicate analysis.

6.3   Queueing Applications

One of the earliest and most elegant applications of dynamic mechanism design has been made within the context of queue operations (Dolan 1978). In these environments randomly arriving, heterogenous customers need to share one or more processing devices that can only be used sequentially. Since customers can only be served one at a time, queues may form and the customers incur a waiting cost until their job is completed. Examples include communication in congested networks, job processing by capacity constrained computers (including services provided via the internet), and the usage of various industrial production units.

In a queueing system where all customers can be eventually served, the allocation problem reduces to a determination of the order in which customers' jobs are processed. There are two main reasons for awarding priority to some customers:

1. Giving priority (e.g., to those with shorter processing times) can lead to a decrease in overall (expected) queuing costs, and thus to overall higher welfare.

2. Since customers are willing to pay a price for being served earlier (which means avoidance of waiting costs), it is revenue-increasing for the service provider to charge customers for priority.

6.3.1   Dynamic VCG Mechanisms for Queue Management

Kleinrock (1967) pioneered the study of the allocation of priorities based on payments made by customers—this small strand of the literature, together with many other strategic issues arising in queues, is surveyed by Hassin and Haviv (2002). The earliest work on priority assignment based on payments that includes an equilibrium condition is due to Balachandran (1972). Incentive problems that arise with privately informed customers have been studied in the context of queues by Ghanem (1975). In his model, customers have linear delay costs and are privately informed about the marginal cost. Ghanem assumed that there is a fixed, finite, and exogenously given set of priorities, and calculated incentive compatible prices ensuring that customers sort themselves according to a constrained efficient rule.

Dolan (1978) is the first paper that uses standard mechanism design analysis for queue management. The designer needs to elicit private information in order to implement an efficient priority system that minimizes total waiting cost. To our knowledge, this is the first known instance of an explicit calculation of a dynamic VCG mechanism.

The considered model is as follows: users arrive at a service facility according to a Poisson process with a known arrival rate (assumed to be less than the service rate, thus ensuring that the queue length does not explode to infinity). Service is nonpreemptive, meaning once a user's service started, it is not interrupted upon arrivals of users with possibly higher priority. All users require the same service time (normalized to be one unit). A user's constant cost of delay per unit of time, c_i, is private information. These costs are drawn from a known distribution F, independently of each other.

In a model with heterogeneous waiting costs per unit of time and with heterogeneous service times, Cox and Smith (1961) have shown that the queue discipline that minimizes total waiting costs is to serve users in descending order of the ratios between delay cost per unit of time and service time (this is the so called $C\mu$ rule). Since in Dolan's model all users share the same service time, it is optimal to serve users in descending order of their costs per unit of time. The designer's task is therefore to truthfully elicit these costs—possibly by using transfers—in order to implement the $C\mu$ rule. The utility of a user with cost per unit c who waits t units until his service is completed (this includes time in the queue and time in service), and who pays p is given by $V - ct - p$, where the common value V is assumed to be high enough so that all users decide to join the queue.

Dolan considers direct revelation mechanisms where users declare a waiting cost per unit of time, and where the designer allocates places in the queue while charging externality payments. Calculating these payments requires the probabilistic computation of expected waiting times and so-called busy periods. These are more or less standard exercises in queueing theory, but these require too many prerequisites for our purposes here. Therefore we illustrate Dolan's approach with two simpler examples adapted from his paper.

Example 17 *Consider first a scheduling example where all n users are already present, and where no other arrivals are expected. Assume that (after relabeling users) true costs per unit of time are given by $c_1 > c_2 > c_3... , > c_n$, which implies that the optimal queue is to serve users according to the order $1, 2, ..., n$. Consider then user i: his presence imposes no externality on users $1, 2, ..., i - 1$—these are anyway served before her—but increases by one time unit the waiting time of users $i + 1, ..., n$. Thus the externality payment of user i is simply $\sum_{j=i+1}^{n} c_j$. In other words, under incomplete information each user reports his marginal cost, users are served in decreasing order of marginal costs, and each user pays a fee equal to the sum of the marginal costs of all users who have a lower marginal cost.*

Example 18 *Let us now consider a slightly more complex example, where there are new arrivals but these are at deterministic times. Suppose that at $t = 0$, users $1, 2, 3$ are already in queue, while user 4 arrives at $t = 1$ and user 5 arrives at $t = 2$. Consider, for example, the following realization of unit time costs: $c_4 > c_1 > c_2 > c_5 > c_3$, and let us compute here the externality* *payment that needs to be paid by user 4. Since this user only arrives at $t = 1$, he imposes no externality on user 1 who still can enter service at $t = 0$. Users 2, 3, 5 are delayed by one unit of time by the arrival of 4. Thus user 4's external-ity payment is here $c_2 + c_5 + c_3$. In the full stochastic model these calculations need to take into account both the probabilistic arrival times and the proba-bilistic nature of the ordered vector of costs pertaining to later agents.*

6.3.2   Auctions for Slots in the Queue

Glazer and Hassin (1986), Lui (1985), and Afeche and Mendelson (2004) re-visit Kleinrock's model but introduce strategic users that make bids in order to minimize total cost (which is the sum of the delay cost and the bid). In their model, customers have privately known, heterogeneous marginal costs of delay and costs are linear in waiting time. This yields "private values" auctions. These authors then derive bidding equilibria, and show that a higher marginal cost leads to a higher bid. Thus the efficient $C\mu$ rule is implemented also by this auction.

Kittsteiner and Moldovanu (2005) analyze auctions in a situation where the own processing time is privately known to customers. In their model randomly arriving customers face a cost of waiting that is an increasing function of their total waiting time: a customer with *processing time* t_i who has to queue for T_i time units before being served incurs a cost $C(t_i + T_i)$, where $C : \mathbb{R}^+ \mapsto \mathbb{R}^+$ is strictly increasing and differentiable with $C(0) = 0$. All agents have the same cost function C. The processing time t_i of customer i is drawn from a distri-bution F with support $[\underline{t}, \overline{t}]$, $\underline{t} \geq 0$, independently of other processing times. The realization t_i is only known to i, whereas the distribution F is common knowledge. Each customer i derives a value of V_i if his task is processed. Cus-tomer i's utility is given by $U_i = V_i - C(t_i + T_i) - m_i$, where m_i denotes a monetary payment.

Note that the queuing time T_i depends here on the processing times of the customers served before i. Therefore it depends on other customers' private information, yielding a model with *interdependent* values. The main role in the analysis is played by the curvature of the cost function. The point is that the increase in waiting cost that is incurred by a customer who waits one additional time unit depends on his own processing time: if the cost function is convex [concave] the magnitude of this dependence is increasing [decreasing] in own processing time, and this influences the incentives agents face for information revelation.

A main insight is that the ubiquitous case of convex cost functions yields higher willingness to pay for priority to agents with longer processing time which implies that the queue service in the bidding equilibrium is according to *longest processing time first* (LPT discipline). In particular, the efficient queue cannot be implemented using online mechanisms; that is, mechanisms that do not condition on information that is being revealed after service is completed. Again, we illustrate this insight in a simpler scheduling framework where all agents arrive at the same time. A simple permutation argument shows that in this case the efficient queue discipline—that minimizes the costs of delay—is to serve users with *shorter processing time first* (SPT discipline).[10]

Example 19 *Assume that two agents arrive simultaneously, and that no other user arrives until those two are served. It is efficient to serve user 1 first if $t_1 < t_2$, which yields total waiting costs $C(t_1) + C(t_1 + t_2)$, and to serve user 2 first if $t_1 > t_2$, in which case total waiting cost is $C(t_2) + C(t_1 + t_2)$. This is the shorter processing times first (SPT) queue discipline, which is the efficient queue discipline in any similar scheduling situation, with any number of users. Assume now that the cost function C is strictly convex. Let us also assume that user 2 truthfully reveals her processing time. We can then focus on the incentives of user 1 who is faced with a menu of choices consisting of allocation and payments: he has to pay $m(t_2)$ if $t_1 < t_2$ (1 is served first), and $m^*(t_2)$ if $t_1 > t_2$ (2 is served first). In order to implement the efficient SPT discipline we need to have*

$$V_1 - C(t_1) - m(t_2) \geq V_1 - C(t_1 + t_2) - m^*(t_2), \text{ for } t_1 \leq t_2,$$
$$V_1 - C(t_1) - m(t_2) \leq V_1 - C(t_1 + t_2) - m^*(t_2), \text{ for } t_1 \geq t_2.$$

By setting $t_1 = t_2$, this yields

$$m^*(t_2) = C(t_2) - C(2t_2) + m(t_2).$$

For $t_1 < t_2$ the first inequality above becomes

$$V_1 - C(t_1) - m(t_2) \geq V_1 - C(t_1 + t_2) - C(t_2) + C(2t_2) - m(t_2) \Leftrightarrow$$
$$C(t_1 + t_2) - C(t_1) \geq C(2t_2) - C(t_2).$$

This yields a contradiction to the strict convexity of C, and implies that the efficient SPT discipline cannot be implemented here in ex post equilibrium (this discipline can be implemented if costs are concave!).

Finally, note that in order to reach full efficiency both the allocation should be optimal and no money should be wasted on the implementation of the respective allocation. Hain and Mitra (2004) and Gershkov and Schweinzer (2010) studied various scheduling problems (when no additional agents arrive) and gave sufficient conditions ensuring that the efficient allocation can be implemented via budget-balanced mechanisms.

6.4 Privately Known Deadlines

In the previous section we looked at queueing models where the private information pertained to time preferences. Here we look at another interesting environment where the cost of delay is "extremely convex": agents are potentially long lived and have an individual, privately known deadline after which they no longer value the objects. By faking the deadline—claiming urgency—agents try to induce an immediate allocation rather than a "wait and see" policy which may be detrimental to them if another agent with a higher value arrives in the meantime.

We illustrate the potential difficulties that arise in this environment in a simple example with two periods. The designer seeks to allocate a single object to one of two agents. At every period only one agent arrives. The agents' valuations are represented by IID random variables according to function F, with density f on support $[0, 1]$. The special feature in this model is that the agent who arrives at the first period may be either long lived—in which case he will still be present in the second period—or he may be short lived, meaning that he will not be available for the allocation next period.[11]

6.4.1 The Efficient Allocation

The complete information solution to this problem is simple. If the first agent is long lived, he should not get the object at the first period. The object should be allocated to the agent with the highest value at the second period. If, in contrast, the first-period agent is short lived, then he should get the object if and only if his value exceeds the expected value of the agent that arrives at the second period, that is, $v_1 \geq E[v]$.

Let us now add incomplete information to this problem. Assume first that only the values for the objects are private information (thus the designer knows whether or not the first agent is short lived). It is easy to implement the efficient allocation: if the first agent is long lived, both agents participate in a second-price auction at the second period; if the first agent is short lived, he faces a take-it-or-leave-it offer of $E[v]$ at the first period. In case of refusal, the object is allocated to the second-period agent at a price of zero.

Interestingly, such a payment scheme implements the efficient allocation even if the time preferences of the first agent are her private information! To show this, we only need to consider the potential deviations of the first agent in case he is long lived. Obviously, if the value of the first agent lies in the interval $[0, E[v]]$, this agent reports truthfully his type (including deadline). So consider the utility of the long-lived agent who arrives at the first period and who has value $v_1 > E[v]$. It is easy to see that for any report about his deadline, the agent prefers to report truthfully his type. If he reports his deadline truthfully, then his expected utility is

$$F(v_1)(v_1 - E[v|v \le v_1]) = \int_0^{v_1} (v_1 - v) \, dF(v).$$

If he misreports his deadline claiming that he is short-lived, then his utility is $v_1 - E[v]$. Since $\int_0^{v_1} (v_1 - v) \, dF(v) \ge v_1 - E[v]$, this is not a profitable deviation.

6.4.2 Revenue Maximization

Private information about deadlines is more problematic when the goal of the designer is revenue maximization, as shown by Pai and Vohra (2013) in a setting with discrete types and by Mierendorff (2010B) in a setting with a continuum of types.

Consider first, as above, the case where the deadlines are known to the designer. Moreover, assume that the virtual value $J(v) = v - (1 - F(v))/f(v)$ is monotone increasing.

Assume first that the first period agent is short lived. Then, if the object was not already allocated to the first agent, the second agent gets a take-it-or-leave-it offer at a price p^* that satisfies $J(p^*) = 0$. Solving the problem backward, we get that the optimal mechanism at the first period is a take-it-or-leave-it offer at a price p^{**} that satisfies

$$J(p^{**}) = \frac{(1 - F(p^*))^2}{f(p^*)}.$$

Therefore the first-period's agent utility is $v_1 - p^{**}$ if $v_1 > p^{**}$ and zero otherwise. It is easy to see that $p^{**} > p^*$.

Assume now that the first-period agent is long lived. Then the optimal mechanism is to run a standard optimal static mechanism at the second period, namely a second-price auction with reserve price of p^*. In this case, the expected utility of the first-period agent, conditional on his value being $v_1 > p^*$ is equal to

$$F(p^*)(v_1 - p^*) + \int_{p^*}^{v_1} (v_1 - v) f(v) \, dv.$$

This solution is implementable under privately known time preferences if and only if for every $v_1 > p^{**}$ it holds that

$$F(p^*)(v_1 - p^*) + \int_{p^*}^{v_1} (v_1 - v) f(v) \, dv \geq v_1 - p^{**}. \tag{6.1}$$

Since

$$\frac{\partial}{\partial v_1} \left[F(p^*)(v_1 - p^*) + \int_{p^*}^{v_1} (v_1 - v) f(v) \, dv \right] = F(v_1) \leq 1$$

if the inequality holds for some v_1, it holds for any lower value as well.

Example 20 *Assume that values distribute uniformly on* $[0, 1]$. *In this case* $p^* = 1/2$ *and* $p^{**} = 5/8$. *Therefore inequality (6.1) boils down to*

$$\frac{v_1 - 1/2}{2} + \int_{1/2}^{v_1} (v_1 - v) \, dv \geq v_1 - \frac{5}{8},$$

which holds as equality for $v_1 = 1$. *The previous argument implies that the inequality is always satisfied.*

As was shown by Mierendorff, inequality (6.1) holds whenever the virtual value is weakly convex. If the virtual value is concave, then both the incentive-compatibility constraint of the long-lived agent and the optimal solution are much more complex, and involve distortions from efficiency that go beyond the mere passage from values to virtual values. Mierendorff shows that revenue maximization calls for favoring the long-lived agent at the second stage.

6.5 Dynamic Information Arrival

All preceding parts focused on settings where there is a dynamic population whose members arrive over time with private information that is fixed and static. Here we consider another, very important class of models where the population itself is fixed and static, while the private information available to the agents evolves dynamically over time. A main difficulty in such models is the fact that types are multidimensional, and thus the incentives constraints are complex. The implementation of dynamically efficient allocations is, nevertheless, less problematic because the allocation that is seeked is completely determined by the complete information dynamic optimization problem where incentives are absent. Revenue maximization is much more difficult, since it is not a priori clear how the revenue-maximzing allocation would look.

6.5.1 Dynamic Efficiency

Allocative Efficiency   In chapter 2 we presented a dynamic generalization of the Vickrey–Clarke–Groves scheme to a specific environment with arriving agents. The implementability of the dynamically efficient allocation with a payment scheme based on externalities extends to much more general environments, as long as the agents's values are private and types are independent. For reference, we present below a model due to Bergemann and Valimaki (2010).

Assume that the time is discrete. There are I agents. All agents are long lived and present in all periods. The type of agent i at period t is $x_{i,t} \in X_i$. In every period the social planner has to make an allocation decision $a_t \in A$, where A is the set of possible allocations. The per-period utility of agent i is given by

$$u_i(a_t, p_{i,t}, x_{i,t}) = v_i(a_t, x_{i,t}) - p_{i,t}.$$

Note that this is a *private values* model; that is, the utility of agent i does not depend on private information of other agents. All agents and the designer have the same discount factor $\delta \in (0,1)$. Agents' types evolve according to a Markov process, such that the distribution of types at period $t+1$ is given by $F_i(x_{i,t+1}; x_{i,t}, a_t)$, *independently* across the agents. That is, the distribution of the agent i's type in a given period depends on his type and chosen action at the previous period.

The designer wishes to maximize welfare. Starting at period t given a current state $x_t = (x_{1,t}, ..., x_{I,t})$, the designer solves the program

$$W(x_t) = \max_{\{a_s\}_{s=t}^{\infty}} \mathbb{E}\left[\sum_{s=t}^{\infty} \delta^{s-t} \sum_{i=1}^{I} v_i(a_s, x_{i,t})\right].$$

The program in the absence of agent i is

$$W_{-i}(x_t) = \max_{\{a_s\}_{s=t}^{\infty}} \mathbb{E}\left[\sum_{s=t}^{\infty} \delta^{s-t} \sum_{j \neq i} v_j(a_s, x_{j,t})\right].$$

As in the static case the *marginal contribution of agent i* is given by

$$M_i(x_t) = W(x_t) - W_{-i}(x_t).$$

Denote by a_t^* the optimal (socially efficient) allocation at period t, and by $a_{-i,t}^*$ the optimal allocation at period t without agent i. The *flow marginal contribution* of agent i is recursively defined by

$$m_i(x_t) = M_i(x_t) - \delta \mathbb{E} M_i(x_{t+1})$$

$$= \sum_{j=1}^{I} v_j(a_t^*, x_{j,t}) - \sum_{j \neq i} v_j(a_{-i,t}^*, x_{j,t})$$

$$+ \delta \left[\mathbb{E}_{a_t^*, x_t} W_{-i}(x_{t+1}) - \mathbb{E}_{a_{-i,t}^*, x_t} W_{-i}(x_{t+1}) \right],$$

where $\mathbb{E}_{a_t^*, x_t}$ is the expectation conditional on the current decision being a_t^* and the current state being x_t. Let the transfer made by agent i at period t be

$$P_i(x_t) = v_i(a_t^*, x_{i,t}) - m_i(x_t).$$

Analogously to the static environment, this payment scheme is based on the externality that agent i imposes on the other agents. But it also takes into account also the effect of this externality on the future periods payoffs. These payments are non-negative, so that at each period a budget surplus is achieved.

Let $\mathbf{P}(x_t) = (P_1(x_t), \ldots, P_I(x_t))$ denote the vector of transfers at state x_t. The main result of Bergemann and Valimaki states that this payment scheme implements the dynamically efficient allocation a_t^* at every period. Due to similarity to the static Vickrey–Clarke–Groves mechanism, the current mechanism is called the *dynamic pivot mechanism*.

Theorem 28 *The dynamic pivot mechanism $\{a_t^*, \mathbf{P}\}_{t=1}^{\infty}$ is incentive compatible and individually rational.*

Proof By the one-shot deviation principle, it is enough to show that, for any agent i and period t, if i receives his marginal values as continuation value then he finds it optimal to report truthfully given that he reports truthfully at all other periods. We have to show that

$$v_i(a^*(x_t), x_{i,t}) - P_i(x_t) + \delta \mathbb{E}_{a_t^*, x_t} M_i(x_{t+1})$$
$$\geq v_i(a^*(x_{i,t}', x_{-i,t}), x_{i,t}) - P_i(x_{i,t}', x_{-i,t})$$
$$+ \delta \mathbb{E}_{a^*(x_{i,t}', x_{-i,t}), x_t} M_i(x_{t+1})$$

for any agent i, period t and types $x_i', x_i' \in X_i$ and $x_{-i,t} \in X_{-i}$. Note that by the construction of the payments, the left-hand side of the inequality above is exactly $M_i(x_t) = W(x_t) - W_{-i}(x_t)$. Thus we have to show that

$$W(x_t) - W_{-i}(x_t)$$
$$\geq v_i\left(a^*\left(x'_{i,t}, x_{-i,t}\right), x_{i,t}\right) - P_i\left(x'_{i,t}, x_{-i,t}\right)$$
$$+ \delta\left(\mathbb{E}_{a^*\left(x'_{i,t}, x_{-i,t}\right), x_t} W(x_{t+1}) - \mathbb{E}_{a^*\left(x'_{i,t}, x_{-i,t}\right), x_t} W_{-i}(x_{t+1})\right).$$

Plugging the expression for $P_i(x'_i, x_{-i,t})$ yields

$$W(x_t) - W_{-i}(x_t)$$
$$\geq v_i\left(a^*\left(x'_{i,t}, x_{-i,t}\right), x_{i,t}\right) + \sum_{j \neq i} v_j\left(a^*\left(x'_{i,t}, x_{-i,t}\right), x_{j,t}\right)$$
$$- \sum_{j \neq i} v_j\left(a^*_{-i,t}, x_{j,t}\right)$$
$$+ \delta\left[\mathbb{E}_{a^*\left(x'_{i,t}, x_{-i,t}\right), x_t} W_{-i}(x_{t+1}) - \mathbb{E}_{a^*_{-i,t}, x_t} W_{-i}(x_{t+1})\right]$$
$$+ \delta\left(\mathbb{E}_{a^*\left(x'_{i,t}, x_{-i,t}\right), x_t} W(x_{t+1}) - \mathbb{E}_{a^*\left(x'_{i,t}, x_{-i,t}\right), x_t} W_{-i}(x_{t+1})\right),$$

which reduces to

$$W(x_t) - W_{-i}(x_t)$$
$$\geq v_i\left(a^*\left(x'_{i,t}, x_{-i,t}\right), x_{i,t}\right) + \sum_{j \neq i} v_j\left(a^*\left(x'_{i,t}, x_{-i,t}\right), x_{j,t}\right)$$
$$- \sum_{j \neq i} v_j\left(a^*_{-i,t}, x_{j,t}\right) - \delta\mathbb{E}_{a^*_{-i,t}, x_t} W_{-i}(x_{t+1})$$
$$+ \delta\mathbb{E}_{a^*\left(x'_{i,t}, x_{-i,t}\right), x_t} W(x_{t+1}).$$

Recall that $W_{-i}(x_t) = \sum_{j \neq i} v_j\left(a^*_{-i,t}, x_{j,t}\right) + \delta\mathbb{E}_{a^*_{-i,t}, x_t} W_{-i}(x_{t+1})$. Therefore we can rewrite the previous inequality as

$$W(x_t) \geq v_i\left(a^*\left(x'_i, x_{-i,t}\right), x_{i,t}\right) + \sum_{j \neq i} v_j\left(a^*\left(x'_i, x_{-i,t}\right), x_{j,t}\right),$$

which holds by the definition of $W(x_t)$.   ∎

It is worth clarifying the equilibrium notion in the result above. In the static environment, the Vickrey–Clarke–Groves mechanism is dominant strategy incentive compatible. This requirement, however, is too demanding in the dynamic environment. Yet the dynamic pivot mechanism is *periodic ex post incentive compatible*, that is, truth-telling is an optimal strategy for any possible history and any current state of the other agents.[12] But the agents may come to regret their strategies at some later point in time when more informations has become available.

Although the model above is formulated as one having a fixed population of agents with varying information, the framework is flexible enough to incorporate agents' arrivals. For example, consider the Derman–Lieberman–Ross model analyzed in previous chapters. Assume, without loss of generality, that in the DLR model agent i arrives in period i with type x_i. That model can be incorporated in the present one as follows: let x_{it}^j denote the type of agent i relevant for good j in period t, and let

$$x_{it}^j = \begin{cases} x_i & \text{if } i = t \text{ and if object } j \text{ is still available at } t, \\ 0 & \text{else.} \end{cases}$$

Budget Balance As mentioned above, the dynamic pivot mechanism generates a nonnegative surplus in every period. Athey and Segal (2013) suggested a dynamic generalization of the *expected externality mechanism* due to Arrow (1979) and d'Aspremont and Gerard-Varet (1979) (AGV mechanism) that besides implementing the optimal allocation a_t^* in a Bayes–Nash equilibrium also balances the budget at every period. The results hold for private, independent values. Of course, the price is that the mechanism may not be individually rational.

The payment in the AGV mechanism has two parts: incentive payment, whereby each agent obtains the expected welfare of all other agents at the efficient allocation, and budget balancing payment, whereby, in order to cover the expense incurred by the incentive payments (and thus balance the budget), each agent pays an equal share of the incentive payments made to all other agents.

The main complication to overcome in dynamic environments is the fact that values may be correlated over time or, more generally, that the agents' preferences may not be separable across periods. Such features may prevent a naive, repeated usage of the static AGV mechanism at every period: on the one hand, the AGV mechanism calculates expected externalities, but expectations change over time as more information becomes available in the dynamic setting; on the other hand, trying to tailor the expectation payment to the available information potentially interferes with the incentives for truthful revelation. Nevertheless, Athey and Segal (2013) show that these difficulties can be overcome under fairly general conditions. In general, the needed payments cannot be "online." We illustrate their construction by an example taken from their paper.

Example 21 *Consider a producer (agent 1) and a buyer (agent 2) who engage in a two-period interaction. In each period $t = 1, 2$ they can trade a quantity $q_t \in [0, 1]$. Before the first period, the producer observes his type*

$x_1 \in [1, 2]$ *that determines his production cost* $\frac{1}{2}x_1 (q_t)^2$. *The buyer's per unit value at the first period is 1, and at the second period it is given by* $x_2 \in [0, 1]$. *The buyer privately learns* x_2 *at the beginning of the second period before contracting with the producer.*

The welfare-maximizing volume of trade at the first and the second periods are given by $Q_1 (x_1) = 1/x_1$ *and* $Q_2 (x_1, x_2) = x_2/x_1$, *respectively. The standard static AGV mechanism generates the correct incentives for the producer who only reports a type once, before the interaction. But, at the second period, the buyer infers the reported producer's type through the first-period traded quantity. Hence in the AGV payment scheme the buyer affects the incentive payment to the producer, and that payment will be charged the buyer himself. As a consequence the mechanism generates incentives for the buyer to mis-report his type, and does not implement the efficient allocation. To correct this situation, the Athey–Segal incentive payment charges the* **change** *in the expectation of the producer's utility due to the buyer's report (conditional on all the previous announcements). The change has zero expected value. In this example the payments that implement the welfare maximizing allocation and balance the budget are given by*

$$P_1(x_1, x_2) = -\frac{1 + \mathbb{E}(x_2)^2}{x_1} - \frac{(x_2)^2 - \mathbb{E}(x_2)^2}{2x_1},$$

$$P_2(x_1, x_2) = \frac{1 + \mathbb{E}(x_2)^2}{x_1} + \frac{(x_2)^2 - \mathbb{E}(x_2)^2}{2x_1},$$

where $\frac{1 + E(x_2)^2}{x_1}$ *is the producer's incentive payment (and the expectation of the buyer's utility) while* $\frac{(x_2)^2 - E(x_2)^2}{2x_1}$ *is the change in the expectation of the producer's costs due to the buyer's report. Note that* $\mathbb{E}_{x_2} \left[\frac{(x_2)^2 - \mathbb{E}(x_2)^2}{2x_1} \right] = 0$.

6.5.2   Sequential Screening and Revenue Maximization

We now illustrate the basic revenue maximization problem under information arrival in the canonical setting of Courty and Li (2000), who considered the problem of a monopolist seller facing buyers that gradually learn about their valuations over time.

In the Courty and Li two-period setting the monopolist could, naively, wait until all values are realized and then charge the standard monopoly price. But, when the first period knowledge of agents is informative about their second-period one, gradually screening buyers according to their current information becomes optimal and the seller is able to extract additional revenue!

Courty and Li build upon earlier insights due to Baron and Besanko (1984) who analyzed the regulation of a firm that obtains information about costs over time. Courty and Li's model is as follows. A monopolist with constant marginal cost of production c faces a population of buyers characterized by types θ distributed according to F in an interval $\Theta = [\underline{\theta}, \overline{\theta}]$. Assume that F has a density $f > 0$. Both monopolist and buyers have quasi-linear utility and do not discount the future.

There are two periods. In the first period the buyers privately learn their type θ. This type determines the buyers' distribution of values for the object (or service) sold by the monopolist. Let $G(v|\theta)$ be this distribution, and assume that for any θ, $G(\cdot|\theta)$ has the same support $[\underline{v}, \overline{v}]$. Let $g(\cdot|\theta)$ denote the density of $G(\cdot|\theta)$, and assume that it is differentiable. In period two, buyers learn their actual value for the object v and decide whether to buy the object or not.

Importantly, Courty and Li assume that the sale contract is written at the end of the first period, when the buyer already knows θ, but before he privately learns his actual valuation v. Although the buyer can be screened here twice (e.g., in a revelation mechanism the buyer sequentially reports θ and v), we can translate this sequential design problem in a particular static problem whereby, in period 1, the buyer chooses from a menu of **contingent** contracts $\{x(\theta, v), p(\theta, v)\}$, where $x(\theta, v)$ is the probability of a sale to this buyer, and $p(\theta, v)$ is the payment to the monopolist. The monopolist solves then the following maximization problem:

$$\max_{x,p} \int_{\underline{\theta}}^{\overline{\theta}} \left(\int_{\underline{v}}^{\overline{v}} [p(\theta, v) - cx(\theta, v)]g(v|\theta)dv \right) f(\theta)d\theta \tag{6.2}$$

subject to

Constraint 1: $\forall \theta, v, \ 0 \leq x(\theta, v) \leq 1$;

Constraint 2: $\forall \theta, \int_{\underline{v}}^{\overline{v}} [vx(\theta, v) - p(\theta, v)]g(v|\theta)dv \geq 0$;

Constraint 3: $\forall \theta, \theta', \ \int_{\underline{v}}^{\overline{v}} [vx(\theta, v) - p(\theta, v)]g(v|\theta)dv \geq \int_{\underline{v}}^{\overline{v}} [vx(\theta', v) - p(\theta', v)]g(v|\theta)dv$;

Constraint 4: $\forall \theta, v, v', \ vx(\theta, v) - p(\theta, v) \geq vx(\theta, v') - p(\theta, v')$.

Constraint 1 is a feasibility constraint. Constraint 2 is the individual rationality constraint at the first period. Constraint 3 is the incentive compatibility constraint at that period, while constraint 4 is the incentive compatibility constraint at the second period. This last constraint is the main addition, reflecting the fact that the buyer is screened a second time. It is important to note here that there is no individual rationality constraint in the second period, which reflects a situation where there are "cancellation fees" if the buyer ultimately decides not to buy.

Using the standard envelope techniques, payments can be eliminated from the objective function, which becomes

$$\max_x \int_{\underline{\theta}}^{\overline{\theta}} \left(\int_{\underline{v}}^{\overline{v}} \left[(v - c) + \frac{1 - F(\theta)}{f(\theta)} \frac{\partial G(v|\theta)/\partial \theta}{g(v|\theta)} \right] x(\theta, v) g(v|\theta) dv \right) f(\theta) d\theta.$$

$$(6.3)$$

Compared with the standard static problem, the new addition is the term

$$\frac{\partial G(v|\theta)/\partial \theta}{g(v|\theta)} = \frac{\partial G(v|\theta)/\partial \theta}{\partial G(v|\theta)/\partial v}.$$

This term measures how informative the agent's (buyer's) initial type is about his final valuation (see also Baron and Besanko 1984). The information rent of the agents in the first period must account for the informativeness of initial types about future types. Note that $\frac{\partial G(v|\theta)/\partial \theta}{g(v|\theta)}$ can be either positive or negative, so that the direction of distortion from efficiency (i.e., from maximization of the social surplus $(v - c)$) is not a priori clear.

Since the constraints involve an element of multidimensional incentive compatibility (where monotonicity alone is generally not sufficient for implementability), the problem above is, in general, very complex. Simplifications can be obtained by assuming some "natural" order on the type space Θ. For example, let us assume here that

$$\theta > \theta' \Rightarrow G(v|\theta) \le G(v|\theta') \qquad \text{for all } v. \tag{6.4}$$

In other words, initial types are ordered such that higher types lead to better distribution of values in the sense of first-order stochastic dominance.[13] In this case the informativeness rate $\frac{\partial G(v|\theta)/\partial \theta}{g(v|\theta)}$ is always nonpositive.

We can then easily solve problem (6.3) by pointwise maximization, while taking into account only the feasibility constraint $0 \le x(\theta, v) \le 1$. The solution $x^*(\theta, v)$ is necessarily deterministic, and it can be implemented by a system of advance payments in the first period, and (partial) refunds at the second. If x^* is monotone in both θ and v, then it can be shown that it also constitutes the solution to the full problem (6.2). But note that x^* may not be monotone even under the first-order dominance assumption. This illustrates the difficulty of finding sufficient conditions for optimality. This difficulty is "endemic" in multidimensional models, and thus also in models such as the present one where agents obtain several pieces of information over time.

Example 22 *Assume that for each θ, $v = \alpha\theta + (1 - \alpha)\epsilon_\theta$, where $\alpha \in [0, 1]$ and where the ϵ_θ are IID random variables on the whole real line with density h and distribution H. The conditional distribution is then given by $G(v|\theta) = H(\frac{v - \alpha\theta}{1 - \alpha})$, which satisfies the first-order stochastic dominance condition (6.4). Moreover note that $\frac{\partial G(v|\theta)/\partial\theta}{g(v|\theta)} = -\alpha < 0$. The solution to the relaxed problem is*

$$x^*(\theta, v) = \begin{cases} 1 & \text{if } v > c + \alpha\frac{1 - F(\theta)}{f(\theta)}, \\ 0 & \text{otherwise.} \end{cases}$$

Under the standard monotone hazard rate condition, whereby $\frac{1 - F(\theta)}{f(\theta)}$ is nonincreasing in θ, x^* is monotonically increasing in both v and θ and thus constitutes the solution to the sequential screening problem. Note that the sale cutoff is lower for buyers with higher initial types. This allocation is implemented by payments of the form

$$p^*(\theta, v) = \begin{cases} p_1(\theta) & \text{if } v > c + \alpha\frac{1 - F(\theta)}{f(\theta)}, \\ p_0(\theta) & \text{otherwise,} \end{cases}$$

where $p_1(\theta) - p_0(\theta) = c + \alpha\frac{1 - F(\theta)}{f(\theta)}$. If $\alpha = 0$ the initial type is not at all informative, and the sequential mechanism achieves perfect discrimination via an efficient allocation: in the first period all buyers buy at a price equal to the expected value (which is identical for all types), and in the second period buyers with realized low values are allowed to return the good while getting a refund of c. If $\alpha = 1$, then values are perfectly correlated with initial types and the optimal sequential mechanism coincides with standard monopoly pricing conducted in the second period, after buyers learn their valuations

6.6   Related Literature

The optimal screening contract with only ex ante participation constraints screens ex ante types by imposing higher ex post losses on lower ex ante types. Since lower ex ante types are less likely to become high ex post types, they are more willing to tolerate higher losses for possible higher ex post types. In a recent contribution, Krähmer and Strausz (2011) show that adding ex post participation constraints eliminates the value of eliciting the agent's information sequentially. Instead, a static contract, which conditions only on the agent's final information, becomes optimal. In this sense the value of dynamic over static contracting in the absence of ex post participation constraints is due to relaxed participation rather than relaxed incentive constraints.

Eso and Szentes (2007) consider a setting in which competing buyers in an auction have an initial estimate of their valuation and the seller is able to control buyers' acquisition of additional refined information. Battaglini (2005) examines an infinite horizon model and characterizes the revenue-maximizing long-term contract of a monopolist facing a buyer whose value follows a two-type Markov process. Pavan, Segal, and Toikka (2014) characterize incentive compatibility and revenue in general settings with dynamic private information. Generalizing most previous insights, they develop a "dynamic payoff formula" that expresses, in incentive-compatible mechanisms, the derivative of an agent's expected payoff (and hence the seller's revenue) with respect to his private information.

A major difficulty in all these studies is the lack of general sufficient conditions for optimality, due to the multidimensional nature of the information and incentive constraints.

While the above-mentioned papers dealt with revenue maximization, Bergeman and Välimäki (2010) focus on welfare maximization. They consider a general infinite horizon model where participants obtain private signals over time, and where a sequence of decisions must be taken in response to these signals. They construct a dynamic pivot mechanism that generalizes the VCG insight to this framework: payments in each period are equal to flow externalities, and each agent receives a flow payoff equal to her flow marginal contribution to social welfare. Therefore each agent's expected discounted payoff is equal to her total marginal contribution to social welfare.[14] An important assumption in this work is that signals are independent across agents. Otherwise, one obtains a model with interdependent values where efficient implementation is not always possible. Athey and Segal (2013) consider a similar setting to that of Bergemann and Valimaki but add the requirement of budget-balanced mechanisms, thus generalizing to the dynamic setting the classical insight due to Arrow (1979) and d'Aspremont and Gerard-Varet (1979). As in the static case, a balanced budget may not be compatible with individual rationality (a condition satisfied by the Bergemann–Välimäki construction). Given dynamic efficiency, these criteria become compatible only in the limit where the horizon is very large and where agents are very patient.

6.7 Outlook

Besides the issues discussed in this last chapter, we briefly discuss here several important topics that have been insufficiently treated so far in the literature, and that require more research:

1. Most of the literature (both static and dynamic) asumes that the designer has full commitment power, meaning she announces a policy and can commit to it. Relaxing this assumption introduces a complex dynamic game between the strategic agents, on the one hand, and a strategic planner, on the other, and the analysis is much more complicated. Several interesting extensions in this direction can be found, for example, in Skreta (2006), Horner and Samuelson (2011), and Chen (2012).

2. In all models considered here there was a unique, monopolistic designer. Of course, in practice there is often competition (e.g., over customers) among various entities that perform dynamic allocation/pricing. The question is whether the particular structure of the dynamic pricing models with uncertain demand analyzed above offer more specific insights into the nature of this competition than those gleaned, say, from the general theory of repeated/stochastic games (e.g., various folk theorems).

3. All models considered here were of the "adverse selection" type. For applications to contracting it is of interest to add to such models a "moral hazard" component.

Notes

1. Said (2012) also considers the possibility that buyers leave the market in each period with a fixed probability.

2. Most textbooks on stochastic processes discuss the construction and properties of counting processes. See, for example, Ross (1983).

3. Since the designer is interested here in implementing the efficient allocation, he never allocates the object strictly after the last arrival in a finite horizon model.

4. Recall that the Poisson process is the special case where G is exponential

5. Although the so-called revelation principle need not hold in settings where some deviations from truth-telling are unfeasible for certain types, this principle does hold for our case of unilateral deviations in the time dimension; see theorem 1 and example 5.a.2 in Green and Laffont (1986).

6. Intuitively, minimizing the information revealed to each agent reduces the available contingent deviations from truth-telling, and therefore relaxes the incentive compatibility constraints for that agent.

7. The equilibrium outcome of any mechanism where at least one agent reports his type (value and the arrival time) after his arrival, can be replicated by another mechanism and equilibrium where all agents reports their types upon arrival.

8. This last component can be thought of as a deadline after which his value for the object drops to zero. This deadline may be either a deterministic or a stochastic function of t_i. The case $d_i = t_i$ for all i corresponds to the case witout recall, while the case $d_i = \infty$ for all i corresponds to the case with perfect recall analyzed above.

9. Gallien offers a solution also for the case where the seller has several identical units: then the revenue-maximizing price jumps up after each sale. Gershkov and Moldovanu (2010) also allow for multiple heterogeneous units. In their no-recall case, the solution has the same form for any renewal process (not necessarily *NBU*).

10. The situation is more complicated when arrivals are not simultaneous.

11. In this illustration we assume that the agent does not discount the future. Adding discounting creates some complications that we wish to abstract from here.

12. This notion sometimes called *within-period ex post equilibrium* (see Athey and Segal 2013).

13. Courty and Li also consider an order in terms of mean-preserving spreads.

14. Cavallo and Parkes and Singh (2009) develop a mechanism similar to the dynamic pivot mechanism in a setting with agents whose type evolution follows a Markov process.

Bibliography

Afeche, P., and Mendelson, H. 2004. Pricing and priority auctions in queueing systems with a generalized delay cost structure. *Management Science* 50: 869–82.

Albright, S. C. 1974. Optimal sequential assignments with random arrival times. *Management Science* 21 (1): 60–67.

Albright, S. C. 1977. A Bayesian approach to a generalized house selling problem. *Management Science*, 24 (4): 432–40.

Armstrong, M. 1996. Multiproduct nonlinear pricing. *Econometrica* 64: 51–76.

Arnold, M. A., and Lippman, S. A. 2001. The analytics of search with posted prices. *Economic Theory* 17: 444–66.

Arrow, K. 1979. The property rights doctrine and demand revelation under incomplete information. In *Economics and Human Welfare*. New York: Academic Press, 23–39.

d'Aspremont, C., and Gerard-Varet, L. 1979. Incentives and incomplete information. *Journal of Public Economics* 11: 25–45.

Athey, S., and Segal, I. 2007. An efficient dynamic mechanism. *Econometrica* 81: 2463–85.

Aviv, Y., and Pazgal, A. 2008. Optimal pricing of seasonal products in the presence of forward-looking Consumers. *Manufacture and Service Operations Management* 10 (3): 339–59.

Babaioff, M., Blumrosen, L., Dughmi, S., and Singer. Y. 2011. Posting prices with unknown distributions. *Innovations in Computer Science* (ICS 2011). Proceedings, 166–78.

Balachandran, K. 1972. Purchasing priorities in queues. *Management Science* 18: 319–26.

Baron, D. P., and Besanko D. 1984. Regulation and information in a continuing relationship. *Information and Economic Policy* 1 (3): 267–302.

Battaglini, M. 2005. Long-term contracting with Markovian consumers. *American Economic Review* 95 (3): 637–58.

Becker, G. 1973. A theory of marriage: Part I. *Journal of Political Economy* 81: 813–46.

Bergemann, D., and Said, M. 2011. Dynamic auctions: A survey. In J. J. Cochrane, ed., *Wiley Encyclopedia of Operations Research and Management Science*, vol. 2. Hoboken, NJ: Wiley, 1511–22.

Bergemann, D., and Välimäki, J. 2010. The dynamic pivot mechanism. *Econometrica* 78 (2): 771–789.

Bertsekas, D. 2005. *Dynamic Programming and Optimal Control*, vol.1, 3d ed. Belmont, MA: Athena Scientific.

Bickhchandani, S., and Sharma, S. 1996. Optimal search with learning. *Journal of Economic Dynamics and Control* 20: 333–59.

Bitran, G. R., and Caldentey, R. 2003. An overview of pricing models for revenue management. *Manufacture and Services Operations Management* 5 (3): 203–29.

Bitran, G. R., and Mondschein, S. V. 1997. Periodic pricing of seasonal products in retailing. *Management Science* 43 (1): 64–79.

Blackorby, C., and Szalay, D. 2007. Multidimensional screening, affiliation, and full separation. Discussion paper. University of Warwick.

Board, S., 2008. Durable-goods monopoly with varying demand. *Review of Economic Studies* 75 (2): 391–413.

Board, S., and Skrzypacz, A. 2010. Revenue managment with forward looking buyers. Discussion paper. UCLA.

Boshuizen, F., and Gouweleeuw, J. 1993. General optimal stopping theorems for semi-Markov processes. *Advances in Applied Probability* 24: 825–46.

Bulow, J., and Roberts, J. 1989. The simple economics of optimal auction. *Journal of Political Economy* 97 (5): 1060–90.

Caplin, A., and Leahy, J. 1996. Monetary policy as a process of search. *American Economics Review* 86 (4): 689–702.

Cavallo, R., Parkes, D., and Singh, S. 2009. Efficient mechanisms with dynamic populations and dynamic types. Discussion paper. Harvard University.

Chamley, C. 2004. *Rational Herds: Economic Models of Social Learning*. Cambridge, UK: Cambridge University Press.

Che, Y. K., and Gale, I. 2000. The optimal mechanism for selling to a budget-constrained buyer. *Journal of Economic Theory* 92: 198–233.

Chen, Y., and Wang, R. 1999. Learning buyers' valuation distribution in posted-price selling. *Economic Theory* 14: 417–28.

Chen, C. H. 2012. Name your own price at priceline.com: Strategic bidding and lockout periods. *Review of Economic Studies* 79 (4): 1341–69.

Chou, C. F., and Talmain, G. 1993. Nonparametric search. *Journal of Economic Dynamics and Control* 17: 771–84.

Courty, P., and Li, H. 2000. Sequential screening. *Review of Economic Studies* 67: 697–717.

Cox, D., and Smith, W. 1961. *Queues.* London: Chapman and Hall.

Cremer, J., and McLean, R. 1985. Optimal selling strategies under uncertainty for a discriminating monopolist when demands are interdependent. *Econometrica* 53 (2): 345–62.

Cremer, J., and McLean, R. 1988. Full extraction of the surplus in Bayesian and dominant strategy auctions. *Econometrica* 56 (6): 1247–57.

Dana, J. 1998. Advance-purchase discounts and price discrimination in competitive markets. *Journal of Political Economy* 106: 395–422.

Dasgupta, P., and Maskin, E. 2000. Efficient auctions. *Quarterly Journal of Economics* 115 (2): 341–88.

Das Varma, G., and Vettas, N. 2001. Optimal dynamic pricing with inventories. *Economic Letters* 72 (3): 335–40.

Deb, R. 2008. Optimal contracting of new experience goods. Unpublished manuscript. Yale University.

Deb, R., and Said, M. 2013. Progressive screening: Long-term contracting with a privately known stochastic process. *Review of Economic Studies* 80: 1–34

De La Cal, J., and Caracamo, J. 2006. Stochastic orders and majorization of mean order statistics. *Journal of Applied Probability* 43: 704–12.

Derman, C., Lieberman, G. J., and Ross, S. M. 1972. A sequential stochastic assignment problem. *Management Science* 18 (7): 349–55.

Dizdar, D., Gershkov, A., and Moldovanu, B. 2011. Revenue maximization in the dynamic knapsack problem. *Theoretical Economics* 6 (2): 157–84.

Doepke, M., and Townsend, R. M. 2006. Dynamic mechanism design with hidden income and hidden action. *Journal Economic Theory* 126 (1): 235–85.

Dolan, R. J. 1978. Incentive mechanisms for priority queueing problems. *Bell Journal of Economics* 9 (2): 421–36.

Elfving, G. 1967. A persistency problem connected with a point process. *Journal of Applied Probability* 4: 77–89.

Elmaghraby, W., and Keskinocak, P. 2003. Dynamic pricing in the presence of inventory considerations: Research overview, current practices, and future directions. *Management Science* 49 (10): 1287–1309.

Eso, P., and Szentes, B. 2007. Optimal information disclosure in auctions and the handicap auction. *Review of Economic Studies* 74 (3): 705–31.

Gale, I., and Holmes, T. 1993. Advance-purchase discounts and monopoly allocation of capacity. *American Economic Review* 83: 135–46.

Gallego, G., and van Ryzin, G. 1994. Optimal dynamic pricing of inventories with stochastic demand over finite horizons. *Management Science* 40 (8): 999–1020.

Gallego, G., and van Ryzin, G. 1997. A multiproduct dynamic pricing problem and its applications to network yield management. *Operations Research* 45 (1): 24–41.

Gallien, J. 2006. Dynamic mechanism design for online commerce. *Operations Research* 54 (2): 291–310.

Gershkov, A., and Moldovanu, B. 2009. Dynamic revenue maximization with heterogeneous objects: A mechanism design approach. *American Economic Journal: Microeconomics* 2: 98–168.

Gershkov, A., and Moldovanu, B. 2009. Learning about the future and dynamic efficiency. *American Economic Review* 99 (4): 1576–88.

Gershkov, A., and Moldovanu, B. 2010. Efficient sequential assignment with incomplete information. *Games and Economic Behavior* 68 (1): 144–54.

Gerhskov, A., and Moldovanu, B. 2012. Dynamic allocation and pricing: A mechanism design approach. *International Journal of Industrial Organization* 30: 283–86.

Gerhskov, A., and Moldovanu, B. 2013. Non-Bayesian optimal search and dynamic implemntation. *Economic Letters* 118: 121–25.

Gershkov, A., Moldovanu, B., and Strack, P. 2013. Dynamic allocation and learning with strategic arrivals. Discussion paper. University of Bonn.

Gershkov, A., and Moldovanu, B. 2012. Optimal search, learning, and implementation. *Journal of Economic Theory* 147: 881–909.

Gershkov, A., and Schweinzer, P. 2010. When queueing is better than push and shove. *International Journal of Game Theory* 39 (3): 409–30.

Ghanem, S. 1975. Computing central optimization by a pricing priority policy. *IBM Systems Journal* 14: 272–92.

Glazer, A., and Hassin, R. 1986. Stable priority purchasing in queues. *Operations Research Letters* 4: 285–88.

Glosten, L., and Milgrom, P. R. 1985. Bid, ask and transaction prices in a specialist market with heterogeneously informed traders. *Journal of Financial Economics* 17: 71–100.

Green, J., and Laffont, J. J. 1986. Partially verifiable information and mechanism design, *Review of Economic Studies* 53: 447–56.

Guo, M., and Conitzer, V. 2009. Worst-case optimal redistribution of VCG payment in multi-unit auctions. *Games and Economic Behavior* 67 (1): 69–98.

Hain, R., and Mitra, M. 2004. Simple sequencing problems with interdependent costs. *Games and Economic Behavior* 48 (2): 271–91.

Hansen, R. 1985. Auctions with contingent payments. *American Economic Review* 75 (4): 862–865.

Hardy, G., Littlewood, J. E., and Pólya, G. 1934. *Inequalities*. Cambridge, UK: Cambridge University Press.

Harris, M., and Raviv, A. 1981. A theory of monopoly pricing schemes with demand uncertainty. *American Economic Review* 71 (3): 347–65.

Hassin, R., and Haviv, M. 2002. *To Queue or Not to Queue: Equilibrium Behavior in Queueing Systems*. Boston: Kluwer Academic.

Horner, J., and Samuelson, L. 2011. Managing strategic buyers. *Journal of Political Economy* 119 (3): 379–425

Iyengar, G., and Kumar, A. 2008. Optimal procurement auctions of divisible goods with capacitated suppliers. *Review of Economic Design* 12: 129–154.

Jaynes, E. T. 2003. *Probability Theory: The Logic of Science*. Cambridge, UK: Cambridge University Press.

Jehiel, P., Moldovanu, B., and Stacchetti, E. 1999. Multidimensional mechanism design for auctions with externalities. *Journal of Economic Theory* 85: 814–29.

Jehiel, P., and Moldovanu, B. 2001. Efficient design with interdependent valuations. *Econometrica,* 69 (5): 1237–59.

Kincaid, W. M., and Darling, D. 1963. An inventory pricing problem. *Journal of Mathematical Analysis and Applications* 7: 183–208.

Kittsteiner, T., and Moldovanu, B. 2005. Priority auctions and queue disciplines that depend on processing time. *Management Science* 51 (2): 236–48.

Kittsteiner, T., Nikutta, J., and Winter, E. 2004. Declining valuations in sequential auctions. *International Journal of Game Theory* 33 (1): 89–106.

Kleinrock, L. 1967. Optimal bribing for queue positions. *Operations Research* 15: 304–18.

Kleywegt, A. J., and Papastavrou, J. D. 2001. The dynamic and stochastic knapsack problem with random sized items. *Operations Research* 49 (1): 26–41.

Kohn, M., and Shavell, S. 1974. The theory of search. *Journal of Economic Theory* 9: 123.

Krähmer, D., and Strausz, R. 2011. The benefits of sequential screening. Discussion paper. University of Bonn.

Kyle, A. 1985. Continuous auctions and insider trading. *Econometrica* 53: 1315–35.

Lavi, R., and Nisan, N. 2000. Competitive analysis of incentive compatible on-line auctions. *Theoretical Computer Science* 310 (1): 159–80.

Lazear, E. P. 1986. Retail pricing and clearance sale. *American Economic Review* 76 (1): 14–32.

Lin, G. Y., Lu, Y., and Yao, D. D. 2008. The stochastic knapsack revisited: Switch-over policies and dynamic pricing. *Operations Research* 56: 945–57.

Lippman, S. A., and McCall, J. 1981. The economics of uncertainty: Selected topics and probabilistic methods. In K. J. Arrow and M. D. Intriligator, eds., *Handbook of Mathematical Economics*, vol. 1. Elsevier, 211–84.

Lui, F. 1985. An equilibrium queueing model of bribery. *Journal of Political Economy* 93: 760–81.

Marshall, A., and Olkin, I. 1979. Inequalities: The theory of majorization and its applications. *Mathematics in Science and Engineering*, vol. 143. New York: Academic Press.

Marschall, A., and Proschan, F. 1965. An inequality for convex functions involving majorization. *Journal of Mathematical Analysis and Applications* 12: 87–90.

Mason, R., and Välimäki, J. 2011. Learning about the arrival of sales. *Journal of Economic Theory* 146: 1699–1711.

McAfee, P., and McMillan, J. 1988. Search mechanisms. *Journal of Economic Theory* 44: 99–123.

McAfee, P., and te Velde, V. 2007. Dynamic pricing in the airline industry. In T. J. Hendershott, ed., *Handbook on Economics and Information Systems*. Amsterdam: Elsevier, vol. 1, 527–70.

McAfee, P., and te Velde, V. 2008. Dynamic pricing with constant demand elasticity. *Production and Operations Management* 17 (4): 432–38.

McAfee, P., and Wiseman, T. 2008. Capacity choice counters the coase conjecture. *Review of Economic Studies* 75 (1): 317–32.

Mezzetti, C. 2004. Mechanism design with interdependent valuations: Efficiency. *Econometrica* 72 (5): 1617–27.

Mezzetti, C. 2007. Mechanism design with interdependent valuations: Surplus extraction. *Economic Theory* 31 (3): 473–88.

Mierendorff, K. 2013. The dynamic vickrey auction. *Games and Economic Behavior* 82: 192–204.

Mierendorff, K. 2010. Optimal dynamic mechanism design with deadlines. Discussion paper. University of Bonn.

Milgrom, P. 1981. Good news and bad news: Representation theorems and applications. *Bell Journal of Economics* 12 (2): 280–391.

Milgrom, P. 2004. *Putting Auction Theory to Work*. Cambridge, UK: Cambridge University Press.

Morgan, P. B. 1985. Distributions of the duration and value of job search with learning. *Econometrica* 53: 1199–1232.

Mortensen, D. T. 1986. Job search and labor market. In O. Ashenfelter and R. Layard, eds., *Handbook of Labor Economics*, vol. 2. Amsterdam: Elsevier, 849–919.

Moulin, H. 2009. Almost budget-balanced VCG mechanisms to assign multiple objects. *Journal of Economic Theory* 144 (1): 96–119.

Mussa, M., and Rosen, S. 1978. Monopoly and product quality. *Journal of Economic Theory* 18: 301–17.

Myerson, R. 1986. Multistage games with communication. *Econometrica* 54 (2): 323–58.

Myerson, R. 1981. Optimal auction design. *Mathematics of Operation Research* 6: 58–73.

Nocke, V., and Peitz, M. 2007. A theory of clearance sales. *Economic Journal* 117: 964–90.

Nocke, V., Peitz, M., and Rosar, F. 2011. Advance-purchase discounts as a price discrimination device. *Journal of Economic Theory* 146: 141–62.

Pai, M., and Vohra, R. 2013. Optimal dynamic auctions and simple index rules. *Mathematics of Operations Research* 38: 682–97.

Papastavrou, J. D., Rajagopalan, S., and Kleywegt, A. J. 1996. The dynamic and stochastic knapsack problem with deadlines. *Management Science* 42: 1706–18.

Parkes, D. C., and Singh, S. 2003. An MDP-based approach to online mechanism design. *Proceedings of 17th Annual Conference on Neural Information Processing Systems.* (NIPS 03). In S. Thrun, L. K. Saul, and B. Schölkopf, eds., *Advances in Neural Information Processing Systems*, vol. 16. Cambridge: MIT Press.

Pashigian, B. P. 1988. Demand uncertainty and sales: A study of fashion and markdown prices. *American Economic Review* 78 (5): 936–53.

Pashigian, B. P., and Bowen, B. 1991. Why are products sold on sale? Explanations of pricing regularities. *Quarterly Journal of Economics* 106 (4): 1015–38.

Pashigian, B. P., Bowen, B., and Gould, E. 1995. Fashion, styling, and the within-season decline in automobile prices. *Journal of Law and Economics* 38 (2): 281–309.

Pavan, A., Segal, I., and Toikka, J. 2014. Dynamic mechanism design: A Myersonian approach, Manuscript. Northwestern University, forthcoming in *Econometrica* 82 (2): 601–54.

Pecaric, J. E., Proschan, F., and Tong, Y. L. 1992. *Convex Functions, Partial Orderings, and Statistical Applications.* Boston: Academic Press.

Pratt, J. W., Raiffa, H., and Schlaifer, R. 1995. *Statistical Decision Theory.* Cambridge: MIT Press.

Puterman, M. L. 2005. *Markov Decision Processes.* Hoboken, NJ: Wiley.

Riley, J., and Zeckhauser, R. 1983. Optimal selling strategies: When to haggle, when to hold firm. *Quarterly Journal of Economics* 98 (2): 267–89.

Rochet, J. C. 1985. The taxation principle and multitime Hamilton Jacobi equations. *Journal of Mathematical Economics* 14: 113–28.

Rochet, J.-C., and Stole, L. A. 2003. The economics of multidimensional screening. *Advances in Economics and Econometrics, Theory and Applications, Eight World Congress*, vol. 1 edited by M. Dewatripont, L. P. Hansen, and S. Turnovsky. Cambridge, UK: Cambridge University Press, 150–97.

Rob, R. 1991. Learning and capacity expansion under demand uncertainty. *Review of Economic Studies* 58: 655–75.

Rosenfield, D., and Shapiro, R. 1981. Optimal adaptive price search. *Journal of Economic Theory* 25: 1–20.

Ross, K. W., and Tsang, D. H. K. 1989. The stochastic knapsack problem. *IEEE Transactions on Communications* 37: 740–47.

Ross, S. M. 1983. *Stochastic Processes*. New York: Wiley.

Rothschild, M. 1974. Searching for the lowest price when the distribution of prices is unknown. *Journal of Political Economy* 82 (4): 689–711.

Said, M. 2012. Auctions with dynamic populations: Efficiency and revenue maximization. *Journal of Economic Theory* 147 (6): 2419–38.

Segal, I. 2003. Optimal pricing mechanisms with unknown demand. *American Economic Review* 93 (3): 509–29.

Skreta, V. 2006. Sequentially optimal mechanisms. *Review of Economic Studies* 73 (4): 1085–1111.

Scierstad, A. 1992. Reservation prices in optimal stopping. *Operations Research* 40: 409–14.

Shaked, M., and Shanthikumar, G. 2007. *Stochastic Orders*. New York: Springer.

Stadje, W. 1991. A new continuous-time search model. *Journal of Applied Probability* 28: 771–78.

Su, X. 2007. Inter-temporal pricing with strategic customer behavior. *Management Science* 53 (5): 726–41.

Talluri, K. T., and van Ryzin, G. 2004. *The Theory and Practice of Revenue Management*. New York: Springer.

Vickrey, W. 1961. Counterspeculation, auctions, and competitive sealed tenders. *Journal of Finance* 16 (1): 8–37.

Vulcano, G., van Ryzin, G., and Maglaras, C. 2002. Optimal dynamic auctions for revenue management. *Management Science* 48 (11): 1388–1407.

Wang, R. 1993. Auctions versus posted-price selling. *American Economic Review* 83 (4): 838–51.

Wilson, C. A. 1988. On the optimal pricing policy of a monopolist. *Journal of Political Economy* 96 (1): 164–76.

Yokoo, M., Sakurai, Y., and Matsubara, S. 2004. The effect of false-name bids in combinatorial auctions: New fraud in internet auctions. *Games and Economic Behavior* 46: 174–88.

Zuckerman, D. 1986. Optimal stopping in a continuous search model. *Journal of Applied Probability* 23: 514–18.

Zuckerman, D. 1988. Job search with general stochastic offer arrival rates. *Journal of Economic Dynamics and Control* 12: 679–84.

Index

Adaptive learning based on empirical
  distribution, 128–32
Adverse selection, 179
Afeche, P., 165
Agents. *See also* Long-lived agents
  continuous-time model with stochastic
    arrivals, 14–29, 70
  delayed purchases by, 71
  density of waiting time till arrival of first,
    47–48
  discrete-time model, 12–14
  expected welfare, 13–14
  nonperishable goods and, 153–62
  perishable goods and long-lived, 151–53
  privately known deadlines, 167–69
  queueing management, 162–67
  time of arrival, 47–48, 145–46, 158, 165–67
  types, 11, 145–46
AGV mechanism, 173–74
Airline Deregulation Act of 1978, 1
Albright, S. C., 3, 11, 15, 25, 105, 109,
    125, 146
Allocation, dynamic, 2–3
  assortative, 13
  budget-balancedness and, 33–37
  comparison of efficient and revenue
    maximizing policies, 59–64
  deterministic and Markovian, 30, 39n5,
    43–44, 75–78
  expected utility after, 140–42
  implementable Markovian, 30, 39n5, 41
  incomplete-information model and, 29–37
  infinite horizon model, 24–29
  learning and, 6–7
  maximizing total expected welfare, 15–17
  private information and, 29–33
Armstrong, M., 103
Arnold, M. A., 70, 71
Arrow, K., 36, 173, 178
Assortative matching, 13, 22

Asymptotically optimal and time-independent
    pricing, 90–92
  deterministic problem, 92–96
  simple policy for stochastic problem,
    96–102
Athey, S., 8, 38, 173, 178, 180n12
Auction/mechanism design, 1
Auctions, queue slot, 165–67
Aviv, Y., 71

Babaioff, M., 147
Balachandran, K., 163
Baron, D. P., 175
Battaglini, M., 178
Bayesian learning, 106–107, 135–36
Bayes–Nash equilibrium, 156, 173
Becker, G., 109
Bergemann, D., 8, 9n1, 38, 161, 170, 171, 178
Bertsekas, D., 154
Besanko, D., 175
Bickhchandani, S., 106, 131, 146
Bitran, G. R., 55, 70, 71, 72n8, 81
Blackorby, C., 103
Blumrosen, L., 147
Board, S., 155
Bowen, B., 67, 70, 72n6
Budget-balancedness, 33–37
  dynamic pivot mechanism and, 173–74
Bulow, J., 72n3

Caldentey, R., 70, 71
Caracamo, J., 24
Cavallo, R., 180n14
Che, Y. K., 103
Chebychev's inequality, 99–100
Chen, C. H., 179
Chen, Y., 146
Chou, C. F., 106, 132
Clearance sales, 42, 67–69
Coase conjecture, 72n10

Compatibility, incentive, 48, 54, 84n4, 160
  periodic ex post, 172
  second-best policy, 136–45
Complete information
  continuous-time with stochastic arrivals,
    14–29
  discrete-time, 12–14
  learning under, 108–10
  long-lived agents/nonperishable goods,
    153–55, 156–59
  sufficient condition for implementation of,
    114–26
Concavity, 81–90
Conitzer, V., 38
Continuous-time model with stochastic
  arrivals, 11, 14–29, 70
  long-lived agents/nonperishable goods,
    156–62
Courty, P., 8, 9n1, 174–75, 180n13
Cox, D., 164
Cremer, J., 145
$C\mu$ rule, 164
Cutoff policy. *See* Revenue maximization,
  dynamic

Darling, D., 70, 102
Dasgupta, P., 147
D'Aspremont, C., 36, 173, 178
Das Varma, G., 70, 72n9
Deadlines
  privately known, 167–69
  revenue maximization with, 162, 168–69
  sequential assignment with, 15–24
De La Cal, J., 24
Decreasing failure rate (DFR), 20
Delayed purchases, 71
Density of waiting time till arrival of first
  agent, 47–48
Derman, C., 3, 6, 11, 12, 105
Derman–Lieberman–Ross model. *See*
  Sequential assignment of heterogeneous
  objects
Deterministic allocation policy,
  30, 43–44
  expected utility and, 142
  stochastic knapsack model, 75–78
Direct mechanisms, 30, 37, 75, 110, 145,
  159–160
Dirichlet process, 131–32, 148n9
Discounting, infinite horizon with, 58–59,
  70–71
Discrete-time model, 12–14
  long-lived agents/nonperishable goods,
    153–55
Dizdar, D., 5
Dolan, R. J., 8, 9n1, 38, 163, 164
Dughmi, S., 147

Dynamically efficient online redistribution
  mechanism (DEON), 34–36
Dynamic information arrival, 169–70
Dynamic mechanism design, 2, 8
  offline mechanisms, 37–38
Dynamic models, 2
Dynamic pivot mechanism, 171–72
Dynamic revenue maximization. *See* Revenue
  maximization, dynamic

Elmaghraby, W., 70
Elving, G., 38
Eso, P., 178
Euler–Lagrange equation, 49, 51, 95
Expected externality mechanism,
  173–174
Expected revenue. *See* Revenue maximization,
  dynamic
Expected utility, 140–42
Expected welfare/welfare maximization
  continuous-time model, 15–29
  discrete-time model, 13–14
  infinite horizon model, 24–29, 178
  learning and, 6–7, 70
  linearity, 144–45
  loss due to sequentiality and, 21–24
  quality choices and, 65–66

First-best policy, 111–14, 148n7
  sufficient conditions for implementation of,
    114–26
Fixed allocation policy and incomplete
  information, 110–11
Flow marginal contribution of agents, 171

Gale, I., 103
Gallego, G., 6, 55, 64, 70, 72n10, 91, 100, 102,
  103
Gallien, J., 58, 70–71, 72n9, 162, 180n9
Gerard-Varet, L., 36, 173, 178
Gershkov, A., 2, 4, 5, 6, 161, 162, 166,
  180n9
Ghanem, S., 163
Glazer, A., 165
Glivenko–Cantelli theorem, 106, 149n13, 128
Gould, E., 70
Green, J., 180n5
Guo, M., 38

Hain, R., 166
Hansen, R., 147
Hardy, G., 13, 38
Harris, M., 72n10
Hassin, R., 163, 165
Haviv, M., 163
Hazard rate stochastic ordering, 80–81
Horner, J., 179

Implementable Markovian allocation policy, 30, 39n5, 41
stochastic knapsack model, 75–78
Incentive compatibility, 48, 54, 84n4, 160
periodic ex post, 172
Incentive efficient (second-best) policy, 136–45
Incomplete information, 29–37
learning and, 110–26
long-lived agents/nonperishable goods, 155, 159–62
Increasing failure rate (IFR) assumption, 20–21, 59, 61–64
Indirect mechanisms, 30, 75, 145
Induction hypothesis, 130–31
Infinite horizon model, 24–29, 178
with discounting, 58–59, 70–71
Information
complete, 12–29, 108–10, 153–55, 156–59
dynamic arrival, 169–77
incomplete, 29–37, 110–26, 155, 159–62
learning and dynamic efficiency, 6–7, 108–26
long-lived agents/nonperishable goods, 153–55
private, 29–33
Interdependent values, 105, 112, 147, 165, 178
Iyengar, G., 103

Jehiel, P., 147

Keskinocak, P., 70
Kincaid, W. M., 70, 102
Kittsteiner, T., 103, 147, 152, 165
Kleinrock, L., 163, 165
Kleywegt, A., 73, 74, 78, 81, 83, 102, 103
Knapsack problem. *See* Stochastic knapsack model
Kohn, M., 127
Krähmer, D., 178
Kumar, A., 103

Lazear, E. P., 67, 70, 71, 72n6
Laffont, J. J., 180n5
Laplace transform, 24–25, 27, 159, 160
Laplace transform order, 27–28
Learning and dynamic efficiency, 6–7, 70
adaptive, 128–32
Bayesian, 106–107, 135–36
under complete information, 108–10
first-best policy, 114–26, 148n7
incentive efficient (second-best) policy, 136–45
incomplete information and, 110–26
introduction to, 105–107
maximum entropy/quantile preserving, 132–36

model, 108
non-Bayesian, 106–107, 128–36, 135–36
offline mechanisms, 145–46
related literature, 146–47
search for lowest price and the reservation price property in, 126–28
Li, H., 8, 9n1, 174–75, 180n13
Lieberman, G. J., 3, 6, 11, 12, 105
Lin, G. Y., 74, 102
Lippman, S. A., 70, 71, 72n9
Lipschitz function, 111–12, 116
Littlewood, J. E., 13, 38
Longest processing time first (LPT discipline), 166
Long-lived agents, 7–8
dynamic information arrival, 169–77
nonperishable goods and, 153–62
outlook, 179
perishable goods and, 151–53
privately known deadlines, 167–69
queueing management, 162–67
related literature, 177–78
sequential screening and revenue maximization, 174–77
Loss due to sequentiality, 21–24
Lu, Y., 74, 102
Lui, F., 165

Majorization, 11–12, 14, 38, 107
sub-majorization, 14, 22
Marginal contribution of agents, 171
Markovian allocation policy, 4, 30, 39n5, 41, 43–44
stochastic knapsack model, 75–78
Maskin, E., 147
Matsubara, S., 39n7
Maximum entropy/quantile preserving learning, 132–36
McAfee, P., 38, 63, 70, 72n10, 155
McLean, R., 145
McMillan, J., 155
Mendelson, H., 165
Mezzetti, C., 147
Mierendorff, K., 168, 169
Milgrom, P., 1, 148n8
Mitra, M., 166
Moldovanu, B., 2, 4, 5, 6, 103, 147, 161, 162, 165, 180n9
Monetary transfers
offline mechanisms, 34, 36–37
online mechanisms, 33–36
private information and, 29–33
Monopolists, 174–77
Morgan, P. B., 146
Mortensen, D. T., 158

Moulin, H., 38
Mussa, M., 3, 64, 66
Myerson, R., 4, 41, 44, 72n3, 79

New better than used (NBU), 158–59, 162,
    180n9
New better than used in expectation (NBUE),
    20–21, 28–29
Nikutta, J., 152
Nocke, V., 71
No-haggling argument, 137
Non-Bayesian learning, 106–107, 135–36
    dynamic implementation and, 128–36
Nonperishable goods and long-lived agents
    search with recall: continuous time, 156–62
    search with recall: discrete time, 153–55

Objects
    assortative matching, 13, 22
    dynamic revenue-maximizing allocation
        curve with one remaining, 48–53
    dynamic revenue-maximizing allocation
        policy independence from quantities of,
        44–45
    implementable Markovian allocation policy
        for, 30, 39n5
    infinite, 23
    loss due to sequentiality, 21–24
    monopolists and, 174–77
    perishable, 151–53
    pricing dynamics for single, 57, 58
    quality and pricing, 65–66, 68–69
    salvage value of, 43–44
Offline mechanisms, 34, 36–37, 145–46
Online mechanisms, 33–36
Optimal inventory choice and dynamic
    pricing, 64–66

Pai, M., 103, 162, 168
Papastavrou, J. D., 73, 74, 78, 81, 83, 102, 103
Parkes, D. C., 38, 180n14
Pashigian, B. P., 67, 70, 72n6
Pavan, A., 178
Payoff equivalence theorem, 41
Pazgal, A., 71
Peitz, M., 71
Periodic ex post incentive compatible, 172
Perishable goods, 151–53
Pólya, G., 13, 38
Pricing
    asymptotically optimal and
        time-independent, 90–102
    clearance, 42, 67–69
    decisions in revenue management, 1
    dynamics with one object available, 57, 58
    no-haggling, 137

nonlinear, 6
optimal, 41–42
optimal inventory choice and dynamic,
    64–66
quality and, 65–66, 68–69
reservation price property, 7, 107, 126–28
revenue maximizing, 4–5
salvage value, 43–44
Vickrey–Clarke–Groves (VCG) mechanism,
    3, 12
Private information and dynamic allocation,
    29–33
Privately known deadlines, 167–69
Puterman, M. L., 39n3, 43, 78

Quality choices, 65–66, 68–69
Quantity decisions in revenue management, 1
Queueing management, 162–63
    dynamic VCG mechanisms for, 163–65
    slot auctions, 165–67

Rajagopalan, S., 73, 74, 78, 81, 83, 102
Raviv, A., 72n10
Reliability theory, 20
Renewals, 24, 158, 160–62, 180n9
Reservation price property, 7, 107, 126–28
Revenue management (RM), 70
    basic issues in, 1
    dynamic models in, 2
    long-lived agents and, 7–8
Revenue maximization, dynamic, 4–5, 43–57,
    58
    clearance sales and, 42
    comparison of efficient and, 59–64
    concavity and, 82–90
    with deadlines, 162, 168–69
    dynamic pricing and optimal inventory
        choice, 64–66
    increasing failure rate (IFR), 61–64
    infinite horizon with discounting, 58–59,
        70–71
    introduction to, 41–42
    model, 43
    multi-unit demand and, 5–6
    quality choices and, 65–66, 68–69
    related literature, 70–71
    Schur convexity and, 64–65
    sequential screening and, 174–77
    stochastic knapsack model, 78–90
    waste and, 42
Riley, J., 9n1, 70, 104n6, 137, 139
Roberts, J., 72n3
Rochet, J.-C., 103
Rosar, F., 71
Rosen, S., 3, 64, 66
Rosenfield, D., 127–28, 146

Ross, K. W., 5
Ross, S. M., 3, 6, 11, 12, 47, 105, 180n2
Rothschild, M., 106, 126–27

Said, M., 9n1, 151, 152, 153, 180n1
Sakurai, Y., 39n7
Salvage valued, 43–44
Samuelson, L., 179
Schur-convexity, 14, 64–65, 137–38
Schweinzer, P., 166
Screening, sequential, 174–77
Search with recall: discrete time, 153–55
Search with recall: continuous time, 156–62
Second-best policy, 136–45
Segal, I., 8, 38, 146, 173, 178, 180n12
Seiderstad, A., 127–28, 146
Sequential assignment of heterogeneous
      objects, 2–3, 108
  continuous-time model with stochastic
      arrivals, 14–29
  introduction to, 11–12
  loss to due to sequentiality, 21–24
  models with complete information, 12–29
Sequential screening and revenue
      maximization, 174–77
Shaked, M., 27
Shantikumar, G., 27
Shapiro, R., 127–28, 146
Shavell, S., 127
Sharma, S., 106, 131, 146
Shorter processing time first (SPT discipline),
      166
Singer, Y., 147
Singh, S., 38, 180n14
Single-crossing, 105, 112, 125
Skreta, V., 179
Skrzypacz, A., 155
Smith, W., 164
Stacchetti, E., 103
Stieltjes integral, 129–30
Stochastic knapsack model, 5–6
  asymptotically optimal and time-independent
      pricing, 90–102
  deterministic problem, 92–96
  dynamic revenue maximization, 78–90
  hazard rate stochastic ordering, 80–81
  implementable policies, 75–78
  introduction to, 73–74
  periods, 74–75
  related literature, 102–103

role of concavity in, 81–90
  simple policy for stochastic problem and,
      96–102
Stole, L. A., 103
Strack, P., 161, 162
Strausz, R., 178
Structural decisions in revenue management, 1
Su, X., 71
Szalay, D., 103
Szentes, B., 178

Talluri, K. T., 1, 70
Talmain, G., 106, 132
Te Velde, V., 38, 63, 70
*Theory and Practice of Revenue Management,
      The*, 1
Toikka, J., 178
Tsang, D. H. H., 5

Uniformization procedure, 39n2
Utility, expected, 140–42

Välimäki, J., 8, 38, 161, 170, 171, 178
Van Ryzin, G., 1, 6, 55, 64, 70, 72n10, 91, 100,
      102, 103
Vettas, N., 70, 72n9
Vickrey, W., 4, 41
Vickrey–Clarke–Groves mechanism, 8, 12, 38,
      161
  dynamic information arrival and, 170
  dynamic pivot mechanism and, 171
  incomplete-information model and dynamic,
      29–37
  for queue management, 163–65
Vohra, R., 103, 162, 168

Wang, R., 9n1, 71, 146
Waste in revenue maximization, 42
Wilson, C., 72n10
Winter, E., 152
Wiseman, T., 72n10
Within-period ex post equilibrium, 180n12

Yao, D. D., 74, 102
Yield management, 70
Yokoo, M., 39n7

Zeckhauser, R., 9n1, 70, 104n6,
      137, 139
Zuckerman, D., 158–59, 162

Printed in the United States
by Baker & Taylor Publisher Services